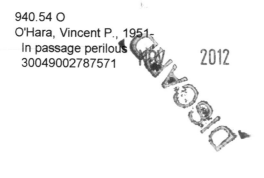

D1593464

IN PASSAGE PERILOUS

⚓ ⚓ ⚓

TWENTIETH-CENTURY BATTLES

Edited by Spencer C. Tucker

IN PASSAGE PERILOUS

Malta and the Convoy Battles of June 1942

VINCENT P. O'HARA

INDIANA UNIVERSITY PRESS

Bloomington & Indianapolis

This book is a publication of

INDIANA UNIVERSITY PRESS
601 North Morton Street
Bloomington, Indiana 47404-3797 USA

iupress.indiana.edu

Telephone orders   800-842-6796
Fax orders   812-855-7931

⊖ The paper used in this publication
meets the minimum requirements of
the American National Standard for
Information Sciences—Permanence of
Paper for Printed Library Materials,
ANSI Z39.48-1992.

Manufactured in the United States of America

Library of Congress Cataloging-in-
Publication Data

O'Hara, Vincent P., [date]
In passage perilous : Malta and the
convoy battles of June 1942 / Vincent P.
O'Hara.
    p. cm. — (Twentieth-century battles)
    Includes bibliographical references and
index.
    ISBN 978-0-253-00603-5 (cloth : alk.
paper) — ISBN 978-0-253-00605-9
(electronic book) 1. Malta—History—
Siege, 1940–1943. 2. World War, 1939–1945—
Campaigns—Malta. 3. World War, 1939–
1945—Campaigns—Mediterranean Sea. 4.
World War, 1939–1945—Naval operations,
British. 5. Naval convoys—Mediterranean
Sea—History—20th century. 6. Great
Britain. Royal Navy—History—World War,
1939–1945. I. Title.
    D763.M3O38 2013
    940.54′5091822—dc23
                                    2012015993

1 2 3 4 5   18 17 16 15 14 13

TO MARIA

For your patience and support

⚓ ⚓ ⚓

Contents

Tables

Maps

Preface

Wars teach us not to love our enemies, but to hate our allies.

W. L. George

ON 26 JUNE 1942, against a backdrop of warships with elevated guns, two columns of sailors massed on a quay on the Neapolitan waterfront and witnessed Benito Mussolini, Italy's premier and supreme military leader, and Admiral Arturo Riccardi, the Regia Marina's chief of staff, present medals to the officers and men of the fleet's 7th Division. The ceremony marked a battle fought two years and five days after Italy's entry into World War II. The British Royal Navy had tried to pass large convoys from Gibraltar and Egypt to the island bastion of Malta in the central Mediterranean. Air strikes and Italian battleships repulsed the eastern convoy. The 7th Division intercepted the western group and applied, in Mussolini's words, "the sharp teeth of the Roman Wolf into the flesh of Great Britain."[1]

The campaign fought in the Mediterranean and North Africa from June 1940 to September 1943, principally between the armed forces of Great Britain and its empire and the Kingdom of Italy, with strong assistance from Germany, has inspired study and passion. A central perception in the English understanding of this campaign is that British air and naval forces operating from Malta choked the Axis sea-lanes and denied German General Erwin Rommel, the "Desert Fox," the supplies he needed to overrun the Middle East and that this justified the heavy cost of maintaining Malta as a base. In fact, for much of the war the island's impact on Axis traffic to Africa was minimal. By mid-1942 Italian and German forces had Malta tightly blockaded by sea and bombarded by air, and the British chiefs of staff believed that its supplies would be exhausted by July.

In June 1942, in an effort to relieve Malta and restore its offensive capacity, the Royal Navy borrowed heavily from the Home and Eastern Fleets to reinforce its flotillas at Gibraltar and Alexandria—despite other threats such as Germany's Atlantic submarine offensive, a German fleet in Norway interdicting the convoy route to Murmansk, and Japanese carriers that had recently defeated British forces in the Indian Ocean. Great Britain used this borrowed strength to escort strong convoys from Gibraltar and Egypt for beleaguered Malta. In a complex aero-naval battle lasting nearly a week, Axis forces defeated Operation Vigorous, the larger eastern effort, and eliminated two-thirds of the western convoy, Operation Harpoon. Seventeen merchant ships set out, but only two reached Malta, and one of those was damaged. The defeat of the mid-June convoys forced the British to immediately organize a repeat operation while their global position continued to deteriorate.

An author recently noted that "Harpoon has been called the 'forgotten convoy,' but a better name might be 'disowned convoy.'" The official British history, following a terse summary of the two convoys, commented, "The enemy's success was undeniable." One British historian titled his chapter on Operation Vigorous "An imperial balls-up." Another tried to paint Harpoon as a success: "the 15,000 tons discharged was little short of munificence to a population faced with starvation or capitulation." Winston Churchill, in his six-volume history of the Second World War, completely ignored the June 1942 convoys after spending a chapter detailing Malta's peril in March, April, and May, 1942.[2]

The Harpoon and Vigorous convoys of mid-June 1942 are the subjects of this work. The conduct of these operations and the Axis response are examined in great detail because the records contain ambiguities and even distortions that justify close scrutiny. This work relies heavily on reports filed during and shortly after events by the Italian and British units and commands involved. It strives to follow the facts and maintain a dispassionate point of view.

The mid-June battle illustrates the Mediterranean balance of power after two years of intense combat. Its operational aspects demonstrate the complex relationship between air and naval power and geography's impact on littoral operations. Harpoon/Vigorous also shows how the prime minister and War Cabinet mortgaged the British Empire's worldwide interests to maintain a position in the Mediterranean; especially interesting are the strategic hopes London pinned on this operation. The convoys were part of a gamble that could, if the dice fell right, help conclude the Mediterranean campaign victoriously and strengthen the British Empire's hand in setting Allied grand strategy.

The mid-June operation also presented an interesting conundrum for the German and Italian leadership. They agreed that the capture of Suez was a worthwhile objective but not what to do about Malta. Mussolini, Comando Supremo's chief of staff, Field Marshal Ugo Cavallero, Admiral Riccardi, and Vice Admiral Eberhard Weichold, head of the German naval command in Italy, considered Malta's capture absolutely necessary for victory in North Africa. Others, including Rommel; General Alfred Jodl, chief of the Wehrmacht operations staff; and, most importantly, German chancellor Adolf Hitler, believed that the risks of assaulting the island outweighed the benefits and lacked faith in Italian ability to conduct the invasion.

Malta dominated Mediterranean operations in many respects. As a British bastion directly athwart the Italian sea-lane between the peninsula and Africa, it had great potential to impede Axis traffic. However, maintaining Malta was an expensive and dangerous task, and historians have from the first debated the merits of the Imperial policy of holding the island at all costs. Along with the question of Malta there is the larger matter of Great Britain's and Italy's whole strategic focus. Did Great Britain need to undertake an offensive war in the Mediterranean? What did London sacrifice in the process, and what did it gain? Did Italy need to conduct a campaign in North Africa? How did this campaign serve its vital interests? Believing that context is required for an appreciation of the specific operations that are the subject of this study, these pages include a summary of the Mediterranean war with an emphasis on Malta and the campaign against traffic to the island and to Africa.

This work observes certain conventions. During the Second World War, Italy and Germany employed the metric system of measurement while the Anglo-Americans used the imperial system. Rather than convert yards to meters or kilometers to miles, this study uses the imperial system except when quoting or discussing Axis actions or vessels when the metric system may be used. In a few instances the two values are given side by side. "Miles" always refers to nautical miles unless otherwise stated. Foreign ranks are translated into English. A table of equivalent ranks appears in the appendix. The appendix also contains a list of abbreviations and conversions. Times present a complication as during the mid-June convoys the British used double summer time and their accounts are one hour later than the times cited in Italian reports. For consistency, British times are used in Chapters 5, 6, and 7. Subtract one hour to reconcile with Italian times. Quotations from the Italian have been translated by the author.

Acknowledgments

ONE OF THE JOYS OF WRITING is to experience the generosity of authors and enthusiasts who are passionate about naval history, and it is a pleasure to acknowledge here the contributions of family, old friends, and new friends who have contributed to this work.

I would like to thank my friend Enrico Cernuschi, who provided crucial material from the Italian archives and, as always, helped in many other ways. Vincent O'Hara Sr., Karl Zingheim, and Dennis Dove read portions of the manuscript. Michael Yaklich carefully tackled the whole thing and offered many helpful comments. Joseph Caruana and Larry deZeng shared information and insights on several ambiguous matters. Benjamin Kaplan and Jack Greene opened their libraries. Jean Hood, Stephen McLaughlin, Jeffrey Kacirk, and Hannah Cunliffe searched the British National Archives for me. Thank you to Commander Erminio Bagnasco for permission to use images from his extensive photographic collection and his outstanding publication, *Storia MILITARE* magazine, to Stephen Dent for sharing from his photographic collection, and to Andrea Tani for memories of his father, Fabio Tani, *Montecuccoli*'s gunnery officer and architect of the longest-ranged 6-inch hit of the war. Thanks to Spencer C. Tucker for giving me the opportunity to contribute to the Twentieth-Century Battles series, which he edits, and to the editorial director of Indiana University Press, Robert J. Sloan, for undertaking this work.

Of course, all interpretations, omissions, and errors in fact are solely my responsibility.

Finally, and above all else, I thank my beautiful wife, Maria, my son, Vincent, and my daughter, Yunuen, who have supported my passion for naval history and tolerated its impact on their lives.

IN PASSAGE PERILOUS

⚓ ⚓ ⚓

1

THE VITAL SEA

We must look to the Mediterranean for Action.

Winston Churchill to First Sea Lord, 12 July 1940

ON 29 JUNE 1940, as German armies gathered along the English Channel, the giant liners *Aquitania, Mauretania,* and *Queen Mary* departed the Clyde and Liverpool. These fast and valuable vessels carried eleven thousand troops bound for Egypt to bring British formations stationed there up to strength. They formed into convoy WS1 escorted by the heavy cruiser *Cumberland* and, for the first stage, four destroyers. The convoy arrived at Freetown, West Africa, on 8 July and Cape Town, South Africa, eight days later. From there WS1 crossed the Indian Ocean, picking up a second escort, the heavy cruiser *Kent.* Because the Admiralty considered the ships too valuable to expose them to Italian attack in the Red Sea, they docked at Trincomalee, Ceylon, on 29 July, and the men disembarked. The troops sailed up the Indian coast to Bombay. At Bombay they transferred to eight transports that formed a part of Convoy BN3: twenty merchant ships and eight escorts, including a light cruiser and two destroyers. BN3 departed Bombay on 10 August and arrived at Suez on 23 August.

GREAT BRITAIN'S STRATEGIC GOALS

Great Britain committed these troops to a journey of nearly two months at a time when England faced a German invasion. The voyage was so long because Italy had declared war against Great Britain on 10 June 1940. This declaration severed the sea-route from Gibraltar to Suez. The official British history of the war at sea summarized the impact. "The distance round the Cape from the Clyde to Suez . . . is 12,860 [statute] miles. For a convoy to reach the Middle East theater and return to Britain by this route necessitated a journey some 20,000 miles longer than the round voyage using the Mediterranean." Not only were the time and the distance inflated but the convoys required escorts and special shipping such as liners and fast cargo vessels. "If one convoy of about twenty-five ships sailed each month, the new requirement meant that about 150 of our best merchant ships were kept permanently on this service." Adding 8,700 nautical miles (thirty days at twelve knots) to each voyage to Suez was hardly the only problem: the one-way journey to India went from 6,200 to 10,600 miles, and the nearest Australian port became 1,500 miles farther away. Ships carrying troops and supplies to Suez generally had to detour to find cargos for the return trip, further reducing their efficiency and adding to the strain on shipping.[1]

Great Britain faced hard choices after France's unexpected collapse. The first was whether to continue fighting or accept a German-dominated Europe. The new government led by Winston S. Churchill mustered popular support, overcame dissent from within its own ranks, and resolved to fight.[2] This decision had global ramifications because, as in 1778 and 1803, the conflict pitted a world empire against a continental coalition. The British Empire's power resided in a resource-rich network spread throughout Canada, Australia, New Zealand, South Africa, the Empire of India, and the colonies and mandates of Africa, South East Asia, the Americas, and the Middle East. Possession of strategic points such as Suez, Gibraltar, Cape Town, Aden, and Singapore allowed Great Britain to control the world's oceanic trade and choke an enemy nation's maritime traffic.

Merchant shipping unified Britain's empire. Sea power kept the ships sailing or, in the case of enemies, confined them to port. The Broadway of the empire's pre-war sea-lanes was the Mediterranean—a vital shortcut to the lands east of Suez. Italy's entry into the war, however, immediately transformed the Mediterranean from a thoroughfare into a dead end.

Malta had been the Royal Navy's main Mediterranean base since 1800; it lay astride Italy's sea-route to Tripoli, Libya's capital and major port. However, the neglect of Malta's defenses in the decades leading up to war and the proximity of Italian air power—the potency of which the Royal Air Force greatly exaggerated "in the hope that, by so doing, a greater share of the service budget would be committed to the air force"—caused the fleet to abandon the island

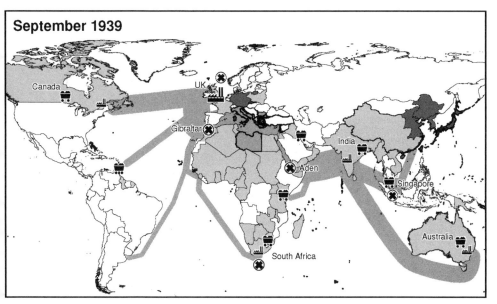

September 1939

Centers of Imperial Power & Britian's Vital Sea Routes

- 🏭 Industrial Center
- ⛏ British controlled Resources
- ✖ Choke point
- ▬ Vital Sea Routes

- ☐ Allied Belligerents
- ■ Axis Belligerents
- ☐ Neutral

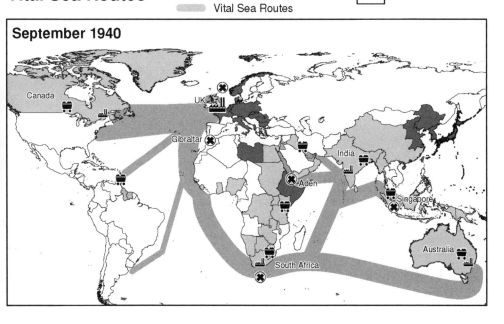

September 1940

by April 1939 for the much less suitable and logistically undeveloped Egyptian harbor of Alexandria.[3]

By the summer of 1940 Malta was an isolated outpost in the midst of a hostile sea. Indeed, the Admiralty even recommended withdrawing the Mediterranean Fleet from Alexandria because "our Atlantic trade must be the first consideration."[4] The Chief of the Imperial General Staff, General John Dill, recognizing that the Far East was of much greater economic value to Great Britain than the Middle East, recommended reinforcing the Far East first against potential Japanese aggression. The other members of the Chiefs of Staff Committee likewise questioned the wisdom of centering Great Britain's war effort on the Middle East. However, keeping a weather eye on a more hopeful future, Churchill and the War Cabinet decided to contest the Mediterranean and reinforce Malta.

A War Cabinet assessment of September 1940 gave the reasons. "Malta should be held. If it could be made secure enough for use as a fleet base we should derive the great advantage of being able to hold the Italians in check with one fleet instead of the two now required (one at each end of the Mediterranean). We should also be able to interrupt Italian communications with Libya much more effectively. From it we could ultimately strike at Italy ..." The War Cabinet's September assessment summarized: "The elimination of Italy and the consequent removal of the threat to our control of the Eastern Mediterranean would be a strategic success of the first importance. Italy's power of resistance is much less than that of Germany and direct attacks on Italy and her possessions in Africa may be the first important step we can take toward the downfall of Germany." Moreover, in the Mediterranean Britain could concentrate its best weapon, the Royal Navy, against its weaker foe: "we should undermine Italian resistance by continued offensive operations with our naval forces." Finally an important if unstated reason was that the Mediterranean was the only place where Britain could realistically assume the offensive. As one historian expressed it, "Churchill owed a perverse debt of gratitude to Mussolini. If Italy had remained neutral ... how else might the British Army have occupied itself after its expulsion from France?" These were the military reasons for the decisions emanating from London in the summer of 1940.[5]

There were also compelling political reasons for Great Britain to retain a Mediterranean presence. Admiral Andrew B. Cunningham, commander of the Mediterranean Fleet, was reflecting common opinion when he observed on 18

June that "Egypt would be untenable soon after the Fleet's departure, Malta, Cyprus and Palestine could no longer be held, the Moslems would regard it as surrender, prospects of Turkey's loyalty would be discounted and even the Italians would be stirred to activity." The Soviets and Americans would certainly have regarded such a withdrawal as a sign of weakness. Furthermore, behind its decision to hold Malta and transfer units of the Home Fleet to form Force H at a time when Great Britain seemed threatened by invasion, the government was confident that the United States would eventually enter the war—secret staff talks between the U.S. and Royal navies were already under way—and it believed that Stalin would distance himself from Hitler, "whose enormous increase of power entailed incalculable risks for the Soviet Union."[6]

War has many consequences, and national leaders sometimes disregard inconvenient ones, especially in the name of politics. Mussolini, with the enthusiastic support of Italy's economic elite, was certainly guilty of this when he elected to enter the war long before his military was ready. Churchill and the War Cabinet likewise failed to fully consider the long-term economic consequences of their strategic and political choices.

The hard truth was that London did not command the shipping required to simultaneously undertake a North African offensive and maintain its economy. According to one scholar, "Britain lacked enough merchant shipping capacity to import the quantities of vital foodstuffs and raw materials required to meet domestic needs, fulfill imperial obligations and sustain offensive warfare at the tail end of a ten thousand mile line of supply. Britain built too few ships, sent them on too lengthy voyages, protected them poorly and unloaded them slowly." In summarizing the impact of a Middle Eastern offensive, another history noted that "the effort to sustain armies in Egypt, Libya, east Africa, and elsewhere in the Near and Middle East, and to maintain naval and air power in the Mediterranean was absorbing, or was soon to absorb, half of Britain's war production, transported at enormous cost over the long route around the Cape of Good Hope."[7]

These assertions raise the question of whether by concentrating its war effort on critical objectives, like maintaining imports and securing the North Atlantic, Great Britain could have won a less costly victory. The answer is almost certainly yes, but given the political imperatives that existed in the summer of 1940, such a strategy was unthinkable to Churchill, who believed that "there must be action, even if not always useful; there must be successes, even if overstated or imagined; there must be glory, even if undeserved." The British government had to fight somewhere, and in the summer of 1940 the Mediterranean was the only choice.[8]

ITALY'S STRATEGIC GOALS

In 1939 Mussolini did not answer the declarations of war made by the western democracies in support of Poland with his own declaration in support of Germany because Italy was unprepared to fight. In January 1940 he spoke of intervening alongside Germany in the second half of 1941. This timetable accelerated as Germany triumphed in Scandinavia, but it was Germany's crushing victory over France that tolled the hour. On 25 May Lord Halifax, the United Kingdom's foreign secretary, met with the Italian ambassador in London to discuss what concessions would be required to maintain Italian neutrality. This initiative confirmed Mussolini's conviction that the British were all but defeated and that the moment to jump in had arrived although his armed forces remained woefully unprepared. When Belgium capitulated on 27 May Italy's foreign minister, and Mussolini's son-in-law, Galeazzo Ciano, terminated the talks, telling Britain's Italian ambassador that "we are on the brink of war."[9]

Italy declared war for several reasons. The country was resource poor, and, like Great Britain, its economy depended upon imports: 86 percent of Italy's pre-war imports, including nearly all of its coal, arrived by sea, and 75 percent of that total passed Gibraltar or Suez. The British blockades imposed in 1914–15, September 1918, September 1939, and again in March 1940, when London restricted Italian shipments of German coal (via the Netherlands), knowing full well the disastrous consequences this would have on Italy's economy, had cemented the general conviction that, as the Duce expressed it to the president of the United States in May 1940, Italy was a "prisoner in the Mediterranean" and required free access to the Atlantic which it did not have "under the guns of Gibraltar."[10]

Mussolini's personal, political, and ideological ambitions required war. He shared power with the king. Victory would give him the prestige to eliminate the monarchy and marginalize the church. He had ideological reasons. Ciano wrote, "it is humiliating to remain with our hands folded while others write history. . . . To make a people great it is necessary to send them to battle even if you have to kick them in the pants." Finally, Mussolini's government had predatory ambitions. These included the annexation of Tunisia, Corsica, Nice, Malta, and portions of Dalmatia. In Mussolini's eyes this constituted the return to Italy of national territory. Rome also sought economic and political domination of the Balkans, an expanded role in the Middle East, and control of Egypt. In short, it sought Mediterranean supremacy.[11]

Such dominance would have benefited Italy—it would have secured the nation's long and vulnerable coastline from attack—but British possession of Gibraltar (or the Canary Islands, if need be) and Aden would still have denied Rome freedom of the seas. A final German victory might have better solved the problem of oceanic access with little effort on Italy's part, but the political consequences of being beholden to Germany in such a case were unpalatable to those segments of Italian society that deeply distrusted German intentions, which included King Victor Emmanuel, the economic elite, many in the government, and most Italians.

Originally, judging that "in the likely event [of] war the colony would be isolated from the *madrepatria*" and that it would face hostile armies on both frontiers, the Italian high command intended its Libyan forces to be self-sufficient for twelve months of defensive warfare. Told it would not need to convoy supplies to Africa, the Regia Marina prepared to face the offensive forays of the French and British fleets. However, the elimination of France transformed the situation, and Mussolini decided to launch an offensive from Libya as soon as possible. This decision presented the Regia Marina with the task of escorting the convoys required to support an army offensive in that inhospitable region, and it elevated Malta from being a minor irritant to an important objective because of the island's location astride the route between Italy and Tripoli.[12]

GERMANY'S STRATEGIC GOALS

In September 1939 Hitler believed that the Mediterranean had limited relevance to his nation's aspirations, and he did not press for an Italian declaration of war. After overthrowing France's defenses, Berlin did not even desire Italian participation. Nonetheless, Mussolini's agenda was not Hitler's, and by July 1940 victory in the west, along with Italy's entry into the conflict, presented German planners with a quandary. What next? Bringing Britain to the peace table was the preferred solution, but Force H's attack against the French fleet at Mers el-Kébir confirmed that Churchill's war party was firmly in control, and the new prime minister scorned the poisoned olive branch Hitler proffered in his Reichstag speech of 19 July.

This left Hitler facing a two-front war come mid-1941 when the invasion of the Soviet Union was scheduled to commence. He was skeptical of Italy's ability to support an army in Africa. Thus, leaving open the future need for some type of Mediterranean operation, the Wehrmacht concentrated on expanding its forces for the eastern campaign and threatening Britain with invasion.

The Kriegsmarine had a clearer view than did the Führer of how an assertive Mediterranean policy could advance German interests. On 6 September 1940 Grand Admiral Erich Raeder argued that the capture of Gibraltar and the Suez Canal would improve Berlin's position in the Balkans, Asia Minor, and the Middle East and guarantee "unlimited sources for raw materials." Germany would also gain strategically vital bases, particularly Gibraltar, which would aid in the Atlantic campaign. Hitler agreed in principle, but he always believed (correctly) that the war would be won or lost on the steppes and forests of Russia. Thus, "Hitler's programmatic policy in the east" dominated planning, and his failure to enlist the active participation of Spain's Generalissimo Francisco Franco and France's Marshal Philippe Pétain in October 1940 ensured that Admiral Raeder's Mediterranean ambitions remained unrealized.[13]

During the last six months of 1940, when the Reich's opportunities seemed unlimited, Germany allowed Mussolini's parallel war to determine its future Mediterranean policy. When Italian misadventures in the Balkans and North Africa threatened the security of Romania's Ploesti oil fields and the southern flank of the forthcoming Russian offensive, Germany acted to protect these vulnerable points. Thereafter, until November 1942 and the unexpected Allied invasion of Algeria and Morocco, the Reich was content to let Britain pour its energies into a remote region far from areas it considered important while supporting its Italian ally with minor forces.

SPAIN, CHOKE POINTS, AND THE IMPACT OF SEA POWER

Spain provided an example of how Great Britain applied sea power. Spain was a second-rank Mediterranean power, but it held the key to control of the Western Mediterranean. Spanish belligerence would render Gibraltar untenable, give Italy an Atlantic gateway, and furnish Germany with bases and a bridgehead in North Africa. Germany and Italy had rendered great assistance to Franco in Spain's recent civil war, and the Axis powers believed they could count on Spanish participation when the time was right. With the defeat of France and the creation of a Mediterranean theater of war, the time was right.

German planners began to seriously study an attack on Gibraltar on 12 July 1940. Admiral Wilhelm Canaris traveled to Madrid on 20 July to secure Spanish permission for transit of the necessary troops. Instead he encountered an unexpected obstacle. Although Franco professed the greatest friendship for Germany and its goals and the strongest desire to help in the fighting, he explained that Spain's situation was difficult; its economy was in ruins, and its army had ammunition for, "at best, a few days of fighting." Therefore, he presented Canaris with a colossal list of aid required before his men could march, not to mention major cessions of French territory in North Africa.[14]

In fact, the biggest factor barring Spanish entry into the war was Spain's absolute dependence upon imported raw materials and food. These imports, which Germany could not provide, came from overseas and were subject to British blockade. London "saw this very clearly and consistently, and exploited their opportunity by conducting a policy of 'conditional assistance.'" Spain could not afford to hazard war unless Great Britain was clearly defeated or Germany would commit to equipping its army and subsidizing its economy. Negotiations dragged on, but in the end, Germany concluded that "a high-priced alliance with a destitute country for the capture of a distant British naval base seemed unnecessary." Thus the Royal Navy won the battle of Gibraltar before it was ever fought.[15]

1942

By June 1942 the Axis controlled the Balkans. The North African war had been going back and forth over empty desert for two years and was close to where it had been when the whole affair started. Spanish nonbelligerency, France's stubborn refusal to succumb to British provocations or German pressures, and Turkey's contented fence-straddling kept the geopolitical situation remarkably static. Given the effort, the losses sustained, and the men and treasure poured into Libya and Egypt, Great Britain and Italy had little to show for two years of warfare. The decisive victory London sought in 1940 had proved a chimera, and the acclaimed aero-naval victories at Taranto and Matapan were only bumps in a long process that had seen Italy and Germany slowly grind the British down.

June 1942 seemed a point of decision. While American participation gave the British government confidence in their ultimate triumph, they needed to win a strategic victory in the Mediterranean on their own. The stakes were high. London sought to massively reinforce Malta, securing it against invasion and reestablishing it as an air and naval base to interdict Axis supply lines to Africa, as in the halcyon days of November 1941. At the same time, Britain's reinforced desert army would drive for Tripoli and complete the conquest of Libya. This would resurrect plans to invade Sicily. At best, the War Cabinet envisioned the French in North Africa returning to the Allied cause, the fleet at Toulon sallying to join the Royal Navy, and Italy's political and military collapse. It foresaw the Mediterranean reopened to traffic, a million tons of shipping released, and the Royal Navy's commitments greatly diminished. By winning such a victory using its own resources, Britain would demonstrate that it was still a great power and able to stand alongside the United States and the Soviet Union: such a victory might sidetrack growing American insistence on a second front in France in 1942. On the other hand, Churchill and the War Cabinet realized that if the United States were obliged to play a large part in resolving Britain's Mediterranean conundrum, their partnership would no longer be one of equals and the United States would insist on an increased role in setting Allied strategy. There was more at stake in the mid-June convoys than simply the resupply of an isolated island.

2

MALTA AND THE
MEDITERRANEAN WAR TO 1942

What to do with the ice-cream vendors. Drown the
brutes is what I should like to do.

Alexander Cadogan, Diary 29 May 1940

PARALLEL WAR JUNE–DECEMBER 1940

When the Mediterranean conflict began on 10 June 1940, the Royal
Navy and French Marine Nationale confronted the Regia Marina with twelve
battleships and carriers against Italy's two battleships. They had twenty-seven
cruisers compared to Italy's twenty-one and a destroyer advantage of seventy-
four to fifty-two. The Allies planned to exploit their superiority by sweeping
Italian coastal waters and bombarding ports, hoping to provoke a fleet action
and stymie any move against Malta. Italy's high command, with a large superiority in submarines and torpedo boats, intended to wage a low-risk, high-
return "all out offensive" with these expendable light forces in cooperation
with air force bombers.[1]

The Italian plan accorded with the *rischio calcolato* (calculated risk) strategy
of naval warfare propounded by the Regia Marina's influential chief of staff
from the First World War, Grand Admiral Paolo Thaon di Revel. Every action
had to be considered in terms of the risk involved and the potential reward. Because Italy had a small industrial base compared to its foes and could not easily
replace losses, any great risk had to be balanced by an even greater reward. In
the beginning of the war, in the eyes of naval staff and the government, there
was no reward that would offset a risk to the battle fleet because the war would

conclude victoriously before the year's end. This point of view was encapsulated by the Italian ambassador in Berlin to the American chargé d'affaires on 27 June 1940. "[The ambassador] remarked . . . that Churchill thought that resistance could be prolonged over a period of months . . . but by virtue of his position as Ambassador of an Allied Power he had been given insight into German plans and preparations and he was convinced no such possibility existed."[2]

The German blitzkrieg on the Western Front forced the Allies to scale back their offensive against Italy to largely symbolic gestures. A pair of Royal Navy light cruisers shelled Tobruk. On 13 June two French heavy cruiser divisions bombarded targets outside Genoa, and French squadrons sortied into the Western Basin four times and the Aegean once. On 21 June the battleship *Lorraine* shelled Bardia. As for Italy's offensive, the Allies had already emptied the Mediterranean and Red seas of all merchant shipping, and Italy's aeronaval efforts were as ineffective as the initial Allied activities and more costly. The Regia Marina lost ten submarines through the end of June in the Mediterranean, Red Sea, and Indian Ocean and only sank a light cruiser, two tankers, and a freighter in return. The Regia Aeronautica lacked operational dive or torpedo-bomber units, and through July, in a series of high-level attacks, it significantly damaged only one British cruiser while inflicting minor or splinter damage on four battleships, two aircraft carriers, five cruisers, and ten destroyers. The air force gave lip service to a doctrine of strategic bombing, although it possessed no aircraft capable of such a mission, and its chief of staff refused to meet the navy's requirements for aerial reconnaissance.[3]

France signed an armistice on 22 June. The next day Churchill, in one of the war's crucial decisions, vetoed the Admiralty's recommendation to withdraw the battle fleet from the Mediterranean, and six days later London activated Force H at Gibraltar to partially fill the void left by the French fleet's departure.[4]

MALTA

Concurrent with the decision to maintain the fleet at Alexandria, the British War Cabinet ordered the Middle Eastern command to reinforce Malta so it could provide a base for offensive operations. At the time 5,500 troops in four British battalions and a Maltese territorial regiment garrisoned the island. There were one radar set, thirty-four heavy and eight light antiaircraft guns, and twenty-four searchlights. Twenty-six coastal artillery pieces ranging from

9.2-inch to modern 6-pdrs defended the coast. The island had three Swordfish, six operational Sea Gladiator fighters, and nine more Sea Gladiators in crates. The Royal Navy contingent included a monitor, a destroyer, a minesweeper, and six submarines. The island's storehouses held a six-month reserve of food for the population and troops, but ammunition stocks were considered low.[5]

Although Italian planners had weighed various schemes to capture Malta, the island's strong coastal defenses and its garrison rendered a *coup de main* risky considering that Italy's amphibious forces consisted of a marine brigade and five semi-specialized landing vessels. Given the short war Mussolini believed he was fighting, an improvised amphibious assault made little sense. Admiral Domenico Cavagnari, the Italian navy chief of staff since 1934, appreciated the British Empire's resilience better than the Duce or the Führer and strongly opposed such an adventure because it would tie the fleet's only two battleships to a specific location for days and expose them to attack from superior forces. Moreover, there seemed little need as the Regia Aeronautica asserted that bombers could neutralize the island. Although the decision to bomb rather than invade Malta has been roundly criticized and many sources characterize Malta as a plum ripe for the picking, the British chiefs of staff believed that the island's defenders could repel "one serious sea-borne assault."[6]

THE WAR CONTINUES

After France signed an armistice with the Axis powers, the disposition of its fleet became such a concern to London that the Royal Navy's newly established Force H attacked the French squadron, demobilizing at Mers el-Kébir on 3 July 1940. In this action the British destroyed one old French battleship and crippled another as well as the modern battleship *Dunkerque*. However, *Dunkerque*'s sister ship, *Strasbourg*, escaped to Toulon, defeating the attack's stated purpose because France retained a powerful fleet in being. British forces also attacked French ships in Great Britain and at Dakar in West Africa. At Alexandria the Mediterranean Fleet's commander, Admiral Cunningham, negotiated an arrangement with the French admiral to intern the battleship, four cruisers, three destroyers, and submarine stranded there.

The reason given for these attacks was to prevent the Axis from seizing French warships. However, "because of British access to French signals before the attack Churchill was aware that French warships were under orders to scuttle or to sail either to Martinique or the United States rather than be surrendered."[7] Nonetheless, the British prime minister felt bitterly betrayed by the French and put little stock in their assurances. Moreover, he wished to send a strong message to his enemies, allies, and potential allies that Great Britain was ruthlessly determined to continue fighting Germany. Mers el-Kébir instigated a cold war against the French that complicated British operations in the Mediterranean for the next two years and occasionally required the commitment of major forces.

London's first opportunity to win a significant victory and fracture Italy's presumably brittle morale occurred when an operation to evacuate shipping from Malta coincided with Italy's first large African convoy. The result was an inconclusive engagement off Calabria involving three of the Mediterranean Fleet's battleships and one carrier against two Italian battleships and a slew of cruisers. The Italians had also hoped to lure the British fleet into a position where it could be subjected to a mass aircraft attack. This happened, but the Regia Aeronautica's high-altitude bombers were ineffective, and worse, they delivered many of the strikes against friendly ships (again ineffectively). It would be months before the Italian air force developed the torpedo and dive-bombing capability needed to reliably attack warships under way.[8]

FIRST MALTA OPERATIONS

After deciding to hold Malta, the British chiefs of staff clearly stated their intentions in a directive dated 22 August: "it is hoped that the reinforcement of the A. A. defence of Malta and its re-occupation by the fleet will hamper the sending of further reinforcements—Italian or German—from Europe into Africa, and that an air offensive may ultimately be developed from Malta against Italy." On the same day Admiral Cunningham wrote to the Admiralty: "until there is greater protection Malta is of little use to us as a base, and its invaluable docking and repair facilities are lost to us." He saw the lack of anti-aircraft defense and proper shelters as being the greatest need and proposed "an energetic and coordinated action . . . to see that requirements are shipped with minimum of delay."[9]

In August Italy commissioned two modern battleships, *Littorio* and *Vittorio Veneto,* giving its battle line superiority over the Mediterranean Fleet. Although these ships were not completely operational until October, the British did not realize that. The Mediterranean Fleet conducted its first major Malta convoy operation, Operation Hats (MF2), at the end of August. This involved a carrier, two battleships, five cruisers, and sixteen destroyers to escort two transports and a fleet oiler from Alexandria to Valletta. On the other end of the

Middle Sea Force H, one carrier, one battle cruiser, one light cruiser, and thirteen destroyers accompanied to the Sicilian narrows reinforcements for the Mediterranean Fleet consisting of a modern carrier, a battleship, two antiaircraft cruisers, and four destroyers. *Ark Royal*'s Swordfish also raided airfields in Sardinia. The Admiralty considered sending four fast transports loaded with vital supplies for the army in Egypt through the Sicilian narrows with the reinforcing warships but concluded it was too dangerous. Instead the transports took the extra five weeks to circumnavigate Africa and reach Egypt via the Red Sea.

The transports sailed late on 29 August, and the fleet departed Alexandria early on the 30th. The Italians learned that British warships were at sea by midday on the 30th. Supermarina decided to let submarines and aircraft confront Force H while, on the morning of the 31st, the entire surface fleet, four battleships, thirteen cruisers, and thirty-nine destroyers sailed to counter the eastern thrust. Supermarina ordered the fleet to reverse course at the latitude of Cape Matapan if, by then, it had failed to contact the enemy.

As the Regia Marina marshaled its response, British cruisers entered the Aegean while the fleet's battleships advanced northwest up the Peloponnesian coast. These feints kept Supermarina guessing the enemy's intentions (it did not learn of the convoy until 1100 on the 31st), and the fleet's initial orders and its relatively northerly turn-about point were intended to repel an attack against the Italian coast, not intercept a convoy. Aerial reconnaissance was poor, and radar-directed carrier fighters shot down two of the lumbering Italian spotters.[10]

At noon on the 31st the British battle fleet abandoned its northwesterly course and turned south to close the convoy, which was heading due west nearly two hundred miles south along the 35th parallel. At 1815 Cunningham learned that Italian battleships were following a hundred miles in his wake. Although the report misidentified these warships as just two of the older *Cavour* class, he continued south, and the Italians never detected the enemy fleet. The Italians headed north during the night and swung south at dawn on 1 September, but the weather had deteriorated, and neither force sighted the other. Force F, the reinforcements from the west, passed through the Sicilian channel undetected. The convoy reached Valetta on the morning of 2 September while Force F entered Malta and then joined the Mediterranean Fleet south of the island. An air raid slightly damaged the Polish destroyer *Garland* on 31 August.

As Italy's first action against a Malta convoy, Operation Hats provides a baseline to measure how capabilities progressed over two years until the 1942 mid-June operations. The Italian response demonstrated three crucial short-

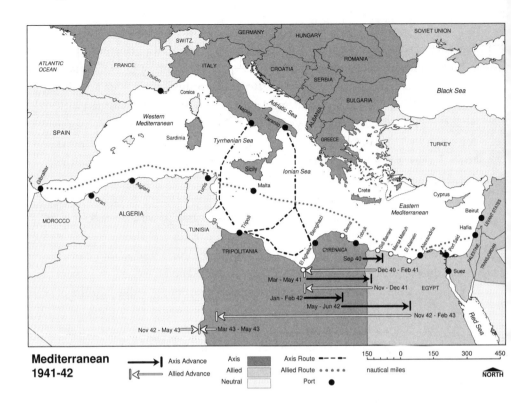

**Mediterranean
1941-42**

→| Axis Advance	
|←══ Allied Advance	

Axis

Allied

Neutral

Axis Route ‑‑ ‑‑

Allied Route ••••

Port ●

nautical miles

NORTH

comings. First, the Regia Aeronautica's attacks and reconnaissance were inadequate. High-level bombers damaged one freighter west of Crete with three bombs at 1205 on the 31st. Admiral Cunningham's report noted that "During 1 September no aircraft were seen at all." Admiral James Somerville, the commander of Force H, wrote that "during this operation the Force was in effective bombing range of Italian air bases for at least 48 hours." The Regia Aeronautica did unveil its first Ju 87–equipped dive-bombing squadron. They attacked the aircraft carrier *Eagle* and the warships that entered Malta to offload stores but failed to secure any hits. Although alerted to a British operation by signals intelligence, the Italians did not determine the mission of either the Mediterranean Fleet or Force H, and Supermarina waited until it had positive information—in other words too long—before it ordered the fleet to sea. Finally, in addition to a slow decision cycle and poor reconnaissance, the fleet's orders did not allow the commander afloat any flexibility. The cumulative effect was that Italy bungled a good opportunity to engage the British with superior forces.[11]

On 13 September five small Italian divisions advanced sixty miles into Egypt against scant opposition. At Sidi Barrani they halted to accumulate supplies and improve roads before continuing the eighty miles to Mersa Matruh, an advance originally scheduled for the end of September and then deferred to October and finally December.

On 8 October the four large transports that had sailed around the Cape of Good Hope rather than risk the narrows during Operations Hats arrived in Suez. They formed convoy MF3 and sailed for Malta the next day covered by four battleships and two aircraft carriers with cruiser and destroyer support. In this instance, Italian intelligence failed completely; the convoy was never sighted and, hence, never attacked. This operation was significant, however, because first three torpedo boats and later four destroyers patrolling east of Malta encountered the light cruiser *Ajax* scouting on the extreme wing of the British formation. In the resulting Action off Cape Passero fought on 12 October, *Ajax* sank two torpedo boats and crippled a destroyer. This defeat caused the Regia Marina's leadership to question its night-fighting doctrine and strategy for blockading the Sicilian narrows with torpedo craft.[12]

TARANTO AND THE THEOREM'S PROOF

On October 24, in an effort to expand his anti-British coalition, Hitler met with France's president, Marshal Pétain, at Montoire in central France. The British were understandably nervous that this meeting portended "[a betrayal of] warships and African and other Colonial harbours to Hitler." However, the outcome was far different. In fact, Pétain "left Hitler in no doubt as to his refusal to allow France to be drawn into a war with her former ally." Nonetheless, on 27 October Winston Churchill addressed a long letter to President Franklin Roosevelt setting forth his nation's intentions and asking for further aid. "We are endeavouring to assemble a very large army in the Middle East, and the movement of troops thither from all parts of the Empire, especially from the Mother country, has for some months past been unceasing. The campaign which will develop there . . . makes demands upon our shipping and munitions output and resources which are enormous and beyond our power without your help to supply to a degree which would ensure victory."[13]

The very next day greeted Churchill with the agreeable news that Italy had invaded Greece and thus that Great Britain, not Germany, had obtained a new ally. This aggression came over the objections of the Regia Marina's leadership, which correctly feared the British would immediately occupy Crete—a strategic location from which the Royal Navy could threaten Taranto and better protect Malta operations.

In November the Mediterranean Fleet ran convoy MW3 to Malta. This consisted of a tanker and four merchantmen escorted by four battleships, a carrier, cruisers, and destroyers. From the west additional reinforcements—a battleship, two cruisers, and three destroyers—slipped unseen past the four destroyers patrolling the 140-mile-wide Sicilian narrows. Supermarina received reports of British ships at sea but once again waited for concrete information on the enemy's location and intentions before responding; again, this came too late for the fleet to intervene. The submarine patrol lines also came up empty-handed. High-level bombing attacks delivered against Force H on 9 November near-missed *Ark Royal, Barham,* and a destroyer.

The Mediterranean Fleet launched an air raid against Taranto as it returned to Alexandria, again undetected, and Swordfish from the carrier *Illustrious* scored hits knocking *Littorio* out of the war for four months, *Duilio* for six, and *Cavour* for the duration. An Allied cruiser and destroyer force confirmed the Royal Navy's night-fighting effectiveness by annihilating a lightly escorted four-ship convoy in the lower Adriatic. As a consequence of the air raid, the Regia Marina withdrew its battleships to Naples while Taranto's defenses were improved. However, for all its success, the raid did not fracture Italian morale as the British War Cabinet had theorized such a victory would. It did not even give the British control of the central Mediterranean as demonstrated two weeks later during Operation Collar, the first Malta convoy from the west. This time reconnaissance was better, and the Italian fleet intervened with two battleships. The fleet fought a tactically inconclusive action with the British escort south of Sardinia in the Battle of Cape Spartivento that resulted in moderate damage to one British cruiser and heavy damage to an Italian destroyer. After the battle the Italian air force failed to damage the convoy in a series of high-level bombing attacks.

That night, after Force H had turned back for Gibraltar, the convoy and its close escort—three cruisers, five destroyers, and four corvettes—continued through the Sicilian narrows. This was another opportunity for Italy to test the effectiveness of using torpedo and MAS boats to guard the restricted passage. However, conditions were too rough for the MAS, and, although all four torpedo boats on patrol made contact separately, only one was able to launch two torpedoes, which missed, while the escort chased the others off.

The convoy's arrival constituted a clear British victory, but the battleship action served a purpose. It demonstrated that Italian capital ships remained a threat and thus that, despite the Taranto raid, convoys still required heavy protection. This helped offset the Royal Navy's growing conviction that the Italian air force was not a serious deterrent.

With the Italian battle fleet temporarily driven from Taranto, the Mediterranean Fleet conducted its largest Malta operation to date in convoys MW5A and 5B, which arrived at Malta on 20 December. There was no effective opposition, in part because eleven days earlier Imperial forces had attacked in Egypt and were in the process of routing Italy's 10th Army. By mid-February 1941, the British had advanced to the borders of Tripolitania. The conquest of Cyrenaica greatly improved London's position in the eastern Mediterranean—especially in conjunction with the occupation of Crete—because it extended the air coverage that could be afforded to convoys and denied the enemy bases from which they could attack.

During the first six months of the Mediterranean war the Regia Marina convoyed to Africa 331 freighters carrying 41,544 men with losses of 0.6 percent and 346,559 tons of supplies with losses of 2.2 percent. It had also kept the direct route from Gibraltar to Suez closed to British mercantile shipping—only one transport sailed directly from Gibraltar to Alexandria. Offsetting these accomplishments, the navy and air force had failed to hinder traffic to Malta. In the first months of the war the Royal Navy delivered twenty-six transports to the island in six convoys—suffering damage to only one vessel en route. They landed 160,000 tons of cargo, which raised stocks to a seven-month consumption level.[14]

British warships also landed substantial numbers of men and much equipment during Operation Hats, Operation MB5 (in September 1940), MW3, and Collar. These included six tanks, twenty-eight heavy and sixteen light anti-aircraft guns, a 25-pounder artillery battery, and more than five thousand army and RAF personnel. Submarines ferried in small quantities of supplies and a few passengers on three occasions. Six convoys returned in ballast from Malta to Egypt or Gibraltar. Italian efforts to block these movements, as well as shipping in the Aegean (thirteen convoys totaling fifty-nine merchant vessels not counting coastal traffic) and the Red Sea, proved unsuccessful.

The Taranto raid and the defeat of the 10th Army were the type of victories Churchill envisioned when he concentrated the British military against Italy in July 1940, but they did not lead to the political collapse London had optimistically anticipated.[15] Nor did the results validate the assumptions behind the War Cabinet's decision to make the Mediterranean the focus of Britain's war effort. Despite the Italian army's failures, the Regia Aeronautica's ineffectiveness at sea, and Rome's shortsighted policies (exemplified by the dispatch of 178 aircraft to participate in the Battle of Britain in August 1940 and the demobilization of 600,000 troops a month before the invasion of Greece), the strategic situation in January 1941 remained much the same as in July 1940. The Axis sea-lanes to Libya were open while Britain's route from Gibraltar to Alexandria was closed. This was the proof that Great Britain's Mediterranean victories had failed to secure sea control. The Royal Navy had failed to stop the reinforcement of Africa or Albania or even isolate the Dodecanese, much less drive Italy from the war. The impact of Malta's submarine and air forces in this campaign had been insignificant. As one author put it, "Malta's few submarines and Swordfish torpedo-bombers rarely sighted an enemy ship and scarcely knew where to look."[16] The Royal Navy had successfully supplied and reinforced Malta, but the effort engaged most of the Mediterranean Fleet's and Force H's resources.

Up to the end of 1940 British submarines operating in the Mediterranean accounted for four warships and fourteen commercial vessels. In return, Italian antisubmarine forces and mines sank nine British, two French, and one Greek boat. On 1 January there were twenty Hurricanes on Malta in 261 Squadron, twenty Wellington ICs in 148 Squadron, twelve FAA Swordfish torpedo-bombers in 830 Squadron, and six RAF Sunderlands and one Glenn Martin for reconnaissance. Opposing them in Sicily were 63 Regia Aeronautica and 141 Luftwaffe aircraft.[17]

GERMAN INTERVENTION JANUARY–JULY 1941

Many histories consider the Mediterranean situation as it existed in January 1941 and conclude that German intervention rescued Italy from defeat. The Germans themselves believed this most of all. As early as 14 November 1940 Raeder was complaining to Hitler that "The Italian armed forces have neither the leadership nor the military efficiency to carry the required operations in the Mediterranean area to a successful conclusion." However, while Germany deployed air units in Sicily in December 1940 and prepared to dispatch two divisions to North Africa (divisions which had been offered before the Egyptian and Grecian disasters), Germany still considered the Mediterranean a backwater.[18]

Fliegerkorp X's deployment to Sicily coincided with Great Britain's first serious attempt to break the Italian blockade by passing four transports from Gibraltar all the way to Greece. Called "Excess," this complicated operation included the passage of three transports to Malta, one from the west and two from the east, and the return of eight freighters from Malta to Alexandria. After an air attack on Naples, the Italian fleet had only one operational battleship, not enough to face the five capital ships and three carriers Force H and the Mediterranean Fleet collectively mustered. Two torpedo boats disputed the passage of the Sicilian narrows, but were easily defeated by the much stronger escort at the cost of one torpedo boat sunk.

Meanwhile, the Regia Aeronautica was assembling dive and torpedo-bomber squadrons. After a domestically produced dive bomber, the S.85, repeatedly proved unable to put bombs on target, Italy purchased a hundred new Ju 87s from Germany. Experiments with torpedo-armed S.79 tri-motored bombers from July 1940 proved encouraging, and between September and December 1940 the first operational torpedo-bomber units damaged three British cruisers. However, these squadrons were at a premium during the war's early months and still working up.[19]

Excess succeeded in delivering the merchant ships to their destinations; the intervention of Fliegerkorp X, however, guaranteed that the blockade remained in force when German aircraft sank a light cruiser and severely damaged the carrier *Illustrious* off Pantelleria. Malta proved a providential refuge for the carrier. The island's defenses defeated repeated German attacks while the dockyards patched *Illustrious* enough to make a break for Alexandria. Nonetheless Malta was still limited as an offensive base despite the largely unhindered arrival of six convoys.

In February Force H bombarded Genoa harbor. Because of heavy fog and misdirection by Supermarina, a superior Italian force, under the battle fleet's new commander, Division Admiral Angelo Iachino, missed a good chance to intercept an inferior British squadron.

Admiral Iachino played a dominant role in Italy's fleet actions through Operation Vigorous in June 1942. Born on 24 April 1889 in San Remo he graduated from the Italian Naval Academy in 1908 as a gunnery specialist. He commanded a torpedo boat in the Adriatic during World War I and was naval attaché to Great Britain from 1931 to 1934. In 1936 Iachino commanded Italian naval forces in Spain. In June 1940 he led the 2nd Fleet and was second in command to Admiral Inigo Campioni at the Battle of Cape Spartivento. On 9 December 1940 Mussolini named Iachino, considered a rising star and a superb tactician as well as a strict disciplinarian who did not tolerate independent subordinates, to replace Campioni as battle fleet (1st Fleet) commander. In this capacity, Iachino led the Italian battleships in all of their major sorties, earning a reputation for caution and hard luck. The Battle of Cape Matapan stood as his greatest failure. Discounting evidence that the British fleet was tailing his damaged flagship, *Vittorio Veneto,* he ordered a pair of heavy cruisers to backtrack and tow their squadron mate to safety over the protests of their commander. British battleships subsequently sank all three cruisers. History has been hard in its evaluations of his handling of the fleet during Operation Halberd in September 1941 and two battles of Sirte on 17 December 1941 and 22 March 1942. He was finally relieved of his command in April 1943.[20]

In February 1941 Athens consented to receive British troops on the mainland, so London decided to ship the best formations fighting in North Africa to Greece. The Mediterranean Fleet's War Diary commented, "The move to Greece so completely absorbed all resources . . . that any question of considered offensive action against the enemy had to be ruled aside." Moreover, it came at a time when air-dropped mines were blocking the Suez Canal. During February and March German aircraft operating from Rhodes closed the canal with magnetic or acoustic mines, either wholly or in part, for thirty-six days. By the end of March 110 ships were logjammed at Suez waiting to head north. February was the first month since August 1940 that Great Britain did not conduct a Malta operation.[21]

The timing of the Grecian diversion was unfortunate because the first convoy carrying German troops to Africa sailed on 8 February. Others followed on 12 and 24 February and 1, 3, 8, 9, and 12 March. On 1 February there were thirteen operational British submarines in the Mediterranean of which seven were Malta-based. From this traffic Allied submarines sank just two merchant ships and the light cruiser *Diaz* and damaged several others. One problem was a shortage of torpedoes. Ordered to economize, submarines often fired just one torpedo against a target. The RAF bombers flying from Malta concentrated on raiding enemy ports, and only an FAA Swordfish squadron went after shipping. The Axis air forces on Sicily began hitting Malta more frequently and with greater force. From August through December 1940 the Regia Aeronautica dropped an average of nearly seventy tons of ordnance a month, and Malta experienced an average of twenty-one air alerts a month. From January 1941 though May 1941 alerts increased to an average of ninety-two. The Luftwaffe averaged 280 tons of bombs a month while the Italians contributed another fifty. This harassment stressed Malta's defenses. In the ten weeks from 16 January to 31 March 1941 heavy batteries fired 21,176 and the light batteries 18,660 AA rounds. They claimed the destruction of forty-six Axis aircraft. From the war's beginning to 15 January 1941 these totals were 9,546 and 1,078 rounds, respectively. Such expenditures rapidly depleted reserves.[22]

GREECE AND MATAPAN

The next Malta convoy, MW6, consisted of four merchantmen. Even though the transports in Operation Excess had passed the Sicilian narrows safely, these vessels were loaded in Great Britain and circumnavigated Africa to reach Suez. They departed Alexandria on 19 March supported by the entire Mediterranean Fleet: three battleships, a carrier, nine cruisers, and twenty destroyers. Once again Italian (and German) reconnaissance failed to detect this movement, and the convoy arrived safely. However, air attacks damaged two of the vessels in port and destroyed some supplies.

Under heavy German pressure to use the fleet offensively against British traffic to Greece, Admiral Iachino sailed on 26 March with *Vittorio Veneto*, three cruiser divisions, and four destroyer squadrons on a mission into the waters south of Crete. The British, who had received hints of an operation from decrypts of Luftwaffe Enigma encoded radio traffic, dispatched three battleships and a carrier to intercept what they suspected might be a convoy bound for Rhodes or an offensive strike against their own traffic.

The Italians flirted with success. Radio intercepts alerted Iachino to the presence of an enemy force south of Crete, allowing him to surprise a British cruiser squadron; but after carrier torpedo-bombers attacked his battleship during the ensuing battle, Iachino turned for home. After four unsuccessful air strikes, an aerial torpedo slowed *Vittorio Veneto* down. Three more unsuccessful strikes followed before the ninth attack, delivered just after dark, immobilized the heavy cruiser *Pola*. Two hours later the Mediterranean Fleet's battleships had just discovered *Pola* when two more cruisers from the same division, returning to tow *Pola* to safety, blundered into the British battle line. In a short and violent melee the Italians lost all three cruisers and two destroyers. This action was named the Battle of Cape Matapan. The British ability to make contact at night, and decrypted messages indicating the existence of radar, spurred Italian interest in this technology, and the fleet's suffering of an entire day of air attacks with no support from land-based fighters finally convinced Mussolini that the navy needed an aircraft carrier. Admiral Iachino wrote, "Supermarina ordered . . . that our battle fleet was not to venture outside land fighter range and was to avoid night battles until it was also equipped with radar."[23] However, Matapan had little impact on the traffic war, and Italian convoys departed for Africa on 1, 2, 8, 9, and 10 April, losing only one merchantman from these sailings.

Events on land greatly influenced naval operations over the next several months. A German mission had determined that only motorized forces were useful in North Africa and that to ensure success, "nothing less than four armoured divisions would suffice," and, more importantly, that this was the maximum that could be effectively supplied in an advance across the desert.[24] The High Command designated General Erwin Rommel to command a German expeditionary force of one light and one armored division and gave him the mission of defending Tripoli. By the end of February most of the 5th Light Division had arrived. On 24 March the division's reconnaissance battalion easily penetrated the forward British positions, and General Rommel decided to exploit this success. By 11 April the German division along with an Italian armored division and elements of two infantry divisions had isolated Tobruk and reached the Egyptian border. Then Germany invaded Yugoslavia and Greece on 6 April, forcing those countries to sue for armistices on 17 and 23 April, respectively. These events forced the Royal Navy to evacuate the expeditionary force it had just transported to Greece.

After Luftwaffe Enigma disclosed that elements of the 15th Panzer Division were scheduled to sail for Libya in April, Admiral Cunningham dispatched a destroyer flotilla to Malta. A few hours after midnight on 16 April this flotilla intercepted a five-ship convoy escorted by three Regia Marina destroyers. The British sank every transport and two of the escorts, losing one destroyer in exchange. The Italian command regarded this event as an unfortunate anomaly based on lucky air reconnaissance. Meanwhile, staggered by its Balkan and North African defeats, London considered desperate measures to dam the flow of enemy supplies reaching Africa. Churchill, via the First Sea Lord, ordered the Mediterranean Fleet to scuttle *Barham* and an old cruiser to block the port of Tripoli. Cunningham refused and instead bombarded the city in conjunction with Operation MD2, which involved dispatching the naval auxiliary tanker *Breconshire* to Malta and evacuating an empty freighter. These ships reached their destinations unmolested while the bombardment occurred on 21 April. It sank two empty freighters and damaged some docks although a convoy of four steamers that had arrived the day before finished unloading that afternoon.

At the beginning of May the British conducted major Mediterranean operations simultaneously from the east and west: MD4 and Tiger. MD4 included a fast convoy with four transports (MW.7A) and a slow convoy of two tankers (MW.7B). They cleared Alexandria by 6 May with the entire Mediterranean Fleet either in direct escort or as distant cover. *Breconshire* and the fast minelayer *Abdiel,* both loaded with fuel and stores, accompanied the fleet. A sandstorm covered the convoy the first day out of Alexandria followed by occasional rain and poor visibility. This hampered Axis reconnaissance, and no attacks against MW.7 developed. Once again Supermarina determined British intentions too late to dispatch the fleet. After a strenuous effort to clear German air-dropped mines that had closed Grand Harbour, the convoy arrived safely at Malta on 9 May with 24,000 tons of oils and 40,000 tons of general cargo.

Tiger, the western operation, was the second large-scale effort to pass transports directly through the Mediterranean and was conducted on Churchill's determination "not to be governed by Admiralty reluctance" and to rush tank and aircraft reinforcements directly to Egypt. Force H, along with *Queen Elizabeth* and two cruisers being sent to reinforce the Mediterranean Fleet, escorted the convoy of five fast transports to the Sicilian narrows. Although thick cloud cover and poor reconnaissance diminished their response, the Regia Aeronautica's Sardinian air command launched high-level, torpedo, and dive-bombing strikes on the third day. Admiral Somerville reported, "the scale of attack was very much less than had been anticipated." Nonetheless, there were a few close calls: Somerville observed one torpedo end its run just yards short of *Renown* while *Ark Royal,* already in a turn, barely managed to comb a pair of torpedoes dropped from two hundred yards.[25]

After Force H turned back at the entrance to the Sicilian narrows, the convoy, the reinforcements, and a cruiser/destroyer escort transited the straits at night, losing one freighter to mines and suffering damage to another. *Queen Elizabeth* barely avoided an air-launched torpedo. Supermarina misjudged British intentions and dispatched a cruiser division to forestall an anticipated night bombardment of Palermo. After these adventures, the Tiger Convoy met the Mediterranean Fleet south of Malta and reached Alexandria on 12 May. Churchill proclaimed this operation a "brilliant success," but the British did not attempt another trans-Mediterranean convoy until May 1943.[26]

Following Tiger, the ground war continued to set the naval war's tempo. London had ordered strong forces to hold Crete. Signals intelligence, mainly from Luftwaffe Enigma, disclosed full details of the forthcoming German attack. The British command calculated that paratroopers alone could not capture such a strongly held objective and that the Royal Navy could shield the island from sea attack. This assessment proved half right. Although cruiser/destroyer squadrons forced one small-craft convoy to turn back and decimated another, German paratroopers captured the island anyway. Another evacuation conducted under enemy-dominated skies followed. The Royal Navy lost three cruisers (Gloucester, Fiji, and Calcutta) and six destroyers (Juno, Greyhound, Kashmir, Kelly, Imperial, and Herward) and suffered damage to three battleships (Warspite, Valiant, and Barham), the carrier Formidable, six cruisers (Ajax, Carlisle, Naiad, Dido, Orion, and Perth), and three destroyers (Nubian, Kelvin, and Napier)—mostly to German air attacks. With these losses and the Axis advance into Egypt, the pendulum in the eastern Mediterranean swung sharply against the Allies, and Malta convoys from Egypt had to run a gauntlet of enemy air bases to the north and south for the majority of their passage.

The Cretan fiasco crippled the Mediterranean Fleet, and on 2 June 1941 Admiral Cunningham advised the Admiralty that "the supplying of Malta from Egypt by convoy was impracticable at the moment." He suggested that submarines and blockade runners shuttle materiel in and that Force H take up some of the slack. In April through June 1941 Force H focused on reinforcing the island's fighter squadrons conducting fly-off operations on 3 and 27 April; 21 May; and 6, 14, 27, and 30 June. These delivered 224 Hurricanes, 93 percent of the number dispatched. Many of the Mark I Hurricanes delivered continued on to Egypt while Malta retained the Mark II models. Despite these reinforcements the Vice Admiral Malta, Rear Admiral W. Ford complained to Churchill on 16 May that "I am getting extremely perturbed with the state of our air defences." He further stated that the enemy were becoming "bolder every day" and had gained complete air superiority.[27]

During May and June 1941 sixty Axis transports arrived in Africa, and just one was lost in route. The Regia Marina had exhausted much of its fuel reserves, and Supermarina was becoming increasingly selective about how it used its large warships, although at this point, it faced little opposition from the Mediterranean Fleet. A British destroyer flotilla kept the besieged port of Tobruk supplied while the Imperial invasion of Syria engaged significant naval assets to counter a French flotilla based there.

In the first half of 1941 five convoys totaling fourteen cargo vessels arrived at Malta without loss. One unescorted merchantman sailed for Malta on 29 April but was mined en route. Warships transported 2,300 men and materiel to the island in five operations. Submarines made twelve supply runs in May and June.

With respect to the war against Axis traffic to North Africa, Allied forces sank thirty-seven transports, displacing 118,592 tons in the six months ending June 1941. Submarines accounted for slightly more than half. On 1 June 1941 there were eight submarines based at Malta, seven at Gibraltar, and fourteen at Alexandria. Aircraft sank four. The April *Tarigo* convoy action represented nearly ten percent of the total Axis losses. Considering all sinkings and not just those involving North African traffic, Malta-based forces accounted for twenty-five ships. Submarines sank fifteen of these vessels, surface warships six, and aircraft three, and a combined attack by submarine and air accounted for the last.[28]

In the January–June period the Italians dispatched 529,957 tons of materiel to North Africa, including fuel, vehicles, ammunition, and general cargo of which 496,899 tons or 93 percent arrived.[29] Despite the narrow waters, the obvious destinations, and the strong forces employed, as the Mediterranean war completed its first year each side was still unable to stop the other's traffic.

STRATEGIC ASSUMPTIONS

In September 1940 the British War Cabinet made several strategic assumptions to justify their decision to reinforce the Middle East, retain Malta, and build up the island as an offensive base. It assumed that a blockade of Europe could, by the winter of 1941, degrade Germany's morale and ability to wage war; that the British position in the Middle East and the ability to interdict shipments of oil from Romania to Italy in the Eastern Mediterranean were critical to the success of said blockade; and, finally, that significant military victories over Italy would destroy Italian morale and further weaken Germany.

By June 1941 it was clear to the War Cabinet that its original assumptions regarding economic warfare and the entire rationale of its Middle Eastern and

Malta policy were invalid. In an assessment of the strategic situation made that month, the Cabinet acknowledged that while withdrawal from Egypt could open the Eastern Mediterranean to Axis control, such a withdrawal "would not be catastrophic, so long as Abadan itself could be protected and naval control preserved in the Red Sea and the Persian Gulf." Moreover, from the "military points of view it would come as an immense relief to abandon the Middle East and re-deploy naval forces and shipping, to say nothing of troops and aircraft, which were urgently needed elsewhere." Not only were the sheer distances in-volved tying up shipping tonnage Great Britain could ill afford to lose, but the inefficiencies that greeted the ships once they arrived in theater were stagger-ing. In May 1941 cargo ships were being unloaded at Suez at the rate of one ev-ery two days while 117 vessels waited in queue for their turn.[30]

Nonetheless, despite the military and logistical advantages of withdrawal, the Cabinet resolved to continue its goal of conducting offensive warfare from Egypt and to further reinforce Malta. "Since wars cannot be won without fight-ing, the only course was to continue, even though it might be at a disadvan-tage or in vain." To this end, men and supplies had been rushed into Egypt in the Tiger and several WS convoys in preparation for an offensive code-named Battleaxe that was designed to relieve Tobruk and reconquer Cyrenaica.[31]

CONVOY WAR JULY–DECEMBER 1941

In June Germany withdrew its air corps from Sicily, and on the 22nd its forces invaded the Soviet Union. Then, on 23 June the British broke, for the first time, C 38m, the mechanical cipher system used by the Italian navy since December 1940 for administrative purposes. During the second half of 1941 re-inforcements of submarines and aircraft increased Malta's offensive capabili-ties, and surface warships returned to the island in October. These forces en-joyed an important advantage because, according to the official British history, "it was as a result of its reading of the C 38m that [Britain] was able from July 1941 to give . . . advance notice of virtually every convoy and important indepen-dent ship that sailed with troops or supplies across the Mediterranean. . . ."[32]

The Mediterranean Fleet had suffered greatly evacuating the army from Greece and Crete, and during the second half of the year it was reduced to three missions: supporting the army in the Western Desert, maintaining the Tobruk garrison, and attacking the Italy–Libya sea-route. As for the Italians, their fuel reserves were nearly exhausted; reverses like Matapan had demonstrated the enemy's superiority in radar and night-fighting ability, and cooperation between the navy and air force remained inexcusably poor. Germany's attack on the Soviet Union had gifted London a new and powerful ally while eliminating Italy's most promising future source of oil. After one year a resolution to Mussolini's brief and victorious war was receding into an uncertain future.

Although pleased to have the Soviet Union on their side, British planners believed that Moscow would fall and that the Germans would advance into Turkey and then Iraq as early as November 1941. This worry, as well as the failure of the June Battleaxe offensive to relieve Tobruk, made Churchill eager for a renewed desert thrust. "To this end, [Churchill] poured reinforcements into Egypt and brushed aside his military's advisers' reminders about the longstanding decision that the defence of the Far East, and particularly of Singapore, was the second priority after the defence of Britain itself, and before the Middle East." He relieved his Middle East commander in chief, General Archibald Wavell, and replaced him with General Claude Auchinleck. However, the shipping losses suffered in the North Atlantic and elsewhere had rendered London's effort to sustain its Middle Eastern position all the more difficult. For example, "In order to send two divisions from the United Kingdom to the Middle East the Prime Minister had had to beg transport from [President Roosevelt] in September 1941 . . ." The magnitude of British requests provoked one American admiral to warn: "If we do not watch our step, we shall find the White House en route to England with the Washington Monument as a steering oar." Nonetheless, by November 1.6 million deadweight tons of American shipping was committed to British routes, mainly to the Middle East.[33]

During the summer of 1941 Malta-based submarines and bombers began to inflict increasing losses on Axis convoys. By 1 July the torpedo shortage was over, and there were sixteen submarines at sea in the Mediterranean. During July British submarines operating from all bases expended sixty-nine torpedoes in forty-one attacks. Greek and Dutch boats made two attacks each. Allied submarines sank seven ships of 19,618 tons and one Italian submarine at the cost of two of their own. Aircraft dispatched four vessels, displacing 19,467 tons. Malta-based submarines and aircraft accounted for six of these vessels.[34]

Starting on 21 July Force H, reinforced by Home Fleet units to the strength of a carrier, two capital ships, four cruisers, and seventeen destroyers, conducted Operation Substance, which involved escorting six transports to Malta (a seventh vessel, a troopship, ran aground and had to drop out) while six empty transports and *Breconshire* were to break out for Gibraltar. Concerned by the possibility of an airborne attack on the island, the reinforcements included two infantry battalions, field artillery, and two antiaircraft units.

Once again, Supermarina misjudged the situation, believing that Force H was conducting a fly-off mission to Malta. When headquarters realized it was dealing with a convoy, the British were already north of Bône and it was too late for the battle fleet to intervene. However, in conjunction with a high-level bombing attack, six Italian S.79s torpedoed the light cruiser *Manchester* and the destroyer *Fearless*, which later sank. *Ark Royal*'s Fulmars and then long-range Beaufighters from Malta contested subsequent air raids, but an Italian high-level attack disabled the destroyer *Firedrake*. Three cruisers and eight destroyers, commanded by Rear Admiral E. N. Syfret, then shepherded the merchantmen through the Sicilian narrows. Syfret skirted Pantelleria to the north rather than following the obvious route along the African shore. During this passage Italian MAS boats attacked and torpedoed the large transport *Sydney Star*, which nonetheless made Malta independently. This was the first success obtained by Italy's small motor torpedo boats in the Mediterranean and the first casualty inflicted by torpedo craft in the Sicilian narrows.[35]

All six transports arrived at Malta on 24 July. The empties likewise escaped to Gibraltar with one vessel damaged in an air attack. Italy tried to offset its failure by sending X MAS commandos to attack the transports before they could unload. However, radar exposed the raiders' approach, and they suffered a stinging defeat.

Following Substance, Malta's garrison stood at 22,297 men and 112 heavy and 118 light antiaircraft guns. There was an eight-month stock of military supplies, and civilian supplies were expected to last seven and a half months.[36]

On 22 August Force H sortied to support the minelayer *Manxman* in sowing a field off Livorno and to launch an air strike against Sardinia. This time, expecting another Malta convoy, Supermarina ordered the fleet to sea early. Italian aircraft failed to catch Force H's turn to the north, and the British accomplished their objectives while the frustrated Italians burned precious fuel south of Sardinia searching for the enemy.

In August British submarines expended sixty-two torpedoes in twenty-seven attacks, and Dutch boats made seven attacks. Allied submarines sank six ships of 24,830 tons, two of which were carrying supplies to North Africa. Aircraft dispatched five Axis vessels of 20,365 tons, four of which were involved in African traffic. Malta-based submarines and aircraft accounted for eight of these vessels.[37]

After the success of Operation Substance London decided to mount another large Malta convoy from the west. On 24 September eight transports and *Breconshire* departed Gibraltar in Operation Halberd. Force H, reinforced by the Home Fleet to a strength of three battleships, *Prince of Wales, Rodney,* and *Nelson;* the aircraft carrier *Ark Royal;* five cruisers, *Sheffield, Euryalus, Kenya, Edinburgh,* and *Hermione;* and eighteen destroyers, covered the convoy.

Churchill still wanted a decisive fleet action, and so did Mussolini. The Duce and Comando Supremo had decided in May 1941 to spend much of Italy's remaining oil reserves at the first good opportunity to seek a strategic victory in the Western Mediterranean by coordinating a fleet action with strong air strikes. Italian intelligence learned of Force H's departure on the 25th and then sighted the convoy on the 26th south of the Balearic Islands. The Italian fleet, commanded by Admiral Iachino, sailed with the two modern battleships, *Littorio* and *Vittorio Veneto;* the heavy cruisers *Trento, Trieste,* and *Gorizia;* the light cruisers *Abruzzi* and *Attendolo;* and fourteen destroyers. The three older battleships would have provided a decisive superiority, but lack of fuel kept them in port, and in any case, the Italians expected to face no more than two battleships.

Once the fleet was at sea, Italian reconnaissance again broke down. Iachino did not receive reports of the British location and strength, although an S.79 torpedoed *Nelson* south of Sardinia shortly after noon. When some information did trickle in, it erroneously implied that three enemy battleships were only forty miles to the southwest. Given the poor visibility in that direction, Iachino believed that the British were setting a trap and that his force was in danger of being suddenly bracketed by 16-inch salvos before he even had the enemy in view. Unaware of *Nelson's* predicament, the Italians turned away. Iachino wrote, "in such conditions of visibility, without air protection, and given the probable superiority of the enemy force, to engage in combat would have been an error on my part."[38]

Replicating the pattern of Substance, the main fleet turned back at the Sicilian narrows while the convoy, accompanied by three cruisers and nine destroyers, took the northern route through the strait. Before dark torpedo-bombers attacked again and sank one of the transports. The torpedo boat squadron patrolling in the narrows did not sight the enemy, and the convoy arrived on 28 September. Halberd delivered fifty thousand tons of supplies and armaments and ensured stocks through May 1942.[39] As soon as the escort made Gibraltar, most of the ships returned to the Home Fleet as quickly as possible, being needed on the Arctic convoy route. By the end of September ten infantry battalions and seventy-five Hurricanes garrisoned Malta.

At the beginning of September eight Allied submarines were on patrol in the Mediterranean. During the month British, Dutch, and Greek boats made twenty-four, seven, and one attack, respectively. The British boats fired ninety torpedoes. Collectively the Allied boats achieved one of their best months, accounting for ten ships of 63,008 tons, four of which were Africa-bound including the 19,000-ton liners *Neptunia* and *Oceania*. Aircraft dispatched five merchant vessels displacing 22,847 tons, including four engaged in African traffic. Malta-based agents accounted for nine of these vessels.[40]

In September German submarines entered the Mediterranean following complaints by General Rommel that the Italians "were not concentrating their forces on protecting the supply shipments to North Africa." Admiral Karl Dönitz, Commander in Chief U-Boats, strongly protested that this deployment diluted Germany's Atlantic traffic war for the sake of a secondary theater. These commanders had different priorities, and their complaints, in part, served to explain the lack of success achieved by their pet strategies.[41]

THE BLOCKADE OF TRIPOLI

Halberd delivered sufficient fuel and ammunition for Malta to supply the forces required to seriously impact Axis traffic. This facilitated preparations for the next ground offensive, code-named Crusader. In Churchill's eyes Crusader would not just relieve Tobruk but would lead "as a matter of course, to Tripolitania, and if possible to French North Africa or even Sicily." Rommel, meanwhile, was preparing his own strike against Tobruk and Egypt.[42]

On 1 October there were thirty British, Dutch, Polish, and Greek submarines in the Middle Sea. Twelve boats operated from Malta. During the month British submarines fired ninety-four torpedoes and made thirty-four attacks. The Polish unit *Sokol* attacked four times and the Dutch *O 21* and *24* once. Throughout the Mediterranean and excluding neutral vessels, Allied boats sank five ships of 18,109 tons, including one carrying supplies to North Africa. Aircraft dispatched another seven vessels, displacing 33,800 tons, of which five were in transit to or from Africa. Malta-based forces accounted for ten of the twelve vessels lost.[43]

By late summer 1941 Churchill was pushing admirals Pound and Cunningham to base a surface force at Malta. Decrypts of C 38m and Luftwaffe Enigma kept the Prime Minister informed of arrivals in North Africa. The docking of one tanker prompted him to minute Pound, "Please ask specifically what if anything [Cunningham] is going to do. We are still at war." The admirals questioned the value of such a force. Cunningham felt that he lacked enough destroyers and cruisers to risk any in Malta, and Pound doubted that they could achieve enough to justify their probable loss. However, Churchill continued to insist. On September 13 he sarcastically responded to Cunningham's assessment of the situation by asking, "All this looks rather gloomy . . . Will it not make [Cunningham] curl up? . . . [He] has not done any fighting since Crete." After Halberd, Pound finally decided "with great reluctance" to meet Churchill's demands because "should Crusader fail, which I sincerely hope it will not, then I think there would have been lasting criticism because we had not made any attempt to cut the communications to Africa by surface forces."[44]

On 21 October two small cruisers from the Home Fleet and two destroyers from Force H arrived at Valletta and formed Force K, the first Malta-based surface strike force since May 1941. On 18 October Force H flew off to Malta two Swordfish and eleven Albacores fitted with auxiliary tanks to give them extended range. To supplement their decryption successes, the British based additional reconnaissance and photographic aircraft at Malta to scout convoy routes and confirm signals intelligence, which was necessary for reasons of security and also because the Regia Marina often changed departure times or routes after they had been communicated.[45]

In October Italy dispatched ten convoys totaling thirty vessels to Africa from Italian ports, but only twenty arrived. The three largest contained six ships each and sailed from Naples on October 2, 8, and 16, respectively. C 38m decrypts disclosed the sailing and route of the last two, but aircraft sighted all three convoys, permitting Malta-based torpedo-bombers to attack every one. Aircraft sank four merchantmen; a submarine accounted for a fifth and damaged another, although it arrived. One freighter turned back, and one broke down. Thus, only eleven of the eighteen ships in these convoys reached Africa.

Six of eight vessels that sailed for Benghazi made port, as did three of four from Trapani to Tripoli. Seventeen merchantmen returned to Italy from Africa of the eighteen that sailed, with one damaged in an air attack. A heavy coastal traffic between Tripoli and Benghazi saw all twenty-eight ships that sailed reach their destination with one damaged by air attack.[46]

The Axis powers made strenuous efforts to restore the situation. On 29 October, after he learned that surface ships had returned to Malta, Hitler ordered twenty-one more submarines and the Luftwaffe's II Fliegerkorps to the Mediterranean.The German 3rd S-Boat Flotilla deployed to Sicily to assist in the blockade of Malta. The Führer also appointed Field Marshal Albert Kesselring as commander in chief, Southern Area (Oberbefehlshaber Süd), under Comando Supremo. Kesselring's mission was to suppress Malta and "achieve air and sea mastery in the area between Southern Italy and North Africa and thus ensure safe lines of communications with Libya and Cyrenaica." The number of Axis air raid alerts on Malta jumped from 76 in November to 169 in December.[47]

Nonetheless, in November, the Axis situation took a dramatic turn for the worse. Nineteen convoys totaling thirty-eight vessels departed Italian and Greek ports for Africa. Only fourteen ships arrived. On the critical Naples to Tripoli route, thirteen vessels set out but not one reached its destination. The Royal Navy obtained its greatest anticonvoy success of the war when Force K, relying on signals intelligence, intercepted the seven-ship-strong Beta Convoy on 9 November. In a brilliant action fought at night, the British warships, light cruisers *Aurora* and *Penelope* and destroyers *Lance* and *Lively,* sank the entire convoy and one of the escorting destroyers despite the distant escort of two heavy cruisers and four destroyers and the close escort of six destroyers.[48]

A slight offset came several days later. On 10 November Force H put to sea and delivered thirty-four of thirty-seven Hurricanes to Malta. While returning from this mission *U 81* scored the Kriegsmarine's first major Mediterranean success by torpedoing *Ark Royal.* The carrier foundered on 14 November twenty-nine miles east of Gibraltar. A board of inquiry attributed the loss to inefficient damage control.[49]

CRUSADER

The British Middle East command finally launched its long-delayed and meticulously prepared Crusader offensive on 18 November, preempting by three days the Axis blow against Tobruk. London held such high expectations for Crusader that on 18 October the chiefs of staff advised Cairo that they planned to exploit the victory and the resultant collapse in Italian morale by invading Sicily in December with four divisions from the United Kingdom.[50]

Crusader disappointed, however. Instead of a lightning blow, it degenerated into a back-and-forth slugfest that burned through painstakingly stockpiled fuel and ammunition on both sides. At sea, Axis losses continued to mount. Force K destroyed the two-ship *Maritza* Convoy on 24 November, and on 1 December it eliminated the tanker *Mantovani* and its escorting destroyer. In balance, a German submarine torpedoed and sank the battleship *Barham* on 25 November.

In November Force K sank nine Axis merchantmen, displacing 44,539 tons. Aircraft dispatched another five, totaling 10,609 tons, of which three were Africa-bound. Allied submarines sank a destroyer, a submarine, and five merchant vessels, displacing 14,380 tons, including one in transit to Africa, in twenty-one attacks using sixty-four torpedoes. Dutch boats executed seven of these attacks, Polish three, and Greek three. All nine Axis merchantmen returning to Italy from Africa arrived safely, as did thirty of the thirty-one vessels plying the coastal route. Malta-based warships, submarines, and aircraft accounted for fourteen of the nineteen merchantmen lost.[51]

In December the Regia Marina effectively abandoned the Naples route as it desperately tried expedients to fight supplies through to Africa, including the use of warships to carry gasoline and ammunition and the formation of small convoys or solitary sailings from minor ports like Trapani and Palermo. The Admiralty, meanwhile, was so pleased with Force K's depredations that it sent two more cruisers to Malta and planned another operation to bring the fuel oil and ammunition these extra warships required.

On 9 December the submarine *Porpoise* defeated December's first sailing from Africa by evading an escort of two destroyers and a torpedo boat and torpedoing the motorship *Sebastiano Venier* (6,311 GRT) in transit from Benghazi to Taranto with two thousand prisoners of war. Two days later *Talisman* sank the motorship *Calitea* (4,013 GRT) en route from Benghazi to Brindisi.

December's next African convoy operation, four motorships and two tankers, sailed from Taranto and Argostoli on 13 December. Twelve destroyers escorted the convoy while three battleships, five cruisers, and twelve destroyers provided distant support. However, in a submarine ambush off Taranto, *Urge* damaged *Vittorio Veneto* and *Upright* sank two of the large motorships, forcing Supermarina to abort the operation. Concurrently, two light cruisers, *Alberico da Barbiano* and *Alberto di Giussano,* loaded with aviation fuel headed for Tripoli. In the Battle of Cape Bon on 13 December four Allied destroyers sailing from Gibraltar to reinforce the Mediterranean Fleet intercepted and sank both cruisers.

By 15 December the Italo-German armies were in retreat. It had been two weeks since a cargo ship had arrived in Africa.[52] However, the Regia Marina restored the situation in the month's third week with three important victories. Iachino and the battle fleet put to sea once again on the 16th to support another Tripoli convoy. At the same time, light elements of the Mediterranean Fleet were shepherding the fleet auxiliary *Breconshire* to Malta in Operation MF1. The First Battle of Sirte followed on 17 December when the Italian fleet with three battleships engaged the British escort just as night fell. The British turned away and then sought to intercept the Italian convoy. However, they failed, and one merchantman reached Benghazi while three anchored off Tripoli in the mistaken belief the harbor's entrance had been mined. Albacores from Malta damaged one of the merchantmen, and Force K raced to finish the job with three cruisers and three destroyers.

On 19 December Force K ran into a minefield off Tripoli, lost a cruiser and a destroyer, and suffered two cruisers damaged. The same day Italian X MAS commandos attacked Alexandria and sank the battleships *Queen Elizabeth* and *Valiant*. These victories transformed the situation. The official British history concluded, "it was the arrival of these supplies [after the Sirte battle] which permitted Rommel to mount his successful counter-offensive of 21 January 1942. Meanwhile, Imperial forces finally reached El Agheila on 6 January but did not clear the last Axis enclaves at Sollum and Bardia until 17 January 1942. By that time, their 'blow was spent.'"[53]

The British had thirty submarines in the Mediterranean by 1 December, of which sixteen were on patrol. Throughout the month they made thirty attacks expending eighty-two torpedoes while the Dutch boat *o 24* made one. Submarines sank seven merchant ships displacing 31,624 tons, including one bringing supplies to North Africa and two ferrying materiel from Tripoli to Benghazi. Aircraft sank three vessels displacing 12,442 tons, of which one, the tanker *Lina* (1,235 GRT), was engaged in the African traffic. Force K sank one vessel of 10,540 tons. Malta-based agents accounted for six of the eleven losses. Between August and December the Royal Navy lost five submarines in the Mediterranean.[54]

SUMMARY OF TRAFFIC OPERATIONS

In the second half of 1941 three convoys arrived at Malta. Of the six-teen transports in these convoys one was sunk and one damaged. An indepen-dent merchant ship arrived at Malta from the west on 19 September, but air-craft, alerted by Regia Marina spy ships disguised as French fishing vessels, sank three others in October and November, causing the British to suspend this type of traffic. Warships landed materiel and some troops or passengers on four occasions in the later half of 1941, and cargo-carrying submarines con-ducted twenty-three missions to the island with only one lost en route. Cargos varied greatly, but a large load might consist of a dozen passengers and up to eight tons of stores or thirty thousand gallons of aviation fuel.

In the war against traffic to North Africa in the period of July through De-cember 1941, Allied forces claimed to have sunk fifty-six Axis transports and tankers, displacing 256,215 tons: thirteen by submarine, thirty by air, eleven by surface warships, and two shared. Compared to the January–June 1941 pe-riod, the number of ships sunk increased 51 percent, but the tonnage lost rose 117 percent. British aircraft were deadlier (tonnage sunk by aircraft rose by 440 percent) due to the operational use of signals intelligence and, after Septem-ber 1941, to the installation of radar in some Wellington bombers. Malta-based surface warships greatly impacted traffic; in addition to the ships they sank, their very presence was disruptive. Between July and December 1941 the Axis dispatched 486,485 tons of materiel to Africa, of which 73 percent, or 356,294 tons, arrived. Loads were down by 8 percent compared to the January through June 1941 period, but deliveries were off by 28 percent. November was the deadliest month for Axis traffic during the whole war, with only 38 percent of the shipped materiel arriving.[55]

THE WORLD SCENE

The British Empire conducted offensive operations in the Mediterra-nean and North Africa at the expense of its other interests. One German ad-miral noted, "The defense of Malaya and Singapore had to bear the cost of the [June Battleaxe] offensive." The Hurricanes, radar stations, and antiaircraft batteries that were to have been emplaced in Malaya in 1941 ended up in Egypt, the Middle East, and Malta instead. Likewise, on the eve of Pearl Harbor, the

British naval forces facing the Regia Marina outnumbered those facing the far more powerful Japanese Imperial Navy—even though from June 1941 the War Cabinet realized that a crisis with Japan was brewing. Britain's global strategy had been derailed by the failure to win the meaningful victories that Churchill and War Cabinet expected when they designated Italy as the focus of the Imperial war effort, and they compromised their ability to import the food and raw materials necessary to meet Britain's domestic requirements in order to conduct offensive war in the Middle East and North Africa.[56]

Churchill's immediate reaction upon hearing the news of the Japanese attack on Pearl Harbor was "the greatest joy." "Hitler's fate was sealed. Mussolini's fate was sealed. As for the Japanese, they would be ground to powder. All the rest was merely the proper application of overwhelming force."[57] He was right, but the process was not always proper and proved long, difficult, and bloody. Indeed, the United States' entry into the conflict negatively impacted Great Britain's position in the short term. With the attack on Pearl Harbor Great Britain had to face a new and powerful enemy on multiple and logistically expensive fronts and with insufficient force to defend its vital interests. German submarines extracted a heavy toll of shipping off the North American coast, and the British access to American resources was constricted by other demands. The situation pleased Hitler and Mussolini and over the next six months it seemed their satisfaction was well founded.

3

THE MEDITERRANEAN WAR
JANUARY TO MAY 1942

Although we could never prove it, we suspected that
the times of our convoy sailing were betrayed.

Field Marshal Albert Kesselring

THE BIG PICTURE

Despite America's entry into the conflict, Great Britain remained the true foe in the mind of most Italians. On 27 December Mussolini spoke to his Council of Ministers and admitted that the war would continue three or four more years. "Russia will be liquidated as an opponent. To win the war, Great Britain must be defeated; either by invasion or the capture of her world bases. The key is the Suez Canal." From Rome's perspective the United States seemed fully occupied by Japan's "amazing victories," and even better, the Far Eastern war was siphoning off British strength. Conditions seemed ripe for an Axis victory in the Mediterranean.[1]

In January, Italian convoys began docking in Tripoli regularly following the successes at Sirte, at Alexandria, and off Tripoli. The Italo-German army was holding the El Agheila line on the border between Tripolitania and Cyrenaica, the high-water mark of the last British offensive in the winter of 1940–41. Churchill was anxious for his desert army to regroup and capture Tripoli, but an assessment by the Chiefs of Staff Committee dated 10 January recognized that supply difficulties might "retard or even prevent" the occupation of Tripoli and recommended a deeper study of operation "Super-Gymnast."[2]

In mid-January the leaders of the Italian and German navies, Admiral Arturo Riccardi and Grand Admiral Eric Raeder, met to discuss strategy. The admirals agreed that the Mediterranean theater of war was "of decisive importance" and that strengthening the army in Libya was their primary objective. They characterized the occupation of Gibraltar "as a goal that should be aimed for" but for which the economic and military conditions were currently absent. Unlike Rommel, the Grand Admiral endorsed the Regia Marina's handling of the Libyan convoys. Raeder further suggested that the French be allowed to rearm so they could defend against British and "*degaullisti*" attack, but Riccardi demurred. He mistrusted the French and did not want to compete with their fleet for German fuel allotments. The admirals saw Malta as a major problem and agreed that the way to neutralize the island was with an air offensive, mine barrages, and special forces. Riccardi, citing the support of Field Marshal Kesselring, also wanted to occupy the island and asked Admiral Raeder for assistance. The Grand Admiral agreed to consider the matter.[3]

The British worried about an Axis descent on Malta although a 3 January assessment by the Joint Intelligence Committee concluded, "We believe that a combined operation against Malta would be of such difficulty that it is improbable that the enemy would attempt it, at any rate until he could judge whether the attempt to neutralize Malta by air attack is likely to succeed." This assessment was essentially correct, as shown by discussions between the chief of staff, Field Marshal Ugo Cavallero, and Riccardi the next month. Cavallero acknowledged that Italy lacked the means to conduct an amphibious assault but that by August the garrison should be sufficiently weakened. Then, "we must do the operation even if we need to come [ashore] in life preservers."[4]

TRAFFIC WAR: MALTA CONVOYS JANUARY–FEBRUARY 1942

At the beginning of 1942 it had been three months since Operation Halbard, the last Malta convoy. Nonetheless, the island's supplies remained adequate. An inventory determined that flour would last until May, coal to the end of March, benzene and kerosene until the end of April, and aviation fuel through the summer. Shortages of fuel oil and ammunition were limiting offensive activities, but the capture of the Cyrenaican bulge and its airfields in Operation Crusader meant that convoys from the east could receive continuous air cover. Based on this advantage the Admiralty ambitiously scheduled a 30,000-ton convoy from Alexandria in January and a 45,000-ton convoy each month thereafter.[5]

At the year's beginning the 10th Submarine Flotilla and Force K, which included the light cruiser *Penelope* and six destroyers, were based at Malta. The air forces consisted of five Hurricane-equipped fighter squadrons: 126, 185, 242, 249, and 605; seven bomber squadrons, 37, 40, 148 (Wellington ICs), 104 (Wellington IICs), 18, 105, and 107 (Blenheim IVs); and the 69 Reconnaissance Squadron. The Fleet Air Arm's 828 and 830 squadrons flew Swordfish and Albacore torpedo-bombers, respectively. Against them the Sicilian airbases held 220 aircraft, two-thirds of them Italian.

Breconshire, loaded with oil, sailed on 24 January in Convoy MF4 escorted by four cruisers and eight destroyers. Simultaneously, Force K shepherded *Glengyle* and another empty transport from Malta. *Breconshire* survived heavy air attacks on 25 January on the way in and *Glengyle* on the 26th on the way out; both arrived at their destinations undamaged.

TRAFFIC WAR: AFRICAN CONVOYS JANUARY–MARCH 1942

The Italian navy's mid-December victories and the renewed air offensive against Malta neutralized much of the pressure on Axis traffic. As early as 3 January 1942 Vice Admiral Malta, Wilbraham Ford, complained to Admiral Cunningham, "I've given up counting the number of air raids we are getting. . . . Something must be done at once." Ford wrote in the midst of a blitz covering the Italian convoy operation M43 during which Axis aircraft made an estimated four hundred sorties against the island during the critical day of 4 January. M43 involved convoying six transports to Tripoli protected by a close escort of six destroyers and five torpedo boats, a distant escort of one battleship, four light cruisers, and five destroyers commanded by Vice Admiral Carlo Bergamini, and a covering group of three battleships, two heavy cruisers, and eight destroyers under Admiral Iachino. Even though signals intelligence disclosed the schedule and route of this convoy and aircraft sighted it several times, bombers dispatched from Malta and Benghazi failed to locate the enemy, and the escort's size kept Force K in port. The convoy, loaded with critically needed supplies, arrived on 5 January in what one English history described as "a serious setback for the British." Five submarines concentrated in an unsuccessful attempt to hit the Italian fleet on its return to port.[6]

The same day M43 arrived, the British operation MF2 got under way. The Mediterranean Fleet's strength was at an all-time low by January 1942. Japan's entry into the war, the loss of the capital ships *Repulse* and *Prince of Wales* off Malaya, and the Home Fleet's commitments in the Atlantic and Arctic oceans precluded replacement of *Queen Elizabeth,* and *Valiant* sunk at Alexandria. Thus, MF2 lacked battleship support. Two cruisers and five destroyers, under the command of Rear Admiral Philip Vian, escorted the assault ship *Glengyle,* which carried oil, while *Breconshire,* escorted by five destroyers, departed Malta in ballast. The two ships swapped escorts on 7 January, and *Glengyle* made Malta the next day while *Breconshire* returned to Alexandria without incident.

The next Malta convoy, MF3, sailed on 16 January. It consisted of four freighters escorted by a cruiser and eight destroyers and covered by three cruisers and five destroyers. The German submarine *U 133* sank the destroyer *Gurkha* en route, and German aircraft picked off the transport *Thermopylae,* which had straggled. However, Beaufighters, which leapfrogged from base to base along the newly conquered Cyrenaican coast, protected the main force. After being met by Force K, the convoy arrived safely on 19 January. The 21,000 tons of cargo landed included eight tanks, twenty antiaircraft guns with their crews, and most of an infantry battalion. The Regia Marina learned of the operation too late for the battle fleet to intervene.

Simultaneously with MF3, two Italian transports escorted by three destroyers and a torpedo boat arrived at Tripoli while two freighters returned to Naples from Tripoli. On 22 January the Italians ran operation T18: five transports escorted by Admiral Bergamini with one battleship, three light cruisers, fourteen destroyers, and two torpedo boats. C 38m decrypts disclosed Italian plans, and "the Chiefs of Staff urged the Cs-in-C [Middle East] to do their utmost to destroy this convoy." FAA Albacores operating from a field near Benghazi sank the ex-liner *Victoria* (13,098 GRT), but the escort rescued 1,046 of the 1,400 troops embarked, and they reached their destination. Unable to penetrate the screen, two British submarines attacked unsuccessfully from long range. Four transports arrived at Tripoli on 24 January. In January British submarines made twenty attacks, firing sixty-nine torpedoes. They sank one German and two Italian submarines and six other vessels displacing 26,021 GRT, none of which were involved in the African traffic. Aircraft sank two ships displacing 18,839 tons, one bound for Africa and one returning. Malta-based boats accounted for three of the eight lost merchantmen.[7]

The Italians ran fourteen convoys to Africa during January. These were mostly one-ship affairs that sailed from seven different ports in an effort to confuse the enemy. Nineteen of twenty-one ships arrived. Aircraft attacked four of these convoys and submarines one. *Victoria* was the only ship lost, although another returned for mechanical reasons. The Axis delivered 66,170 tons of fuel, vehicles, arms, and general cargo to Libya, 99.9 percent of the amount dispatched.[8]

THE GROUND WAR

Both sides raced to prepare for the ground war's next round. General Auchinleck recognized that an Axis counteroffensive was possible, "but he did not think this likely, or likely to succeed." On January 12 he told Churchill that he believed a renewed offensive to capture Tripoli was the proper course, although three days later he accepted his army commander's recommendation that it be deferred until 11–15 February due to administrative difficulties.[9]

These difficulties allowed Rommel to reclaim the initiative. On 21 January the German general launched an aggressive reconnaissance in force from El Agheila that captured Benghazi on 29 January. By 6 February the front had solidified west of Tobruk, and once again the Cyrenaican airfields were in Axis hands. The Royal Navy, however, deserved credit for conducting three Malta operations from the east during the army's brief possession of Benghazi.

Despite this setback, the first of the envisioned 45,000-ton monthly convoys, MF5 with three large, fast transports, departed Alexandria on 12 February. The escort consisted of an antiaircraft cruiser, one fleet destroyer, and seven Hunt-class escort destroyers. Cover included the three cruisers of Rear Admiral Vian's 15th Squadron and eight fleet destroyers. Nine Ju 88s of LG 1 flying from Crete damaged the merchantman *Clan Campbell* off Tobruk on the evening of the 13th and forced her return. The next afternoon five Ju 88s from LG 1 hit *Clan Chattan* southwest of Cape Matapan, igniting her load of ammunition and forcing the transport's abandonment. After swapping escorts with Force K, which was bringing *Berconshire* and three other empties from Malta for the return voyage to Alexandria, air attacks delivered by German and Italian units continued. Finally at 1804 an He 111 of II./KG 26 damaged the last transport, *Rowallan Castle*.[10] The destroyer *Zulu* took her under tow, but then word arrived that Vice Admiral Bergamini had sallied from Taranto with a battleship, two light cruisers, and seven destroyers. Division Admiral Angelo

Parona was bringing two heavy cruisers and five destroyers from Messina. The British warships scuttled *Rowallan Castle* and fled in the face of this threat. After it had turned for home, Bergamini's force evaded an attack by Malta-based Albacores. However, the Malta-based submarine *P36* damaged the destroyer *Carabiniere* off Messina on 16 February.

The Italians continued to run frequent convoys to Tripoli. Despite the increasing intensity of the Axis aerial offensive, Force K remained at Malta with *Penelope* and five to six destroyers. On the night of 7 February Force K achieved its last offensive success when, west of Sicily, *Lively* and *Zulu* overcame the small Italian transports *Grongo* (316 GRT) in local service in the Pelagie Islands and *Aosta* (500 GRT) sailing from Pantelleria to Tripoli.

On 21 February in Operation K7, three transport convoys departed Messina and Corfu, each with a close escort of five destroyers and a torpedo boat. A battleship, two heavy and one light cruiser, and seven destroyers provided distant cover. German fighters repelled an air attack on 22 February, and a submarine attack the next day failed. The transports docked at Tripoli on 23 February.

The intensifying air offensive against Malta finally prompted Britain's chiefs of staff to order Spitfires to the island. On 27 February, Force H sortied with seventeen of these more modern and effective aircraft. However, the tanks designed to give the planes the range to reach Malta proved defective, and the carrier's air officer refused to authorize their launch. Admiral Somerville "nearly exploded" and promptly ordered Force H back to Gibraltar.[11]

During February the Italians ran eleven convoys to Africa of which British forces contested five. Of the fifteen vessels dispatched to Africa, thirteen arrived. Submarines sank three of the eleven ships returning from Africa to Italy while fourteen vessels transited between African ports without loss. Axis merchantmen delivered 58,965 tons of materiel, 99.2 percent of the amount dispatched. Throughout the Mediterranean, Allied submarines attacked twenty-eight times, firing sixty-seven torpedoes. They sank six ships, displacing 29,359 GRT, including the tanker *Lucania* (8,106 GRT), which was on a humanitarian mission to East Africa with a British safe conduct, and two vessels previously damaged by aircraft. Malta-based boats dispatched four vessels and aircraft one, and Force K accounted for two small vessels as related above.[12]

On 6 March, after fixing the auxiliary tanks, Force H successfully delivered fifteen Spitfires to Malta. By this time only thirty-two Hurricanes remained operational. Fifteen more Spitfires arrived at the end of the month as the result of fly-offs conducted by Force H on 21 and 26 March.

The British continued to strike from Malta with mixed results. Wellingtons raided Palermo on 3 March. Their bombs detonated the German ammunition ship *Cuma* (ex-*Australien* 6,652 GRT), and splinters from the explosion slightly damaged seven other vessels in the port including two destroyers, four freighters, and a yard tanker.[13]

Italy's next large convoy operation was V5. The support group, led by Division Admiral Raffaele De Courten, had three light cruisers and five destroyers covering three convoys with a total of four transports that departed southern Italian ports on 7 March escorted by four destroyers and two torpedo boats. Sailing in three groups, six transports and a tug departed Tripoli for Italy the next day. Their escort included three destroyers and four torpedo boats. Aircraft from Malta unsuccessfully attacked elements of V5 but had better luck on 9 March when they hit a small convoy near Pantelleria and damaged the torpedo boat *Centauro*.

On 10 March Admiral Vian sailed from Alexandria with the 15th Cruiser Squadron and nine destroyers in response to a report that Malta Beauforts had crippled two enemy warships and a large merchantman. In fact no ships had been hit. Returning to base, Vian's force, assisted by long-range Beaufighters, repelled a series of air attacks. However, *U 565* sank *Naiad,* his flagship, north of Mersa Matruh on 11 March. A destroyer fished the Admiral from the sea "cold and oily" while the submarine escaped.[14]

Operation Sirio, the next major Italian operation, got under way on 15 March. Four transports in two convoys escorted by four destroyers and five torpedo boats reached Tripoli on 18 March. The distant cover was just one light cruiser and two destroyers. Italian oil stocks, and the suspension of German deliveries, which equaled 142,000 tons between December 1941 and March 1942, did not permit the continuance of the massive escorts provided in the "battleship" convoys of December and January, and the threat had diminished. Four ships left Tripoli for Italy on 17 and 18 March; one was mined off Tripoli, but the rest arrived safely.

THE SECOND BATTLE OF SIRTE

As Malta's food stocks continued to shrink, the British mounted a major convoy in mid-March. At the same time Force H sortied to bolster the island's air defenses with more Spitfires because by 21 March only two remained in service.

46

46IN PASSAGE PERILOUS

On 20 March in Operation MG1, *Breconshire, Clan Campbell* (7,255 GRT), *Pampas* (5,415 GRT), and the Norwegian *Talabot* (6,798 GRT) departed Alexandria accompanied by the light cruiser *Carlisle* and the 22nd Flotilla's six destroyers. Rear Admiral Vian's 15th Cruiser Squadron with *Cleopatra, Dido,* and *Euryalus* and four destroyers of the 14th Flotilla followed eleven hours later. The 5th Flotilla's seven Hunts had already left Alexandria to sweep for submarines along the convoy's route. They found *U 652*, which torpedoed *Heythrop* and then escaped.

The British took measures to minimize air attacks on the merchantmen, including commando raids against airfields and demonstrations by the 8th Army. Although German aircraft spotted the convoy shortly after its departure from Alexandria, it enjoyed a quiet passage through the dangerous zone between Crete and Cyrenaica due to faulty reconnaissance and communications. A contemporary Italian report complained, "Reconnaissance by X CAT (Fliegerkorp X) south of Crete on the 21st would have clarified the situation." That morning, however, no news arrived, and Supermarina assumed the British force had been headed for Tobruk. Later Supermarina learned that the absence of news meant that the Germans had been unable to perform reconnaissance that morning, not that there was no convoy. Finally at 1630 on 21 March the Italian submarine *Platino* reported a cruiser, four destroyers, and three steamers south of Crete, and Supermarina realized there was a Malta convoy at sea after all. Within hours it ordered two surface groups to raise steam. Admiral Iachino departed Taranto at 0027 on 22 March with *Littorio*, escorted by four destroyers. Division Admiral Parona left Messina at 0100 with three cruisers and four destroyers. The Italians believed their movements were unknown to the British, but, while this was true of Parona's cruisers, signals intelligence and the submarine *P36* reported *Littorio's* departure.[15]

The 15th Cruiser Squadron and 14th Destroyer Flotilla met the convoy escort at 0600 on 22 March while *Penelope* and *Legion* joined from Malta two hours later. At 0518 Vian received *P36's* report of "three destroyers and hydrophone effect of heavier ships" and adjusted course to the southwest. His orders were to "evade the enemy if possible until dark, when the convoy—dispersed if it seemed advisable—was to be sent on to Malta with the Hunt class destroyers, and the remaining warships were to attack the enemy."[16]

Axis air attacks commenced after 0930 on 22 March as the convoy passed beyond fighter range. "The forenoon attempts were not dangerous, however, being only a few torpedo shots at long range by Italian S.79 aircraft." Vian realized that the Italian fleet might catch him before dark. If so, he planned to employ his cruisers and fleet destroyers in independent divisions and maintain smoke between the transports and the enemy. He did not consider delaying the convoy or turning back. Admiral Cunningham, who remained ashore at Alexandria, made no effort to direct the operation once his orders had been issued and the ships were at sea, although he did express his concerns in a 15 March letter to Admiral Pound. "If we are lucky with the weather all may be well, but if not, we may easily lose the convoy, and a ship or two as well."[17]

In fact, the weather was "lucky." Heavy seas and gale winds developed as the Italians pressed south with Parona's cruisers ranging fifty miles ahead of *Littorio*. Floatplanes scouted overhead (although their reports were "not always in agreement"), and Parona sighted the enemy at 1422 twelve miles off the port bow. The raising wind was blowing twenty-five knots from the southeast, and visibility was steadily dropping.[18]

Contact had come several hours before Vian anticipated presenting the admiral with a dilemma. His ships had already expended large amounts of antiaircraft ammunition, and if the convoy detoured too far off the direct route to Malta, it would face an additional day in bomber-infested waters. So, the admiral implemented his defensive plan and hoped for the best. Parona's orders helped: he was to make visual contact and then "communicate news without engaging."[19]

The convoy and Hunts turned southwest while *Carlisle* and *Avon Vale* trailed smoke. The other warships formed columns by divisions and headed west by northwest, also spewing white chemical and black funnel smoke. The wind drove the dense clouds directly toward the Italian cruisers as they labored southwest in a line of bearing. At 1429, with the British columns advancing toward him, Parona turned north in accordance with Admiral Iachino's instructions. Iachino assumed the British would pursue Parona right into range of his big guns.

The two forces traded long-range salvoes from 1435 until 1513, when Vian swung back toward the convoy. While the cruisers were engaged, Ju 88s of II./ KG 77 and twelve S.79s out of Sicily attacked the transports. Seventy-two German bombers had lifted off, but in the stormy conditions only thirty made contact. A unit of Ju 87s was also scheduled to attack, but the weather grounded their guide units, so the Stukas attacked Malta's airfields instead. The Hunts and *Carlisle*'s 4-inch guns foiled the initial Ju 88 strike in a barrage that Vian described as "impressive, resembling continuous pom-pom fire, even though heard at a distance of 8 to 10 miles." At 1520 the convoy resumed its westerly heading, and fifteen minutes later Vian signaled Cunningham that he had repelled the enemy.[20]

Parona's cruisers, meanwhile, joined *Littorio* at 1530. Shortly after 1617 *Littorio*'s lookouts spotted an enemy cruiser while one of the battleship's floatplanes reported the convoy beyond. Iachino immediately turned due west. Two precious hours had elapsed since first contact, and conditions were deteriorating, with the wind rising to thirty knots. The rough conditions made station keeping difficult, particularly for the destroyers. *Grecale* had already suffered a rudder failure, so Iachino reduced speed to twenty-two knots to minimize the possibility that his other ships might suffer damage.

At 1637 *Zulu* reported four unknown ships eighteen thousand yards to the northeast. After *Euryalus* confirmed, Vian hauled off to the northeast with his four cruisers, *Cleopatra, Dido, Euryalus,* and *Penelope,* and the fleet destroyers, *Sikh, Zulu, Lively, Hero, Havock, Hasty,* and *Legion.* Every vessel commenced generating smoke. The four fleet destroyers *Jervis, Kelvin, Kingston,* and *Kipling* reinforced the convoy's escort because *Carlisle* and the six Hunts were running low on antiaircraft ammunition.

Admiral Iachino had two hours of daylight. He considered working to windward but rejected that option because he wanted to be "absolutely sure that the enemy did not escape to the west" and "because a move to the east would have imposed an upwind turn and then a sharp reduction in speed that would have delayed the encounter with the enemy." By keeping to leeward he could, at the very least, force the convey to detour south. At the best he could achieve decisive gunnery results. "For these reasons, while realizing the drawbacks of a battle with the enemy to leeward, I felt better to insist on a safe course forcing the convoy south."[21]

At 1643 the Italians opened fire. *Bande Nere* hit *Cleopatra*'s bridge with her second salvo, disabling the radar and radio and killing fifteen men. A salvo from *Littorio* straddled *Euryalus* from nineteen thousand yards, spraying the cruiser with large splinters, including one weighing more than two hundred pounds that penetrated nine bulkheads. The British cruisers ducked into their smoke after five minutes as the range slowly narrowed.

Sikh, Lively, Hero, and *Havock* paralleled the enemy until 1705, when they turned south "to avoid punishment." The Italians assumed this turn signified that the British warships had made a torpedo attack, and the destroyer *Ascari* even reported tracks. Iachino maneuvered to avoid and ordered his destroyers to counterattack. Under enemy fire, the Italian destroyers launched torpedoes and turned north. The convoy labored south-southwest, the rising gale on its port beam.[22]

At 1718 Iachino reduced speed to twenty knots as Parona's cruisers fell into line behind *Littorio*. At 1720 a 15-inch shell fired from fourteen thousand yards damaged *Havock* and compelled her withdrawal. Then, at 1730, Vian decided to backtrack with his four cruisers and three of the six engaged destroyers "in search of two enemy ships not accounted for and which I thought might be working round in the rear." Vian later acknowledged that this action was "a serious tactical error." At 1731 Iachino, now closing on a south-by-southwest heading, reengaged. Only *Sikh*, *Lively*, and *Hero* opposed him, although smoke hid this fact from the Italian admiral. The destroyers briefly jogged north answering *Littorio's* fire in what their commander characterized as a "somewhat unequal contest." The torpedo threat, however, kept Iachino cautious. Under heavy fire the destroyers then veered south, spewing billows of wind-whipped smoke. Upon learning of the renewed attack, Vian reversed course and plunged blindly back through his own smoke. Iachino was now twenty-five thousand yards north of the convoy.[23]

At 1748 *Littorio* straddled *Sikh* from twelve thousand yards, and the British destroyer commander ordered the convoy to turn south. *Sikh* fired two torpedoes "in order to avoid sinking with all torpedoes on board and in the hope of making the enemy turn away."[24]

At 1752 Iachino ceased fire. He wrote, "the gunnery action had assumed a twilight character, and this had rendered uncertain the fire of our vessels. Moreover, the great inundation of seawater coming aboard our ships shrouded the fire control optics so that both measuring instruments (inclinometers and rangefinders) . . . were practically useless." Nonetheless, he was slowly blocking the convoy from its destination.[25]

At 1803 *Cleopatra* engaged *Littorio* from thirteen thousand yards and fired three torpedoes. *Littorio* dodged northwest to avoid these. Then, still concerned that he had lost track of some enemy vessels, Vian again turned east and steamed away from the action with four cruisers and three destroyers, leaving just three destroyers to stand off the entire enemy force. At 1808 Captain A. L. Poland, the commander of the four fleet destroyers assigned at the start of the battle to supplement the convoy's antiaircraft firepower, received an alarming message that the enemy was only sixteen thousand yards away. On his own initiative, he led his four destroyers northwest to intervene. Meanwhile, Iachino steered 280 degrees until 1820, when he came to 220. At 1827 he pointed his ships due south. In his words, "In order to overcome the serious fire control difficulties [presented by the weather] and to achieve a decisive result at any cost, I stubbornly maintained contact with the enemy ships, decreasing the range even into the enemy's torpedo waters."[26]

The Italian column resumed fire at 1831, and at 1834 Poland's division, *Jervis, Kelvin, Kingston,* and *Kipling* reinforced by *Legion,* spotted *Littorio* just twelve thousand yards away. One British sailor recalled, "Looking through my gunlayer's telescope, we seemed to be right alongside the battleship."[27] At 1841 with the range at six thousand yards, Poland's destroyers swung starboard to launch torpedoes. The Italians were firing every gun that could bear. An 8-inch round from *Gorizia* exploded in *Kingston's* boiler room. *Legion* disappeared into a forest of giant geysers as 15-inch shells smashed into the water around her, and Italian and British spectators alike were astonished to see the destroyer emerge on the same course and speed. As the first of twenty-five British torpedoes began hitting the water, Iachino turned 110 degrees to starboard and reduced speed two knots. Lookouts spotted one torpedo passing ahead of *Littorio* and others streaked between the Italian ships.

As Poland attacked, Vian's four cruisers and two destroyers rushed back from their excursion east. They engaged *Littorio* and provoked a response from the battleship. *Euryalus's* captain recorded, "Then, at 6:41 PM . . . I saw flashes from [*Littorio's*] fifteen-inch guns rippling down her side as she fired a salvo at us . . . *Euryalus* shuddered and shook and then rocked so violently that I thought the topmast would come down, while fragments of shell screamed through the air to bury themselves in our ship's sides."[28]

At 1851 Iachino turned northwest and increased speed to twenty-six knots. He wrote, "after the last enemy torpedo attack, led with great courage . . . when the sun had already set and darkness was rapidly adding to the haze on the horizon to cover the whole scene of the action in shadow . . . I pulled out with my ships to avoid being hit."[29] In fact, at 1855 the British made another torpedo attack from eight thousand yards. *Lively* launched eight torpedoes, but *Sikh* and *Hero* held fire, not having a clear shot. *Littorio* replied with her aft turret. A 15-inch shell landed beside *Lively* and splintered her hull and superstructure, causing some flooding. Also at 1855, a 4.7-inch destroyer shell struck *Littorio* on her starboard aft deck. This parting shot was the only hit the British achieved during the entire battle.

By 1858 all guns had fallen silent. The British suffered heavy damage to two destroyers, light damage to two others, and moderate damage to two cruisers, but the convoy survived. Throughout the surface action, the merchantmen recorded twenty-eight air attacks by Ju 88s and S.79s, which enthusiastically, but incorrectly claimed three steamers hit and one sunk. The escort expended much of its remaining munitions, shooting down one Ju 88 and three S.79s in the process.[30]

The weather continued to deteriorate as Iachino put about for home. The destroyers *Lanciere* and *Scirocco* foundered the next morning, and other ships suffered heavy storm damage.

At 1940 Vian headed back to Alexandria, less *Penelope* and *Legion* from Force K and the damaged *Havock* and *Kingston,* which all headed for Malta. Painfully behind schedule the convoy dispersed and proceeded for Malta at each ship's best speed, accompanied by *Carlisle* and the Hunts.

Due to the detour forced by the surface action, even the fastest merchant ships, each escorted by a Hunt or two, remained at sea the next morning and came under heavy air attack. *Talabot* and *Pampas,* hit by two dud bombs, entered Malta's Grand Harbor between 0900 and 1000 on 23 March. *Carlisle* and *Avon Vale* collided trying to avoid bombs in an attack that damaged *Breconshire* at 0920. Attempts to tow the auxiliary into port failed, forcing her to anchor off Marsaxlokk. German aircraft sank *Clan Campbell* twenty miles off the island. A near miss severely damaged *Legion*. She was beached and subsequently towed into harbor. On 24 March while patrolling offshore to protect *Breconshire, Southwold* struck a mine and sank.

Unrelenting air attacks destroyed *Legion, Breconshire, Talabot,* and *Pampas* on 26 March along with much of the 25,900 tons of cargo and oil they carried. A British wartime account painted this disaster in heroic hues, "Sailors and soldiers, with divers in the flooded holds, working night and day regardless of bombs, saved much of the invaluable cargo and many precious tons of oil fuel . . ." In fact, Maltese longshoremen refused to unload the ships during air attacks, and the island's governor, Lieutenant General William Dobbie, was inexcusably slow in ordering soldiers to undertake the task. The ships sat in harbor three days before the deadly raid of 26 March, and in that time 969 of 8,956 tons of embarked cargo were unloaded from *Talabot* while longshoremen removed 799 of 7,462 tons from *Pampas*. Subsequently, troops salvaged another thirty-three hundred tons mostly from *Pampas* before the wreck finally broke up on 13 April—overall a disappointing return for the effort expended.[31]

Admiral Cunningham later boasted that the Second Battle of Sirte was "one of the most brilliant actions of the war, if not the most brilliant."[32] In fact, the battles of the Barents Sea or Leyte Gulf demonstrated how smoke and a few determined, torpedo-armed escorts could stand off vastly superior forces for longer periods and under conditions much less favorable than Vian enjoyed. Although Iachino never engaged the merchantmen, the Italians shot much better than the British (1,480 Italian rounds fired compared to 2,807 British) and forced the convoy to detour south and ultimately to scatter. He forced even the fastest freighters to face another morning of air attacks, which otherwise would not have been the case. And because the escorts had fired off most of their antiaircraft ammunition while the fleet units fought the surface engagement, these extra air attacks were particularly effective. Even more importantly, his battleship established a threat that would have a decisive impact three months later.

The lessons Supermarina drew from this action are relevant as they affected the Italian response to the mid-June operation. At Sirte, Iachino sought battle with high hopes of a decisive result due to Axis air superiority and gunnery strength. Weather and a lack of time frustrated his expectations. Iachino wrote, "the tactic of the smoke screen, which the British have studied and developed with great care and with undeniable skill, we can counter only, if in a future meeting, we will have many hours of daylight before sunset, or a large mass of cruisers, destroyers and possibly MAS boats launched within the curtain of fog to fight a type of night melee without worry of losses incurred."[33]

TRAFFIC SUMMARY, WINTER 1942

In March Allied submarines made fifteen gun and fourteen torpedo attacks and expended fifty-five torpedoes. They sank three Italian submarines and four merchant ships, displacing 18,547 tons at the cost of two boats lost to Italian depth charges. The Malta boats (nine of the thirteen on patrol at the beginning of the month) accounted for two ships of 6,859 tons and aircraft two others of 8,430 tons, including the Cuma mentioned above. The Italians ran fourteen convoys to Africa. The British attacked three, but eighteen of the twenty escorted merchantmen arrived safely. Aircraft sank one of the fourteen steamers on the coastal routes and submarines torpedoed one of the fifteen ships convoyed from Africa to Italy. The Axis delivered 47,588 tons of materiel to Libya, 82.7 percent of the amount dispatched.[34]

During the January through March quarter Allied aircraft flew a thousand antishipping sorties, sinking two vessels of 7,686 tons and contributing to the sinking of three others. Malta boats accounted for 41 percent of the total losses inflicted by submarines. The Axis delivered 172,723 tons of materiel to Libya, 94 percent of the amount shipped. This was a marked improvement over the previous quarter when the Axis had delivered 142,519 tons, or 65 percent of the amount shipped.[35]

SPRING 1942

On 26 February the Chiefs of Staff Committee queried General Auchinleck about his intentions. Their cable began, "Our view is that Malta is of such importance both as an air staging point and as an impediment to the enemy reinforcement route that the most drastic steps are justified to sustain it." Auchinleck replied that he required at least four more months' preparation before launching an offensive and asserted that a premature undertaking to save Malta could jeopardize Britain's whole Middle Eastern position. This response infuriated Churchill. His draft reply (which was toned down before being dispatched) read, in part, "The reputation of the British Army now lays unhappily very low. . . . I was looking to the 8th Army, on which everything has been lavished, to repair the shame of Singapore. . . . No one is going to stand our remaining in deep peace while Malta is being starved out."[36]

The navy shared the prime minister's opinion of Malta's importance. On 15 March Admiral Cunningham, in his final days with the Mediterranean Fleet, wrote Admiral Pound, "I do not find the attitude of the soldiers to this Malta problem much to my liking. . . . I have pointed out that we can't gamble on the convoys getting through and that we may well lose Malta . . . but I am met with the reply that it is better to lose Malta than Egypt." This debate between the Middle Eastern command in Cairo and the chiefs of staff and prime minister in London raged for several months. In essence, Cairo refused to move prematurely while London believed that the Middle Eastern command exaggerated the dangers it faced. In May, Auchinleck even went so far as to express the heresy that in its present neutralized state the loss of Malta would not improve the Axis supply situation or necessarily prove fatal to Egypt's security.[37]

On 2 April Fliegerkorp II and the Regia Aeronautica commenced an aerial onslaught designed to destroy Malta as a base and soften it up for an invasion. They accomplished their first goal, sinking the destroyers *Lance, Gallant,* and *Kingston,* a minesweeper, three submarines, a tanker, and several smaller vessels. The Royal Navy withdrew everything still afloat, including the 10th

Flotilla's last five submarines. The cruiser *Penelope* escaped in such a condition she earned the nickname "HMS *Pepperpot*." The bombing also drove out the RAF's Blenheims and Wellingtons. Although the Spitfires and Hurricanes soldiered on, on some days there were as few as six operational fighters. The consumption of aviation fuel and fuel oil dropped, but the expenditure of antiaircraft ammunition soared, and the guns, "apart from special occasions, were down to a daily ration of fifteen rounds." During April the island's 112 heavy antiaircraft guns fired 72,053 rounds and the 144 light ones 88,176 rounds. In mid-May, the BBC informed its audience that "The bombs dropped on Malta last month totaled a greater weight than during the 1940 blitz on England." In fact, the April total was 6,728 tons, 18 percent of the 1940 Blitz total of 36,844. Nonetheless, the airfields were, by then, "a wilderness of craters, the docks . . . a shambles, Valetta a mass of broken limestone. . . ."[38]

On 3 April Admiral Cunningham hauled down his flag. The reason given was that an admiral of the highest stature was required to serve in Washington to deal with the Americans on the Anglo-American Combined Chiefs of Staff Committee and because, as Pound pointed out when he broke the news, "there is now no fleet to go to sea in." In his reply, Cunningham expressed surprise, reluctance to leave, and doubts around his replacement, but London tactfully ignored all this. As one author noted, "certainly Cunningham did not leave trailing clouds of glory." His last major victory was a year in the past, and since then he had presided over several defeats, the worst being his careless handing of the carrier *Formidable* during the evacuation of Crete and the loss of two battleships at Alexandria after he deferred defensive improvements because they were too expensive. Acting Admiral Henry Harwood, a Churchill favorite since his victory over the German armored ship *Admiral Graf Spee* in December 1939, replaced Cunningham on 20 May.[39]

Cunningham was not the only iconic British leader replaced in this spring of discontent. The March convoy debacle, particularly the unloading fiasco, brought to the forefront concerns about the island's leadership. On 12 April the acting minister of state, Walter Monckton, and Air Marshal Arthur Tedder arrived in Malta on a tour of inspection. About the supply situation they reported that aviation spirits would last well into August; a tanker was needed to bring in black oil, and merchant ships could bring in drummed white oils. There was enough milled flour to last until late May, and additional stocks of wheat and corn would extend the supply into July if rations were cut. They concluded, "it was vitally important to receive a convoy in May, but there must first be many more fighters and more ammunition." However, they also reported that the garrison lacked training, the population was discontented and anxious about food, and Governor Dobbie was becoming "worn out."[40]

Malta's service chiefs, as well as certain influential civilians, had a litany of complaints about Dobbie, including a lack of vigor, excessive concern for civilians, and too much religion (he objected to soldiers working or training on Sundays, for example). They felt that he failed to appreciate the fundamentals of modern warfare, especially the use and impact of airpower, and should be relieved immediately.

This recommendation stunned Churchill, particularly since on 15 April London had tried to improve morale by awarding Malta's inhabitants and garrison the George Cross. He dispatched a War Cabinet member to the island for another opinion and received the advice, "I have no doubt that Dobbie should be replaced . . . as soon as possible." The chiefs of staff acted on this and designated Field Marshal John Vereker, the 6th Viscount Gort, the governor of Gibraltar and former commander of the British Expeditionary Force in France, to replace Dobbie.[41]

London also took to heart the recommendation to fly a strong contingent of Spitfires to Malta. However, because *Eagle* was in dock, *Victorious* could not accommodate Spitfires, and the other carriers that could were in the Indian Ocean, the Royal Navy had no ships able to do the job other than *Argus,* which could handle only nine aircraft. This situation forced Churchill to appeal directly to President Roosevelt for loan of the U.S. Navy carrier *Wasp,* then operating in the North Sea as part of a U.S. task force replacing the British capital ships that had been watching *Tirpitz* while they were off in the Indian Ocean supporting the invasion of Madagascar. On 14 April *Wasp* loaded forty-seven Spitfires in Greenock. Escorted by the battle cruiser *Renown* and four British and two American destroyers, she entered the Mediterranean and flew off the fighters on 20 April.

Forty-six Spitfires arrived at Malta after an uneventful flight. However, Axis radar and radio interceptions had detected their launch. Two hours after they landed enemy bombers appeared overhead. During the course of the day Axis aircraft flew 272 sorties. By the next dawn only twenty-seven Spitfires were serviceable, and by that evening that number had dropped to nineteen. The air officer in command complained that many of the new arrivals had dirty guns and broken radios and that the new pilots lacked experience. He cabled London that "only fully experienced operational pilots must come here. It is no place for beginners." His complaints, however, masked shortcomings in his own command: arrangements for getting the new aircraft airborne or even into protected spaces after landing had been lackadaisical. At least eleven were destroyed or damaged on the ground within hours of arrival and nine more trapped in their pens by debris. Only three were shot down. By 23 April Axis raids had destroyed or severely damaged twenty-five Spitfires on the ground and shot down nine.[42]

On 18 April the chiefs of staff concluded it would be impossible to send a convoy to Malta in May because the world situation did not permit the deployment of any capital ships. They considered that battleships were needed for the escort because "Experience had shown that the Italian Fleet would challenge [the convoy] in strength and it was unlikely that the 'providential escape of the March convoy, which was mainly due to weather' would be repeated." This conclusion confirmed the success of Iachino's March sortie: he had established a viable threat that prevented a May convoy from being sailed at all. At least the delay allowed *Nelson* and *Rodney* to complete a post-refit working-up period.[43]

In May Fliegerkorps II began to transfer aircraft from Sicily to North Africa for the planned offensive against Tobruk. German air strengths fell from fifty-two to forty-two bombers and from eighty-eight to thirty-six fighters. Axis planes dropped only 520 tons of bombs during the month. *Wasp* made another run to the island in company with *Eagle,* which had completed her refit. The two carriers carried sixty-seven Spitfires, and on 9 May they sent their cargo on its long flight east. Sixty planes arrived, and the arrangements to receive them were more efficient than in April—the goal was to have each new fighter serviced and back into the air with an experienced pilot within fifteen minutes of landing. Although German and Italian bombers attacked heavily all day and Axis fighters swarmed to hunt the new arrivals, they only damaged six aircraft on the ground and shot down four. By the end of the day there were still fifty undamaged Spitfires on hand and a dozen more easily repairable.[44]

The large and speedy minelayer *Welshman,* disguised as a French contre-torpilleur and carrying 340 tons of supplies, mostly antiaircraft ammunition, aircraft engines, powdered milk, and foodstuffs, arrived on 10 May. When thirty German bombers accompanied by a heavy fighter escort attempted to attack *Welshman* that morning, thirty-seven Spitfires and thirteen Hurricanes rose in opposition. It was another day of heavy air raids delivered mostly by German bombers, but at the end confirmed losses were five Ju 88s, four Ju 87s, three Bf 109s, one Z.1007bis, and one MC.202. Against this the British lost only three Spitfires with another six damaged.[45]

Striving to create the conditions where the island could receive a large convoy, *Eagle* flew in another seventeen Spitfires on 18 May, thirty-two on 3 June, of which twenty-seven arrived, and thirty on 9 June. Three submarines arrived with aviation fuel, kerosene, and ammunition. The need for a major convoy was rapidly becoming dire. The civilian population was down to a daily diet of twelve to fifteen hundred calories, and the bread ration was slashed to 10.5 ounces on 5 May. Malta's new governor, Field Marshal Gort, warned the chiefs of staff that starvation would compel surrender within two months.

OPERATION C3 (HERCULES)

Rome had long considered plans to invade Malta. By October 1941 studies had evolved into an operation involving 35,000 troops. In January 1942 Comando Supremo ordered that planning be accelerated, giving these studies the code name C3. Army units designated for the operation concentrated in the south and began training. Kesselring advocated an invasion, and Grand Admiral Raeder energetically pitched it to Hitler in March and April. In an unusual case of Axis joint planning, German and even a few Japanese advisors participated. On 17 March the German liaison at Comando Supremo proposed an airborne component with large-scale German participation. Mussolini endorsed this idea, and on 12 April, encouraged by the effectiveness of the air offensive against Malta, he ordered the operation launched "after the end of May."[46]

On 29–30 April Mussolini and Hitler met at Castle Klessheim near Salzburg to review Mediterranean grand strategy and discuss their next objective. Mussolini pressed for Malta, but Hitler (and Rommel) preferred Tobruk. Rommel in particular was worried about Auchinleck's buildup and wanted to preempt his offensive. As Kesselring bitterly complained, "at that period Rommel exercised an almost hypnotic influence over Hitler." In the end the Axis potentates decided that the African panzer army would take Tobruk at the end of May and then pause on the Egyptian border. The air forces would redeploy, and the attack on Malta would occur in June, or, at the latest, during the July full moon. As for the rest of the war, Ciano's diary relates a conversation with Ribbentrop that expressed Germany's belief that once Russia was brought to her knees, "the British Conservatives, and even Churchill himself, who, after all, is a sensible man, will bow in order to save what remains of their mauled empire." And if not, submarines and airplanes as in 1940. The Germans, he stated, acted as if America were a big bluff. "This slogan is repeated by everyone, big and little, in the conference rooms and in the antechambers."[47]

Most of the forces allocated to Operation C3 were Italian. There were to be 222 Italian and 189 German fighters, 474 Italian and 243 German bombers, and 170 Italian and 216 German transports. The airborne forces included the German 7th Fallschirmjaeger and the Italian Folgore divisions. As soon as they secured an airfield, the La Spezia Division would fly in. After these forces occupied the area behind the landing beaches, a heterogeneous force of 151 barges, trawlers, ferries, motorboats, and transports would deliver the Italian Friuli and Livorno divisions and the navy's San Marco marine regiment. Two more Italian divisions would land in a follow-up wave: 96,000 men in total. Admiral Iachino would protect the invasion fleet with the battleships *Vittorio Veneto, Littorio, Duilio,* and *Doria,* four heavy and eight light cruisers, and twenty-one destroyers. Ten destroyers and ten torpedo boats, a sloop, twelve minesweepers, and German S-boat and minesweeping flotillas would screen the amphibious armada. To contest this invasion the British had eleven British and four Maltese battalions, or about 26,000 men.[48]

Whether the capture of Malta would have led to victory in North Africa or whether it would have been a gigantic fiasco was never tested. Hitler did not believe the Italians were serious or, even if they were, that they had the "necessary attacking spirit." Jodl wrote to Kesselring as early as 27 March, "One can hardly tell the Italians they may as well drop their preparations to take Malta because they won't get Malta anyway." On 21 May at a situation conference Hitler suggested that German preparations for the operation continue only in spirit.[49]

SPRING TRAFFIC SUMMARY

In the first five months of 1942 the British conducted five Malta operations, all from the east. Thirteen transports sailed, of which seven arrived. Five were sunk, and one turned back.

Throughout the spring small Italian convoys regularly crisscrossed the Mediterranean suffering light losses. Ultra gave details of twenty-six sailings between Italy and North Africa during April and May, but air reconnaissance only sighted nine. In April the Regia Marina convoyed sixty-two vessels across the Mediterranean in forty-four operations. On 4 April six transports in three convoys escorted by a light cruiser, ten destroyers, and three torpedo boats arrived safely in Tripoli in Operation Lupo. On 16 April six transports in three convoys escorted by five destroyers and two torpedo boats made Tripoli in

Operation Aprilia. During this operation the torpedo boat *Pegaso* sank *Up-holder*, commanded by the Royal Navy's ace submarine captain, Lieutenant Commander David Wanklyn.[50]

With the destruction of Malta's striking power, the British attempted to interdict Axis traffic with submarines based at Alexandria and Gibraltar while aircraft flying from Egypt concentrated on bombing African ports, mostly at night. Benghazi recorded twenty-four attacks in April and twenty-three in May with an average of ten planes in each strike. These caused little damage, the goal being disturbance as much as destruction. In May bombers also hit Trapani, Augusta, and Cagliari. British submarines made twenty-nine attacks and expended fifty-six torpedoes to sink the light cruiser *Bande Nere* and six merchant ships displacing 19,583 tons, of which two were engaged in supplying Africa. Throughout the month the Italians delivered 150,389 tons of materiel to Africa, 99.2 percent of the amount shipped. All but one of the thirty-nine vessels convoyed to Africa arrived safely while nineteen of twenty-one ships on the coastal routes and twenty-two of twenty-three ships bound for Italy made their destinations.[51]

In May the tactic of dispatching swarms of microconvoys reached its height. During the month there were twenty-three escorted convoys to Africa, twenty-six along the coast, and twenty-four back to Italy involving 110 ships. On 10 May Operation Mira commenced. This consisted of Convoy R of two and Convoy G of four transports bound for Tripoli from Naples. On 11 May, on the basis of signals intelligence, Admiral Harwood dispatched the 14th Destroyer Flotilla from Alexandria to intercept, but German aircraft pounced on the destroyers south of Crete. The first attack by fourteen Ju 88s from I./LG 1 based at Heraklion sank *Lively*. A later attack by a different unit was unsuccessful, but before dark I./LG 1 struck again, dispatching *Kipling* and *Jackal*. *Jervis*, the sole survivor, returned to Alexandria, crammed with 650 men. Several convoys sailed on 19 May, and all ships reached their destination except for *Agostino Bertani* (8,329 GRT), which was torpedoed by a bomber and towed back to Tripoli. On 31 May Convoy F of three ships escorted by four destroyers and a torpedo boat reached Benghazi.[52]

Allied forces attacked nineteen of these convoys; British submarines operating out of Alexandria made twenty-four attacks, expending thirty-three torpedoes, and sank a destroyer and five merchant vessels displacing 15,123 tons including, on 31 May, *Gino Allegri* (6,386 GRT), which had been previously damaged by aircraft. Six of the eleven totaling 16,289 tons were engaged in the Africa traffic. Throughout May Italy dispatched 93,188 tons of materiel to Africa of which 86,849 tons arrived. The Italian official history concluded, "Our traffic maintained a sufficient degree of security in the trimester of April through June which allowed the execution of the great Axis offensive in North Africa that began on 26 May." The British submarine history agrees. "By the end of May the offensive against Axis shipping had practically collapsed and the Italian Navy was claiming victory."[53]

The Regia Marina's strong position allowed a more aggressive posture within the confines of its hand-to-mouth fuel situation. Italian destroyers, MAS boats, and German S-boats constantly thickened the minefields surrounding Malta. The 3rd S-Boat Flotilla laid twenty-four fields from 16 December 1941 through the middle of May. The German boats saw little of the British, sinking just a motor launch and a trawler. S 31 hit a mine just off Valletta on 10 May, and S 34 fell victim to a shore battery on 17 May. The rest of the flotilla transferred to Derna on 21 May to support Rommel's offensive.

Italian special forces also participated in the campaign. The submarine *Ambra* launched three "pigs" of X MAS on the night of 14–15 May. Their targets were the battleship *Queen Elizabeth,* which was in a floating dock being repaired after the December 1941 attack, and the submarine depot ship *Medway.* However, the mission failed because of navigational errors, an unexpected westerly current, and incessant searchlights that forced frequent submersions. One team scuttled its weapon after failing to find the port's entrance and was captured ashore. Another could not reach the entrance against the current. After sinking its weapon the crew took refuge on a wreck outside the port. The third manned torpedo broke down. Its crew swam ashore and evaded capture until 29 June.[54]

THE BRITISH DEBATE THEIR OPTIONS

On 18 April the Chiefs of Staff Committee began planning a major Malta convoy operation for June, which they considered the latest possible date to resupply the island.[55] To facilitate the operation London pushed for a ground offensive by mid-May to secure the Cyrenaican airfields before the convoy sailed. On 3 May, however, Cairo flustered London by asking whether efforts should not be devoted toward strengthening the Middle East's defenses and reinforcing India inasmuch as Auchinleck considered the severing of the Indian Ocean supply route by the Japanese a much greater danger to the Middle

East than the loss of Malta. Auchinleck also had his eyes on his northern front, which included Iran and Turkey and which seemed to him threatened by Germany's forthcoming summer offensive in Russia.

On 8 May Churchill warned Auchinleck that the "loss of Malta would be a disaster of the first magnitude to the British Empire and would probably be fatal in the long run to the defence of the Nile valley." Auchinleck, plainly unconvinced by this rhetoric, still refused to move, stating that the destruction of the 8th Army's "armoured forces which may result from a premature offensive may be more serious and more immediate than that involved in the possible loss of Malta, serious though this would be." Cairo also believed that indications of an Axis attack in early June "were not very definite."[56]

This was too much for Churchill. On 10 May he stressed that Rommel was preparing to strike and gave Auchinleck the choice of attacking or resigning. On 19 May, after mulling over Churchill's ultimatum for nine days, Auchinleck agreed to move, although he still resisted committing to a firm date. By 22 May intelligence had made it clear to all that an Axis attack was imminent, and preparations turned to repelling it and following with a counterstroke. The blow fell on 26 May.[57]

After a seesaw struggle, Panzer Army Africa captured Tobruk on 21 June. By 30 June Rommel approached El Alamein only sixty miles west of Alexandria. This was the consequence of six months of continuous Axis control over the Central Mediterranean during which Italy transported 441,878 tons of materiel to North Africa, suffering losses, principally to British submarines, of only 6 percent. Even after this victory Italy still considered the conquest of Malta essential, but the German high command did not. In a conference with Raeder on 15 June 1942 Hitler gave lip service to the importance of Operation Hercules and then listed all the reasons it was unfeasible, including the Eastern Front situation, a lack of transport planes, and distrust of Italian troops. He also rationalized, "the British efforts to get convoys through to Malta from the east and from the west testify the plight of the island. These convoys, by the way, give us an opportunity to inflict much damage on the enemy."[58]

4

GLOBAL SNAPSHOT—JUNE 1942

But even a nation which loves to hail its disasters as triumphs could hardly
look back on the campaign of the first half of 1942 with satisfaction

J. R. M. Butler

ON 10 MARCH 1942 Supermarina issued a strategic assessment. It correctly noted that "above all other considerations the enemy coalition has enormous economic opportunities for sustaining a war of long duration. . . . Their
vulnerability lies in the length and complexity of the maritime communications necessary for exploiting their strategic and economic opportunities and
the relative inferiority of their ground forces." It concluded that while the Russian front was the most important, a vigorous continuation and even intensi-
fication of the war against maritime traffic would be the best way to defeat the
enemy and indeed was the only way the three Axis powers could effectively co-
operate in their separate theaters of operation.[1]

This assessment demonstrated the Regia Marina's appreciation of the war's
economic foundations and worldwide nature. It did not address political issues. Great Britain's mid-June operation to restore Malta's offensive capacity
had global ramifications, but a review of the world situation at the beginning
of June 1942 suggests that London's objectives were as much political as military in light of more serious threats faced elsewhere.

AFRICA

In June 1942 the German army fielded 235 divisions. Three were deployed in Africa. Italy had seventy-eight divisions with eight in Africa. The
British Empire had seven divisions and five independent brigades in Africa

from a total of twenty-five British and twenty-five Commonwealth and Imperial Divisions and fifteen independent brigades. In other words, Germany had 1.3 percent of its field formations in Africa, Italy had 10.3 percent, and the British Empire had 15.7 percent. The British numbers in Africa had even greater significance because many of the formations in the United Kingdom or India were not fully equipped or were territorial units. In nearly two years of campaigning in Africa, Great Britain had not been able to parlay a hard-won material dominance into success. General John Kennedy of the War Office put the problem into a nutshell. "We manage by terrific efforts to pile up resources at the necessary places and then the business seems to go wrong, for lack of generalship and junior leadership and bad tactics and lack of concentration of forces at decisive points."[2]

THE EASTERN FRONT

On 5 June 1942 the Eastern Front was relatively quiet, caught in a moment between the failure of the Soviet Union's spring offensives and the onset of Germany's summer push toward Stalingrad and the Caucasus oil fields. In Russia the German army deployed 139 infantry and 36 armored and motorized divisions. There were, in addition, sixteen Finnish, thirteen Romanian, nine Hungarian, three Italian, one Slovakian, and one Spanish division there. Axis forces totaled about 2.7 million men. Against them the Soviets fielded 5.5 million troops organized into forty-nine field and four tank armies.[3]

THE ARCTIC FRONT

Germany maintained more ground, air, and naval forces in Norway than in the Mediterranean. By June 1942 these included eight divisions to protect against a feared Allied invasion and, to menace Russian-bound convoys, a strong surface fleet and a specialized antishipping Luftflotte with 264 aircraft.

The Arctic convoys strained Great Britain's shipping resources, and London needed the tanks and aircraft it sent more than the Soviets did, but the convoys were a political necessity. The Soviet Union was tremendously popular in Great Britain at the time, and the government was under heavy pressure to support the heroic Russian soldier defending his land against the mighty Nazi army. The convoys also reduced the threat of Stalin signing a separate peace with Hitler—an event which the two foes periodically discussed through the summer of 1943 when Stalin concluded Germany could not defeat him.

Like the Malta convoys, the Arctic operations traversed restricted waters dominated by enemy aircraft and subjected to submarine and surface attack to reach an isolated destination. The British ran six major convoys from March to July 1942. These averaged twenty-eight transports and forty-three escorts each. The first five convoys lost twelve vessels and the last, PQ17, twenty.

THE ATLANTIC

The Royal Navy fought, with Canadian and American assistance, its most important naval campaign in the North Atlantic. The United Kingdom's economy and ultimately its survival were at stake, not to mention the buildup of U.S. forces for the eventual invasion of Europe.

In February 1942 imports shipped to Great Britain dropped to a low of 1,867,000 tons. By June 1942 imports had recovered slightly to 2,091,000 tons, but this was still less than half the wartime high of 4,207,000 tons achieved in March 1940. Great Britain had to devote massive naval resources to keeping even this diminished flow open. Numbers varied, but on 1 August 1942 the British and Canadian navies had 97 destroyers, 26 sloops, 167 corvettes, and 8 "cutters" escorting Arctic and Atlantic convoys.[4]

On 1 June 1942 there were 447 merchant vessels at sea in the North Atlantic in 13 convoys escorted by 130 warships. On 1 June Germany had 318 submarines available, of which 127 were in frontline use. In the vital tonnage war, May and June 1942 were deadly months. Worldwide, the Allies (and neutrals) lost 151 vessels in May displacing 705,050 tons and 173 ships displacing 834,196 tons in June, the month when German submarines were at their most effective, with forty-eight merchantmen sunk for every submarine lost. In the first six months of 1942 the Allies lost 4.15 million tons of shipping worldwide. Losses in the Atlantic and home waters constituted 74.5 percent of this total. The Pacific and Indian Oceans accounted for 22.1 percent and the Mediterranean 3.9 percent.[5]

THE AIR WAR IN THE WEST

Great Britain's strategic bombing campaign was based on the premise "that victory would come to the power which mounted the heaviest and most sustained bombing offensive." In the months immediately before the mid-June operations, the strategic bombing proponents felt that their campaign was finally starting to gain momentum.[6]

On the night of 30–31 May 1942 the RAF threw everything it had into the sky, including training squadrons, and mounted the first of its heavily publicized "thousand-bomber" raids on Cologne; 1,046 aircraft took off, and 898 arrived over the target. The RAF hit Essen three nights later in a raid nearly as large. On 25 June thirteen hundred planes bombed Bremen. In June 1942 Bomber Command delivered the greatest weight of bombs it had managed in the war to date: 6,845 tons in 4,997 sorties—totals that would not be surpassed until February 1943. While this was impressive compared to earlier efforts, it was insignificant compared to what was to come. By June 1944 bomber tonnage dropped on Germany by the British and the Eighth USAAF routinely exceeded 80,000 tons a month, and even under this pounding, German production increased.[7]

The strategic bombing campaign's greatest impact in mid-1942 was that it prevented long-range aircraft from being used to protect convoys. The Admiralty lamented the unsupportable rate at which U-boats were sinking shipping and asserted that the best help would be the "diversion of more long-range aircraft to Coastal Command, and in accepting the inevitable decline in our bombing offensive against Germany."[8] Bomber Command, supported by the War Cabinet and the prime minister, denied the Admiralty's requests in the conviction that even minor diversions of long-range bombers to other uses weakened the critical mass required to achieve victory. In fact, the lost shipping and sunken cargos which small numbers of long-range aircraft could have saved cost the British war effort more than indiscriminate night bombing hurt the Germans.

SOUTHEAST ASIA AND THE INDIAN OCEAN

Following the attack on Pearl Harbor a Japanese corps of 30,000 troops swept through British Malaya and captured Singapore from 85,000 British and Empire soldiers on 15 February. Three weeks later Japan accepted the surrender of the Dutch East Indies. In three months ten Japanese divisions conquered a vast area and secured the resources Tokyo required to become a world power.

These defeats rocked the British government and opened the gates of the Indian Ocean, which bordered two of the Empire's centers of power, Australia and India. Despite alarming losses in the North Atlantic, the need to counter Germany's High Seas Fleet in the Arctic, and the demands in the Mediterranean, Japan's victories forced Great Britain to station its most powerful fleet in the Indian Ocean. By the end of March the Eastern Fleet had three carriers (albeit with less than a hundred aircraft), five battleships, two heavy and five light cruisers (one Dutch), sixteen destroyers, and seven submarines (two Dutch).

Japanese forces occupied the Andaman Islands in the eastern Indian Ocean on 23 March. On 3 April a powerful force that included five large carriers with 350 aircraft and four fast battleships penetrated the Indian Ocean. Over the next week this armada raided Ceylon and hammered the Eastern Fleet. Meanwhile, a light carrier, supported by cruisers and destroyers, swept the Bay of Bengal clean of Allied shipping. Overall the Japanese forays cost the British the light carrier *Hermes*, the heavy cruisers *Cornwall* and *Dorsetshire*, two destroyers, a corvette, an auxiliary cruiser, twenty-five merchantmen, and thirty-nine aircraft. The Japanese lost seventeen aircraft. Reeling from the sheer power of this incursion and shocked by the Eastern Fleet's helplessness, the chiefs of staff confessed, "we are in real danger of losing our Indian Empire."[9] On 5 May Great Britain invaded French Madagascar—an expedition that required a substantial contribution from Force H—to obtain a fallback position should catastrophe overtake India as it had Malaya, Burma, and the East Indies.

On 1 June five Japanese submarines and two auxiliary cruisers were operating in the Indian Ocean and in the Mozambique Channel. In May and June they sank twenty-five vessels, displacing 120,119 tons.

THE PACIFIC

The Pacific war raged on the far side of the world from the Mediterranean, but it also profoundly affected operations there. Easy victories encouraged Tokyo to indulge in offensive actions beyond its planned defensive perimeter. The incursion into the Indian Ocean was the first such expedition, and the results it garnered so cheaply seemed to promise unlimited possibilities. On 25 May the Japanese commenced an intricate operation to seize Midway Atoll and provoke a fleet action with the elusive American carriers. By 1 June 1942 the bulk of the Japanese navy was escorting, supporting, or covering transports bound for United States territories in the Central Pacific and Alaska. However, even as the Harpoon convoy was at sea, American carriers ambushed their Japanese counterparts in the battle of Midway, fought on 4 through 6 June, and sank four fleet carriers at the cost of one of their own. This action relieved much of the pressure on Great Britain's Eastern Fleet and, by extension, on the Royal Navy as a whole and was, arguably, the most significant Allied victory in the war to date.

POLITICS AND THE NEED FOR VICTORY

In February 1942 Churchill wrote to a correspondent, "I can't get the victories. It's the victories that are so hard to get."[10] At this point in the war the record of Great Britain's armed forces, particularly its army, was one of failure. In 1940 defeats in Norway and France were climaxed by evacuations. The successful African campaign against the Italians hardly offset these disasters. In 1941 Imperial forces were driven from Greece and, less excusably, from Crete. The year saw defeat in North Africa followed in November by partial redemption and then, in January 1942, by another reversal. Only along the peripheries against isolated or second-rate foes in East Africa, Iran, Iraq, Syria, and Madagascar did Imperial arms prevail. As 1942 progressed catastrophic collapses in Malaya and Burma stunned the nation and the government. After three years of war the British public had scant reason to cheer their military's performance. True, the navy had brightened the gloom with successful actions against German warships like *Graf Spee* and *Bismarck*. It had knocked the Italians at Taranto in November 1940 and at Matapan in March 1941, and the RAF had triumphed in the Battle of Britain, but in the conflict's larger scheme these triumphs were either defensive or of minor consequence.

The participation of the United States seemed to ensure ultimate victory, but it had a poisonous side as well. The Americans were providing an ever-increasing share of the materiel required to fight, and Britain faced the prospect that it would no longer be able to act in what it believed were its best interests without American approval. This process was under way in the spring of 1942 and would reach its ultimate fulfillment in 1944, when the United States insisted on assaulting northern France over the objections of the British chiefs of staff, and when it scuttled Churchill's schemes for Italy and the Balkans by invading southern France in August 1944.

Thus, in the context of May 1942, a British victory in the Middle East was crucial to the United Kingdom's future standing, to its own morale, and to ensuring that future actions could play out as the British, not the Americans, deemed best.

ALLIANCES AND LOGISTICS

Another influence on the mid-June convoy battles was the way the two grand alliances coordinated their efforts and approached strategy. June 1942 was the nearest the three signatories of the Axis pact came to fighting as a coalition, although, in the case of the Japanese, this was a case of accidental convergence of effort. Italy and Germany, on the other hand, were fighting together on land in North Africa and the Soviet Union; on the sea in the Atlantic, where Italian submarines operated from German bases; in the Mediterranean; and in the air in North Africa and the Mediterranean. Italo-German military cooperation had dramatically improved by June 1942 after a poor beginning. First, Admiral Riccardi, who spoke fluent German, became the Regia Marina's chief of staff in December 1940. In October 1941 Berlin appointed Field Marshal Albert Kesselring Commander in Chief South, and he proved more adept at working with the Italians than the abrasive Rommel. Italian and German planners had devised a large-scale, combined-arms operation to capture Malta. Even Admiral Weichold, a relentless critic of Italian leadership, noted that "With the joint planning and carrying through of the preparations for the Malta operation, a complete joint staff work was achieved in the Mediterranean for the first time."[11]

The Anglo-American relationship was much stronger, given the common language and cultural affinities of the Allied partners. President Roosevelt and Prime Minister Churchill met on a regular basis, and each nation's chiefs of staff combined to coordinate strategy and operations at the highest levels in a body known as the Combined Chiefs of Staff. In the case of the mid-June convoys, the impact of this cooperation was subtle but powerful. The Americans had lent a valuable aircraft carrier to the British to conduct two aircraft ferry missions to Malta. Long-range American bombers operated from Egypt for the first time to attack Italian warships. Most importantly, the June 1942 participation of an American task force in the Arctic, which included the U.S. Navy's newest and best battleships, allowed the British to draw down the Home Fleet, provide escorts for Harpoon, and preserve the appearance of an all-British operation.

The fact that the Americans and British enjoyed a more cooperative relationship than did their foes should not disguise the fact, however, that they had sharp differences as well, and these differences affected operations. The United States still advocated direct landings in France, potentially as early as September 1942, but the British were bitterly opposed to any such adventure. This difference lent extra impetus to a large-scale, successful Mediterranean offensive. The British needed a victory of their own.

CONCLUSION

In June 1942 Great Britain's global position was precarious. The Royal Navy was losing the Battle of the Atlantic while Bomber Command wasted resources to burn German cities. Britain had made a pathetic botch of defending Singapore, which the government had deemed the empire's second most valuable possession after the Home Islands. Japan had further cracked the foundations of Imperial power with its rapid conquest of Burma and its unstoppable rampage through the Indian Ocean. Australia seemed imperiled. In the midst of this maelstrom, the Mediterranean war continued. The British Empire's North African army was larger and required more supplies than ever before, but Malta's position was weaker. The Royal Navy's power in the Mediterranean was diminished and the forces to mount a significant operation, such as the mid-June convoys, could only come through the loan of vessels from other fleets guarding more important assets. Despite this grim situation, North Africa remained the Empire's focus, and the government gave priority to Malta over more critical needs.

HMS *Havock* photographed from an Italian aircraft on 11 April 1942. After being heavily damaged by *Littorio* on 22 March in the Second Battle of Sirte, *Havock* put into Malta for repairs. However, air raids inflicted further damage, and on 5 April she set out for Gibraltar. Unfortunately, *Havock* ran aground near Kelebia Lighthouse south of Cape Bon shortly after midnight on 6 April. At 0317 that same morning, the Italian submarine *Aradam* torpedoed the wreck. The crew detonated the aft magazine the next afternoon to complete the vessel's destruction. This caused the stern (labeled *Poppa* on the photograph) to break away. *Enrico Cernuschi Collection*

Italian troops exercising for the scheduled invasion of Malta during the spring of 1942. They are coming ashore from a *motobragozzi*, a motorized fishing vessel that served as a type of landing craft using long plankways that extended from either side of the vessel. *Courtesy of Erminio Bagnasco*

Victorio Veneto at high speed on the morning of 15 June 1942. Her secondary battery is firing to port fending off an air attack. *USMM*

The Vigorous convoy under air attack. *Storia MILITARE*

Photograph taken by a Cant Z.1007bis of the 35° Stormo showing the Australian destroyer *Nestor* apparently on fire. The ship suffered a severe shock from a near miss and was subsequently scuttled when attempts to tow her to safety failed. *Enrico Cernuschi Collection*

A line of S.79s armed with torpedoes. These tri-motored medium bombers, in service from 1936, were the workhorses of the Italian air force and were most dangerous to ships as torpedo-bombers. The U.S. Army Intelligence Bulletin for January 1943 said, "Torpedo squadrons are believed to have the highest morale of all units of the Italian Air Force. Their efficiency is such that Germany has sent squadrons to Italy for instruction in torpedo tactics." *Storia MILITARE*

The most common German bomber active in the Mediterranean during the mid-June convoy battles was the Ju 88, pictured here. The A-4 variant saw heavy service in these actions. It could reach 317 mph and carry 6,600 pounds of ordnance and served as a level and a low-angle dive bomber. *Storia MILITARE*

Italian Cant Z.506 rescuing downed airmen. These floatplanes, which could accommodate up to a dozen passengers, were the best hope for any aircrew shot down over water. *Storia MILITARE*

HMS *Coventry*. She sailed with the Vigorous convoy. These old cruisers were modified to serve as specialized antiaircraft vessels, *Coventry* being converted in 1936. She carried ten single 4-inch mounts whereas *Cairo*, converted in 1938, received four enclosed twin mounts. Otherwise, their appearances were similar. *Stephen Dent Collection*

HMS *Hasty*. She was a veteran ship that had fought in Norway and then, from June 1940, in the Mediterranean. She met her end in Operation Vigorous when a torpedo fired by *S.55* caught her in the bow just as she was taking station after chasing *S.56*, the boat that had damaged *Newcastle*. *Stephen Dent Collection*

FACING. The battleship *Littorio* entering the inner harbor at Taranto on 26 June 1942 after her sortie against the Vigorous convoy. The torpedo damage is not visible as the weapon struck on the starboard bow. Counterflooding corrected her trim, and she was on her way to the dry dock to make repairs. *Commander Vittorio di Sambuy*

HMS *Matchless*. The M class was larger and presented a more substantial profile than pre-war destroyers like *Hasty*. Her 4.7-inch guns fired a heavier shell to a longer range. Admiral Da Zara mistook these destroyers for cruisers, and given *Matchless'* twin mounts and the unusually large size of the geysers thrown up when her shells hit the water, this was an understandable mistake. *Stephen Dent Collection*

Raimondo Montecuccoli in action at Pantelleria on 15 June. Italy began constructing modern 6-inch gunned light cruisers of the so-called Condottieri type in 1928. *Montecuccoli,* a third-generation ship, displaced two thousand tons more than the first-generation vessels but a thousand tons less than *Eugenio.* Most of the extra weight was given to better armor protection. *Storia MILITARE*

Premuda laying smoke during the Battle of Pantelleria. Armed with 5.5-inch guns and originally constructed as Yugoslavian destroyer leader *Dubrovnik,* she was a powerful vessel but handicapped during the action because she was a late addition to Da Zara's force and there had not been enough time to top her bunkers before the squadron sailed. *Storia MILITARE*

The charge of the 14th Squadron. *Malocello* followed by *Vivaldi.* They closed to within 7,000 yards of the convoy and claimed a torpedo hit on one of the transports. From a painting by the famous Italian maritime artist Rudolf Claudus. *USMM*

Division Admiral Alberto Da Zara, commander of the 7th Division at the Battle of Pantelleria. He felt that he had a historic opportunity to win a victory, and his persistence was key to the success Italian forces enjoyed that day. *Rivista Marittima*

Smoke plumes on the horizon seen from the cruiser *Eugenio di Savoia* on the early afternoon of 15 June. Da Zara called these a "fantastic spectacle" and considered them proof of a successful mission. *Storia MILITARE*

Italy's premier and head of state Benito Mussolini congratulating the crew of *Littorio* on 25 June. The navy's chief of staff, Admiral Arturo Riccardi, is behind and to the right of Mussolini. *USMM*

Mussolini distributing decorations, this time at Naples on 26 June. An Ro.43 can be seen on a catapult in the background. *Storia MILITARE*

84

MS 53, one of the new and more capable Italian *motosiluranti* type MTBs that were so effective against the August convoy. *Storia MILITARE*

FACING ABOVE A souvenir of battle. A splinter from the shell that hit *Montecuccoli*. The inscription reads, "here we are all again still the same as then." *Courtesy of Giancarlo Vivaldi*

FACING BELOW The Pedestal convoy under air attack. *Storia MILITARE*

Risk and reward. The heavy cruiser *Bolzano* torpedoed after being called back from intercepting the Pedestal convoy. *Courtesy of Erminio Bagnasco*

5

OPERATION VIGOROUS

Perhaps we should [have been] grateful that it was the Italians and the
Germans with their equal lack of understanding of how to operate naval
air power that we faced in those waters and not the Japanese.

Commander A. J. Pugsley, HMS Paladin

ON 18 APRIL the Chiefs of Staff Committee concluded that it would
be impossible to send a convoy to Malta in May. Instead they decided to mount
a massive operation during the June dark period—a simultaneous double convoy from Alexandria and Gibraltar. The western operation, dubbed Harpoon,
planned and commanded by personnel from the Home Fleet, would include
five transports and a tanker. The convoy from the east, which was a production of the Mediterranean Fleet's new commander in chief, (acting) Admiral Harry Harwood, and was code-named Vigorous, would have ten merchant
ships and a tanker. Because they were independent operations, these convoys
will be considered sequentially.

AIRPOWER

The Mediterranean Fleet lacked capital ships, which the experiences
of the December 1941, February 1942, and March 1942 convoys suggested would
be needed to protect the operation against the Italian battleships. However,
at the time the convoy was conceived, London anticipated that a desert offensive would have secured airfields near Benghazi, increasing the effectiveness of
the land-based airpower that Admiral Harwood considered a potential offset.
He envisioned "bombers and torpedo bombers to provide the heavy hitting

power, and long-range fighters to give the cover that had previously been provided by battleships and carriers." London also recognized that Malta's fighter squadrons needed to be reinforced if they were to protect two convoys and cover their unloading.[1]

The decision to forgo a May convoy allowed *Eagle* to ferry Spitfires to Malta on 3 and 9 June. Bf 109s based at Pantelleria bounced the thirty-two Spitfires involved in the 3 June operation and shot down four over the water; another crash-landed, leaving a net gain of twenty-seven aircraft. Thirty Spitfires safely arrived in the 9 June operation and nine of ten Beaufighters flew in from Gibraltar the next day. Other reinforcements included six torpedo-armed Wellingtons, fifteen Beauforts, and more Beaufighters. The RAF did what it could to set the stage. Between 24 May and 10 June Malta-based Wellingtons made 104 sorties against airfields in Sicily and the harbors at Naples, Taranto, Messina, and Cagliari.[2]

On 10 June Malta had 146 operational aircraft. The fighter force consisted of ninety-five Spitfires and fourteen Beaufighters. Attack aircraft included four FAA Albacores, six Baltimores, fourteen Beauforts, ten Wellingtons, and three photographic-reconnaissance Spitfires. In Egypt air strength included two FAA Albacore and one FAA ASV Swordfish squadrons, one Beaufort and two Blenheim squadrons (one Greek), a squadron of RAAF Hudsons, a squadron of Marylands, one of Sunderlands, one of Wellesleys, and some ASV Wellingtons. In addition there were fighter and fighter-bomber P-40 and Hurricane squadrons.[3]

Facing the RAF and FAA forces at Malta and in North Africa, the Germans deployed three major units. On 10 June Fliegerkorps II in Sicily had 96 aircraft: 38 Ju 88A-4, 14 Ju 88C-6, 28 Bf 109F-4, and 20 Ju 88D-1 and Bf 109F reconnaissance planes. Fliegerkorps X in Crete and Greece deployed 98 machines including 2 Bf 109F-4 fighters, 59 Ju 88A-4 bombers, 14 He 111H-6 bombers, 5 Ju 88D-1 reconnaissance aircraft, and 23 assorted float- and seaplanes. In Libya Fliegerführer Afrika had 140 aircraft including 57 Bf 109F fighters, 8 Bf 109F-4B fighter-bombers, 46 Ju 87D-1 dive bombers, and 29 reconnaissance Bf 110C-4s, Bf 109Fs, and Hs 126s.

On the afternoon of 12 June the Regia Aeronautica responded to news of a British force departing Gibraltar by ordering several units to redeploy from the mainland to Sardinia. By 14 June the Sardinian command's operational strength was 175 aircraft including 63 torpedo-bombers, 35 level bombers, 9 fighter-bombers, and 68 fighters. Air Sicily deployed 174 machines on Sicily and Pantelleria consisting of 41 level bombers, 17 dive bombers, 14 torpedo-bombers, and 102 fighters. In addition, Superaereo ordered Aegean and North African air units to attack the convoys. The 5ª Air Fleet in Libya allocated a dozen S.79s, five Cant Z.1007bis, twenty-eight MC.202s, and a Stormo of MC.200s to this task. Comando Egeo in Rhodes had an operational strength of ten Cant Z.1007bis bombers, five S.79 torpedo-bombers, twenty-seven CR.42s, and seventeen G.50 fighters, although only the bombers had the range to participate in the campaign.[4] Mindful of the many failures rooted in faulty or inadequate reconnaissance, the Regia Aeronautica and Luftwaffe, in conjunction with the navy's *ricognizione marittima,* implemented a rigorous exploration of the Western Mediterranean beginning on 13 June.

VIGOROUS

Vigorous was the larger and more important of the two operations. It was Admiral Harwood's first task after hoisting his flag on his dry-docked flagship, *Queen Elizabeth,* on 20 May 1942—and not an easy one considering he had just a few weeks to settle into his command, meet his personnel, and finish planning the war's greatest Malta convoy.

Harwood had been a captain since 1928 and had been marked as unfit for flag rank until the onset of war and the appearance of the German armored ship *Admiral Graf Spee* in his command area, the remote South American station. He concentrated the majority of his squadron in the right place at the right time and fought a competent surface action to win the Royal Navy's first significant victory. After the River Plate battle Harwood cooled his heels as Assistant Chief of Naval Staff (Foreign). Churchill, who considered that Britain lacked military leaders with "fire in their bellies," had held up Harwood as an exemplary offensive spirit and had pressed the Admiralty to find a better use for him. Interestingly, Harwood was no fan of Churchill's offensive ideas. General Kennedy recalled one occasion in August 1941 when Harwood telephoned him and "swore heartily for five minutes on end" about the prime minister's suggestion to run another direct convoy through the Mediterranean.[5]

Harwood was so long in getting an active command because the Admiralty did not share the prime minister's enthusiasm for him. "He was seen as a kindly, very robust man, capable of impetuosity but with generally sound if unexciting judgment . . . he was not a great leader, nor a great brain." Harwood succeeded Admiral Cunningham, who made his reputation as a fighter, not as

an administrator. According to two peers, Cunningham "paid so little attention to staff work [and] could never entirely overcome his boredom with administration, which at times caused serious inconveniences to subordinates,
and left difficulties for successors." Nonetheless, the new commander in chief
energetically plunged into his task and crafted a meticulous plan that borrowed
from past operations and included a few wrinkles of his own that he hoped
would improve the convoy's odds.[6]

The vessels for Vigorous were gathered from the Eastern Mediterranean
and, as in the past, some sailed from the United Kingdom. Reports filed by
some participants suggest unease and complain about suspicious characters
who might be spies and sloppy work preparing the ships. For example, the
transport Potaro was entering Alexandria after dark with an Egyptian pilot
when the pilot instructed the master to exhibit recognition lights. The master
refused because he had observed flares being dropped from aircraft eight miles
off. The Examination Service Steamer (the vessel that examined shipping coming into port) accosted Potaro with "a full brilliancy Aldis light" and demanded
the ship show its lights, much to the master's ire.[7]

Harwood was also concerned that spies would betray the gathering of a
large convoy, and to "facilitate the extremely difficult business of disguising
the fact that a convoy was being prepared for Malta," he arranged for Vigorous
to sail from three ports: Alexandria, Haifa, and Port Suez. One convoy would
sail two days before the others and then turn back, hoping to lure the Italian
fleet from base prematurely. Following past practice, Harwood also arranged
for commando raids on Axis airbases. He assigned the Special Interrogation
Group (SIG) three fields around Derna, the Special Air Service (SAS) was to
hit targets at Benghazi and Barce, and he gave the Special Boat Service (SBS)
and SAS four fields on Crete. However, Italian intelligence learned of these
ventures from reports filed by the U.S. Army attaché in Cairo, which it routinely intercepted and read, and the North African ventures failed. The raids
on Crete were a qualified success, in part because the Germans discounted
Italian warnings. The commandos destroyed twenty-eight aircraft at two of
the target fields, including sixteen Ju 88s at Maleme, and more than 26,000 gallons of fuel. However, the Germans flew in replacements from Greece the next
day, and the air formations were at full strength by the time the convoy was in
range.[8]

Harwood noted that "in previous operations, available submarines had
been disposed in the close approaches to Messina and Taranto. Apart from

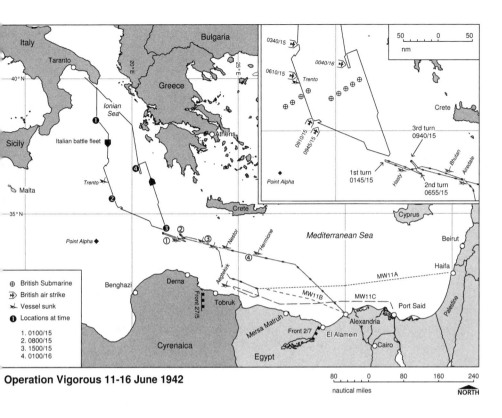

Operation Vigorous 11-16 June 1942

valuable early sighting reports and an occasional attack on returning enemy forces, these dispositions had produced little result." He decided to deploy submarines of the 1st and 10th flotillas north of the convoy's route in a moving picket line that the Italian fleet would need to cross, hoping to inflict damage before battle was joined. On 1 June there were seventeen boats in the Mediterranean. Twelve of these were at sea when the operation began, and nine, *Proteus, Thorn, Taku, Thrasher, Porpoise, Una, P31, P34,* and *P35,* all based at Alexandria, were on patrol in the Ionian Sea or the Gulf of Sirte. The Gibraltar boats, *P42* and *P44,* patrolled off Sardinia and Sicily.[9]

Finally Harwood decided to personally command the operation from Alexandria in conjunction with Air Marshal Tedder from a special room in the RAF Naval Cooperation Group headquarters. He felt that this would improve coordination between the operation's various elements, especially as air striking forces were replacing battleships should the Italian heavy units threaten the convoy.

There were other factors that Harwood needed to consider in his planning. First, sunrise at Cairo on 12 June 1942 was at 0552 and sunset 1954. To this fourteen hours of daylight could be added two hours of twilight, which meant that the convoy would be exposed to air attack for long periods. Second, the weather forecast called for clear and calm conditions, which also worked to the advantage of the attackers. Third, the Italian intelligence network in Egypt had been improved in 1942, and it was not possible to conceal the sailing of a large convoy. To offset these factors, Malta now had enough fighters to protect the convoy as it neared Valletta and to once again allow bombers to base there. The Royal Air Force had pledged complete cooperation. Air Marshall Tedder agreed that should the Italian battle fleet sortie, he would hit it with everything he had: forty Wellington medium bombers, Beaufort torpedo-bombers from Libya and Malta, and American B-24s that happened to be in Egypt. A few RAF B-24s in transit to India were also available.

The escort for Vigorous consisted of eight light cruisers, twenty-six destroyers, four corvettes, two minesweepers, and the ex-target ship *Centurion*, dressed up with wooden turrets and a false superstructure to resemble a modern *King George V* class battleship. Even though its largest warship was a dummy dreadnought, Vigorous was still the Mediterranean Fleet's greatest display of strength since autumn 1941, made possible by the loan of four cruisers and ten destroyers from Somerville's Eastern Fleet. Churchill also asked the Admiralty to assign *Warspite* and the Eastern Fleet's three carriers, but they considered that too risky. Admiral Somerville observed that "it was the sort of party I liked but I reckoned the odds of 1,320 [aircraft] against 120 was such that the prospect of [the aircraft carriers] being usable afterwards was remote."[10]

Harwood's chief lieutenant was Rear Admiral Philip Vian. Vian had commanded a destroyer flotilla and became famous in February 1940 for violating Norwegian neutrality to rescue British prisoners aboard the German supply ship *Altmark*. A year later he was involved in the *Bismarck* action attacking the battleship at night with his flotilla instead of following orders to screen *King George V* and *Rodney*. After that Vian raided Spitzbergen Island in August and then, leading two cruisers, he attacked a German convoy along the Arctic coast in September. The Admiralty posted him to the Mediterranean in October 1941 to command the 15th Cruiser Squadron. Vian led that force in the First Battle of Sirte in December 1941 and in the Second Battle of Sirte in March 1942 as related above.

Vian was known as a loose cannon. He conducted shore bombardments without orders, and Admiral Ramsay wrote of him, "He is d—d temperamental & at times a great annoyance . . . he is always apt to work against rather than with me." On a fitness report written in February 1941 his superior officer noted, "Captain Vian is ambitious and has a very high opinion of himself, somewhat intolerant and prone to rather sudden likes and dislikes." He was not the ideal subordinate for a new and untested commander. Indeed, more than a decade after events Vian wrote that he "lacked confidence in the plan, in the C-in-C, and the C-in-C's ability to carry out the plan."[11]

Harwood's plan called for Convoy MW11C, the antiaircraft cruiser *Coventry*, and the 5th Destroyer Flotilla to depart Port Said at 1630 on 11 June and reach the longitude of Tobruk at dusk on 12 June. There it would reverse course and meet the main convoy west of Alexandria on the afternoon of the 13th. Harwood listed MW11C's objectives as

"(a) drawing the enemy's surface forces and thus exposing
   them to submarine and air attack.

(b) confusing his appreciation of our real intentions.

(c) endeavour to force a heavy expenditure of fuel on the Italian
   fleet so that they will have difficulty in intercepting our main
   convoy."[12]

At 1500 on 12 June MW11A and the 7th Flotilla would depart Haifa. MW11B, sailing from Alexandria, would join MW11A at 0600 on June 13. *Centurion*, heavily armed with antiaircraft weapons and loaded with supplies, would head to Alexandria independently and then, with the 14th and 22nd destroyer flotillas and the 11th Corvette Group, join MW11A and B at 1400 on the 13th. The 14th Minesweeping Flotilla would move to Tobruk and from there rendezvous with the united convoy at 0600 on 14 June. The cruisers of the 15th and 4th squadrons and the 5th Destroyer Flotilla, which would separate from MW11C to refuel in Alexandria, would likewise join the united convoy at 0600 on the same morning.

INTELLIGENCE

Supermarina knew that a large convoy operation was impending and had updated its plans to counter such an event based upon the ships available,

Table 5.1. Operation Vigorous Escort

Name	Commander	Type	Tons Std.	Main Guns	Secondary	Speed
15th CS	R Adm. P. L. Vian					
Cleopatra (F)	Capt. G. Grantham	CLA	5,600	10 × 5.25in	6 × 21in TT	32
Dido	Capt. H. W. McCall	CLA	5,600	10 × 5.25in	6 × 21in TT	32
Hermione	Capt. G. N. Oliver	CLA	5,600	10 × 5.25in	6 × 21in TT	32
Euryalus	Capt. E. W. Bush	CLA	5,600	10 × 5.25in	6 × 21in TT	32
Arethusa	Capt. A. C. Chapman	CL	5,220	6 × 6in	6 × 21in TT	32
Coventry	Capt. R. J. Dendy	CLA	5,240	8 × 4in		29
4th CS	R Adm. W. G. Tennant					
Newcastle (F)	Capt. P. B. William-Powlett	CL	9,100	12 × 6in	6 × 21in TT	32
Birmingham	Capt. H. B. Crane	CL	9,100	12 × 6in	6 × 21in TT	32
7th DD Flot						
Napier (F)	Capt. S. H. Arliss	DD	1,760	6 × 4.7in	5 × 21in TT	36
Nestor	Cdr. A. S. Rosenthal	DD	1,760	6 × 4.7in	5 × 21in TT	36
Norman	Cdr. H. M. Burrell	DD	1,760	6 × 4.7in	5 × 21in TT	36
Nizam	L Cdr. M. J. Clark	DD	1,760	6 × 4.7in	5 × 21in TT	36
14th DD Flot						
Jervis (F)	Capt. A. L. Poland	DD	1,760	6 × 4.7	5 × 21in TT	36
Kelvin	Cdr. M. S. Townsend	DD	1,760	6 × 4.7	5 × 21in TT	36
Javelin	L Cdr. H. C. Simms	DD	1,760	6 × 4.7	5 × 21in TT	36
12th DD Flot						
Pakenham (F)	Capt. E. B. Stevens	DD	1,540	5 × 4in	4 × 21in TT	37
Paladin	Cdr. A. F. Pugsley	DD	1,540	5 × 4in	4 × 21in TT	37
Inconstant	L Cdr. W. S. Clouston	DD	1,335	4 × 4.7in	4 × 21in TT	36
22nd DD Flot						
Sikh (F)	Capt. St. J. Micklethwait	DD	1,959	6 × 4.7in	4 × 21in TT	36
Zulu	Cdr. R. T. White	DD	1,959	6 × 4.7in	4 × 21in TT	36

Ship	Commander	Type	Tonnage	Guns	Torpedoes	
Hasty	L Cdr. N. H. Austen	DD	1,335	4 × 4.7in	4 × 21in TT	36
Hero	Lt. W. Scott	DD	1,335	4 × 4.7in	4 × 21in TT	36
5th DD Flot						
Dulverton (F)	L Cdr. W. N. Patch	DD	1,050	6 × 4in	—	27
Exmoor	L Cdr. L. St. G. Rich	DD	1,050	6 × 4in	—	27
Croome	L Cdr. J. D. Hayes	DD	1,050	6 × 4in	—	27
Eridge	L Cdr. W. Gregory-Smith	DD	1,050	6 × 4in	—	27
Airedale	L Cdr. A. G. Forman	DD	1,050	4 × 4in	2 × 21in TT	27
Beaufort	L Cdr. S. O. Roche-Bart	DD	1,050	6 × 4in	—	27
Hurworth	L Cdr. J. T. Birch	DD	1,050	6 × 4in	—	27
Telcott	Lt. H. R. Rycroft	DD	1,050	6 × 4in	—	27
Aldenham	Lt. H. A. Stuart-Menteth	DD	1,050	4 × 4in	2 × 21in TT	27
2nd DD Flot						
Fortune (F)	L Cdr. R. D. Pankhurst	DD	1,460	3 × 4.7in	4 × 21in TT	36
Griffin	L Cdr. A. N. Rowell	DD	1,335	4 × 4.7in	4 × 21in TT	36
Hotspur	Lt. T. D. Herrick	DD	1,335	4 × 4.7in	4 × 21in TT	36
11th DC Group						
Delphinium (F)	Cdr. R. L. Spalding	DC	900	1 × 4in	—	16
Primula	L Cdr. J. H. Fuller	DC	900	1 × 4in	—	16
Erica	L Cdr. W. C. Riley	DC	900	1 × 4in	—	16
Snapdragon	Lt. P. H. Potter	DC	900	1 × 4in	—	16
14th MS Flot						
Boston	Lt. D. H. Coughlan	MS	605	1 × 3in	—	16
Seaham	Lt. R. E. Brett	MS	656	1 × 3in	—	16
Miscellaneous						
Centurion	Cdr. A. H. Alexander	TS	25,500	A/A only	—	16
Antwerp	L Cdr. J. N. Hulse	RS	2,957	—	—	21
Malines	Lt. J. R. Freeman	RS	2,969	—	—	21

Table 5.2. Operation Vigorous Convoys

MW11A (Hafia)	GRT	Nationality	Fate	Speed
Ajax	7,540	British		16
City of Edinburgh	8,036	British		15.5
City of Pretoria	8,049	British		15.5
City of Lincoln	8,039	British		15.5
Elisabeth Bakke	5,450	Norwegian	Dropped out	16
MW11B (Alexandria)				
Potaro	5,410	British	Damaged by air	15
Bulkoil	8,071	American	Damaged by air	14
MW11C (Suez)				
Aagtekerk	6,811	Dutch	Sunk by air	16
Bhutan	6,104	British	Sunk by air	14
City of Calcutta	8,036	British	Damaged by air	15.5
Rembrandt	7,121	British		

their locations and, most importantly, the amount of fuel oil on hand. On 23 May Admiral Riccardi sent a personal appeal to Grand Admiral Raeder requesting a special shipment of twenty thousand tons of oil because the navy's reserves had dropped to a point where it had become impossible to even maintain normal traffic with Libya. On 7 June the situation was such that two destroyers stationed in Taranto could only be deployed on antisubmarine duties by siphoning 500 tons of fuel from the battleship *Cesare*.[13]

Supermarina's first concrete intelligence about the mid-June operations arrived from the navy general staff's information section, which decrypted radio traffic regarding the arrival of a convoy in Gibraltar bound for Malta. On 4 June Supermarina read in a Tangiers newspaper that a 10,000-ton American tanker had arrived in Gibraltar. The next day agents in Algeciras, across the bay from Gibraltar, reported that several steamers loaded with supplies had docked and would try to reach Malta. British intelligence was able to read traffic generated by German intelligence routed to Berlin via Madrid, but the principal Italian navy code remained secure. Thus, "against the ever present threat of intervention by the Italian fleet it was not possible to rely on advance notice." Moreover, the British were unaware that Italian intelligence was reading routine wireless traffic generated by reconnaissance aircraft with as little as a half-hour delay.[14]

THE OPERATION GETS UNDER WAY

Convoy MW11C sailed from Port Said at 1400 on 11 June—the day the Axis mobile divisions broke out of the position known as the Cauldron and began to advance toward Tobruk. The escort consisted of the light cruiser *Coventry* (Captain R. J. R. Dendy) and the 5th Destroyer Flotilla—the Hunt-type destroyer escorts *Dulverton* (Lieutenant Commander W. N. Patch), *Croome*, *Eridge*, *Airedale*, *Beaufort*, *Hurworth*, and *Aldenham*. *Exmoor* and *Tetcott* joined the next day at 0700 and 1330, respectively.

German aircraft sighted MW11C north of Alexandria at 0715 on 12 June and again at 1815 off Mersa Matruh, but these sightings failed to lure the Italian fleet from port. In fact, Harwood's deceptions were too effective: Supermarina did not initially believe the Mediterranean Fleet was mounting a Malta convoy from Alexandria at all. Instead, they focused on the Western Mediterranean. Admiral Riccardi judged that "the situation at Alexandria was not such as to suggest a major operation." He conceded that the enemy had augmented the number of cruisers at Alexandria but that the general situation there justified such reinforcements. As of 1400 on 12 June Riccardi recommended that the battle fleet transfer to Naples so it could be ready to intervene in the Tyrrhenian Sea. Cavallero supported him affirming that "the Italian fleet cannot remain in port; the consumption of oil is justified." Mussolini added his endorsement. The high command wanted to ensure that it spent its oil for a valid reason because, following a sortie into the Tyrrhenian Sea, it would take twenty days to collect sufficient stocks from German charity and Rumanian deliveries to allow another fleet movement.[15]

Twelve Ju 88s from I./KG 54, the unit raided by the commandos, struck MW11C between 2102 and 2110 on the 12th just when the convoy was scheduled to reverse course. The German flight leader reported three steamers and one escort hit, but in fact the bombers only near-missed *City of Calcutta*. Nonetheless, the shock flooded the vessel's No. 5 Hold and brought her to a temporary halt. When the convoy came about at 2130 Captain Dendy believed the enemy missed his maneuver, but in fact they observed his turn. Eighty minutes later *City of Calcutta* reported defects, so Dendy ordered her to head for Tobruk and detached *Exmoor* and *Croome* to escort.[16]

Convoy MW11A's four transports departed Haifa at 1500 on 12 June escorted by the 7th Destroyer Flotilla, *Napier* (Captain S. H. T. Arliss), *Norman*, and *Nizam* with *Inconstant* and *Hotspur* attached, and the fleet minesweepers *Boston* and *Seaham.*

MW11B left Alexandria in sections on the morning of 13 June. The convoy's commodore, Rear Admiral H. England, sailed in the American tanker *Bulkoil.* The escort included the Eastern Fleet's 12th Destroyer Flotilla, *Pakenham* (Captain E. B. K. Stevens) and *Paladin* with *Fortune* attached. At 1010 the rescue ships *Malines* and *Antwerp,* ex-Channel ferries, with elements of the veteran 14th Flotilla, *Jervis* (Captain A. L. Poland) and *Kelvin,* and the 22nd Flotilla *Sikh* (Captain St. J. Micklethwait), *Zulu, Hasty, Hero,* along with *Tetcott* and the four corvettes got under way. *Javelin* was to sweep ahead of *Centurion,* which was scheduled to cast off by 1040. Boiler troubles delayed the target ship's departure, however, so Captain Poland detached *Javelin, Tetcott,* and the corvettes *Primula* and *Snapdragon* to screen her.

Convoys MW11A and B united off Alexandria at 1205 on the 13th. At 1230 *Malines, Antwerp,* and *Centurion,* accompanied by the 14th Destroyer Flotilla and the four corvettes, joined up. Destroyers of the 7th and 12th flotillas shuttled back to Alexandria to fuel. The 14th Flotilla's Captain Poland assumed command pending Vian's arrival. At this time he ordered *Elisabeth Bakke* to put into Alexandria because her bottom was badly fouled and she was not maintaining the convoy speed of thirteen knots. "As she did not appear to know her way, and was seen to be steaming to the northward, [Captain Poland] sent *Zulu* to escort her to the Great Pass Beacon."[17]

At 1315 on 13 June convoy MW11C hove into view. The 5th Flotilla's ships took their turn to duck into Alexandria to refuel.

At 1330 on 13 June the motor-torpedo boats *MTB 259, 261, 262,* and *264* joined up, and at 1440 the convoy reduced speed to allow these small craft to be taken in tow by a merchant vessel. They were "intended to increase the striking power of the fleet" should a surface action develop. If not, they would assist during the final push for Malta "to counter attack enemy E-Boats" and afterwards reinforce the light craft based on the island. The combined force, *Coventry,* ten destroyers, four corvettes, two rescue ships, four MTBs, and *Centurion,* escorting the tanker and eight steamers, continued west toward Malta.[18]

As the convoys converged and destroyers shuttled back and forth, reports began to flood the situation rooms at Superaereo and Oberbefehlshaber Süd (OBS). At the same time, Harwood's plans started to go slightly awry. A strong, hot wind kicked up a chop and made the going difficult for the MTBs. *MTB 259* lost a man overboard, and at 1945 she slipped her tow and advised that the boats "were being damaged and flooded." Poland immediately ordered them back to Alexandria. The process, however, proved "long and difficult" and was not completed until 2215. *Bhutan's* boat, for example, requested to be hauled in closer, but the ship's winch would not take the strain. The master "ordered the M.T.B. to come up on his engines. This was not obeyed and as, by this time, flares were being dropped astern of the convoy and the M.T.B. was still using an unshaded Aldis lamp and would not stop signaling when ordered to do so, I cut the tow with an axe."[19] *MTB 259* foundered on the return, and the other boats sustained damage.

Early that evening two groups of Ju 88s departed airfields in Crete to hit the large enemy formation that had been reported. Seven Ju 88s of I./KG 54 were unable to locate the target and instead dropped their ordnance near Mersa Matruh. The ships could see the searchlights and flak this attack provoked. Thirteen Ju 88s had better luck and struck between 2120 (an hour and twenty-five minutes after sunset) and 2145. *Conventry* opened fire at one point, and the convoy commander reported that bombs had fallen near screen's port wing and the convoy's port side, but none very close. *Bhutan,* however, reported sticks falling nearby and blamed the MTB's signaling for making her a target.[20]

By the evening of the 13th Supermarina had revised its assessment and concluded that the enemy had two operations under way. Based on past practice, the Italian naval command assumed that in the west the enemy's heavy escort would reverse course rather than risk the Sicilian narrows and thus a cruiser division would suffice to intercept the convoy near Pantelleria on the morning of 15 June. An eastern convoy, on the other hand, provided an excellent opportunity for the battle fleet to intervene in the central basin, just as it had in March. This would avoid the need to redeploy to Naples and save thousands of tons of fuel oil. Accordingly, Supermarina changed its plans, and at 1800 the fleet came to three hours' notice.

Rear Admiral Vian's cover force, the 15th and the 4th cruiser squadrons escorted by *Jervis, Javelin, Sikh, Hasty, Hero, Nestor,* and *Griffin* along with the 7th and 5th flotilla vessels that had refueled—fourteen destroyers in total—departed Alexandria at 1740 on the 13th.

During the night German aircraft shadowed the convoy. British vessels reported flares some distance to the southeast. *Cleopatra* noted small bombs exploding in her vicinity shortly before dawn; these probably came from a Ju 88 of I./KG 54 which reported attacking a vessel at 0500.[21]

At 0600 on 14 June *Boston, Seaham,* and the two Hunts, *Exmoor* and *Croome* that had accompanied *City of Calcutta* into Tobruk, joined MW11. A little more than two hours later Vian's warships overhauled the force. With the convoy finally whole one of the destroyer captains wrote, "The ring of warships round the convoy was a heartening sight and represented a tremendous volume of A-A fire power." However, MW11 did not remain whole for long. The freighter *Aagtekerk* and the corvettes *Erica* and *Primula* began to develop engine problems and fell behind. At 0835 Vian ordered *Aagtekerk* to make for Tobruk accompanied by *Tetcott* and *Primula.* He instructed *Erica* to head for Mersa Matruh. At the same time the main force turned northwest as it approached the enemy-held coast so as to keep an equal distance between Crete and the bulge of Cyrenaica. This route was popularly known as "Bomb Alley." Nonetheless, the 4th Cruiser Squadron's Admiral Tennent described the day as "surprisingly peaceful considering the area in which the large body of ships was situated."[22]

The British believed that their passage was peaceful because, beginning with a flight of six Hurricanes that patrolled overhead from 0600 to 0700, fighters protected the convoy with only small gaps in the coverage. The first shifts were Hurricanes and F4F Martlets, but after 0900, as the range increased, P-40s (Kittyhawks) and Beaufighters took over. However, as Vian noted in his report, "the acid test of the value of a small fighter escort is its ability or otherwise to keep the Fleet clear of shadowing aircraft by day. Under this test, in Operation 'Vigorous,' fighter co-operation failed."[23] Indeed, German reconnaissance aircraft kept the convoy under continuous observation, and air attacks did not develop during the morning only because Fliegerführer Afrika and Fliegerkorps X were preparing their blows. Units of LG 1 and KG 54 transferred from their Cretan airbases that morning and flew to Derna, which was twice as close to the British route. There the Ju 88s refueled and beginning at 1100 the first unit, II./LG 1, lifted off to attack.

At 1210 *Aagtekerk,* with *Tetcott* in attendance, was just twelve miles off Tobruk with *Primula* following six miles behind when thirty-six Ju 87s of II./St.G.3 and Ju 88s of II./LG 1 escorted by Bf 109s from III./JG.53 and I./JG.27 filled the eastern sky. They swarmed *Primula* first. Near misses shook the corvette, and concussions holed two fuel tanks, knocked a boiler off-line, and reduced the ship's speed to ten knots.

Explosions astern were *Tetcott*'s first sign of trouble. Then, as the small destroyer's captain, Lieutenant H. R. Rycroft, reported, "nine to twelve [Ju 87s]

dived on me, in a 'hose-pipe' formation, the remainder attacking *Aagtekerk.*"
The report of II./LG 1 spoke of scoring a direct hit on a freighter north of Tobruk
at 1210, but the Stukas also claimed success. In any case, a bomb detonated on
the Dutch freighter's bridge and ignited a large fire which reached a ready-use
diesel oil tank near the funnel and blazed up out of control. The wheel jammed
to starboard, and the ship began to circle. At this point P-40s of the RAF 250th
Squadron and the South African 5th Squadron piled in. They downed one Bf
109, but each squadron lost two fighters. *Tetcott* shot down two Ju 87s.[24]

As *Aagtekerk* circled in flames, Rycroft radioed Tobruk for help, and several MTBs and MLs and the minesweeping sloop *Aberdare* responded. By this
time "the men were very restless and were slipping over the side on their own."
The rescue flotilla hauled the survivors out of the water, a process they completed by 1430. The master and chief officer reported to Rycroft that there was
little hope of saving the ship while the chief engineer warned that she "might
explode at any minute." Thus, the freighter was left to drift aground and burn
herself out.[25]

At 1005 on 14 June Supermarina's second in command and chief operations
officer, Vice Admiral Luigi Sansonetti, briefed admirals Iachino and Alberto
Da Zara, commander of the cruiser division picked to intercept the Harpoon
convoy. Sansonetti identified the eastern convoy as the main effort and estimated its composition as one battleship, two cruisers, fifteen to eighteen destroyers, fifteen to twenty patrol vessels, and six transports. He offered Iachino
some extra destroyers and the battleship *Duilio.* Iachino accepted the destroyers but not the old battleship.[26] At 1430 Admiral Iachino's battle fleet began
staging from Taranto's Mar Grande led off by the two cruiser divisions and
the 11th Squadron. Gruppo Littorio and its screen, the 7th and 13th squadrons,
followed. *Legionario* carried a German "Dete" radar and acted as the destroyer
flagship.

Meanwhile, the main convoy, now down to seven merchant vessels and
the tanker, pressed on in four columns with the rescue ships in the middle. The
eight cruisers deployed twelve hundred yards beyond the steamers while the
eight remaining Hunts and the two minesweepers formed up two thousand
yards beyond the cruisers. The fleet destroyers patrolled twenty-five hundred
yards beyond the Hunts to keep submarines away and provide the first line of
air defense.

On this day the desert land battle was raging fiercely. The 1st South African
and 50th Infantry divisions were destroying their supply depots and preparing

Table 5.3. Italian Strike Force

Name	Commander	Type	Tons Std.	Main Guns	Torpedoes	Speed
Gruppo Littorio	Vice Adm. A. Iachino					
IX Division	Div Adm. G. Fioravanzo					
Littorio	Capt. Vittorio Bacicalupi	BB	41,377	8 × 15in	—	29
Vittorio Veneto	Capt. Corso Pecori Giraldi	BB	41,167	8 × 15in	—	29
7th Squadron	R Adm. Carlo Giartosio					
Legionario		DD	1,830	44.7in	6 × 21in	34
Freccia		DD	1,520	4 × 4.7in	6 × 21in	30
Folgore		DD	1,540	4 × 4.7in	6 × 21in	30
13th Squadron						
Alpino		DD	1,830	4 × 4.7in	6 × 21in	34
Bersagliere		DD	1,830	4 × 4.7in	6 × 21in	34
Mitragliere		DD	1,850	5 × 4.7in	6 × 21in	34
Attached						
Pigafetta		DD	2,125	6 × 4.7in	3 × 21in	28
Saetta		DD	1,520	4 × 4.7in	6 × 21in	30
Gruppo Garibaldi	Div Adm. R. de Courten					
VIII Division	De Courten					
Garibaldi		CL	9,195	8 × 6in	6 × 21in	33
Aosta		CL	8,450	8 × 6in	6 × 21in	33
III Division	Div Adm. A. Parona					
Gorizia (F)		CA	11,900	8 × 8in	8 × 21in	30
Trento		CA	10,511	8 × 8in	8 × 21in	31
11th Squadron						
Aviere		DD	1,830	4 × 4.7in	6 × 21in	34
Geniere		DD	1,850	5 × 4.7in	6 × 21in	34
Camicia Nera		DD	1,850	5 × 4.7in	6 × 21in	34
Corazziere		DD	1,830	4 × 4.7in	6 × 21in	34

to retreat to Tobruk and the Egyptian border. Dust storms hampered aerial activity over land, and the convoy attracted air units from both sides.

At 1639 nine Ju 88s of I./KG 54, which had staged to Derna that morning, attacked from astern followed six minutes later by Ju 88s from LG 1, which approached from the port quarter in ones or twos. The escorts met the diving aircraft with intense antiaircraft fire. *Paladin's* captain, Commander A. F. Pugsley in from the Eastern Fleet, noted that "the Germans did not display the technique we had learnt to fear from the Japanese; for the formations were small—ten or twelve at a time—and the fire of the ships enough to put them off their aim." Bombs fell within two hundred yards of *Centurion* and near *Hermione*. Aboard *Paladin* "one [bomb] burst right abreast the bridge. A shower of splinters made ragged holes all round the bridge plating and caused the only casualty we suffered." The German airmen reported intense flak and claimed two hits on the bow of a freighter. Two Junkers were lost, including one that ditched returning to base.[27]

At 1730, in the day's heaviest strike, twenty-seven Ju 88s of I./LG 1, reinforced by units of IV./LG 1 from Crete, attacked the port wing column, *Bulkoil, Potaro,* and *Bhutan*. Six Beaufighters intercepted, but most of the bombers broke through and dived in sub-flights of three through long-range antiaircraft fire from the port beam and quarter. Near misses rocked *Potaro* and sprang leaks in her hull. The pumps seized, and two holds flooded to a depth of nine feet, forcing the crew to jettison some cargo. The light cruisers *Euryalus* and *Dido* and the freighter *City of Edinburgh* reported bombs dropping within two hundred yards. A stick of bombs exploded closer than that off *Bulkoil's* port quarter and caused a temporary loss of speed. A Royal Navy gunner serving aboard *Ajax* recalled, "All the ships were tacking; continually changing course in an effort to avoid the bombing, there must have been many near collisions. The tanker was close to us, and I watched with interest as a Stuka aimed a stick of three bombs at it. Spray from the exploding bombs hid the tanker from view, but not for long. The bows of the tanker came ploughing through the spray, no damage done. I felt the urge to cheer."[28]

Bulkoil was more fortunate than *Bhutan*. Three bombs hit the 6,000-ton freighter in the engine room and in holds 2 and 3. A fire erupted, and within five minutes *Bhutan* began to settle. The two rescue ships raced into action and pulled from the water 153 of the 169 crew and passengers embarked. *Malines's* captain recalled that his ship "appeared to be in the middle of a sea of oil fuel and bobbing heads." Thereafter Vian, who never intended that the rescue ships should accompany the convoy beyond the afternoon of the third day, ordered *Antwerp* and *Malines* to Tobruk. Antiaircraft fire downed one Ju 88 while another returned to Iraklion riddled with holes.[29]

The next air strike arrived at 1904 when twelve Ju 88s from I./KG 54 flying out of Tympakion in southern Crete swooped down on the convoy. They claimed a hit on one freighter. Flak damaged several aircraft and one, on its return to base, crashed short of the runway with the loss of its crew.[30]

At 1945 five Cant Z.1007bis bombers from Comando Egeo's 47° Stormo passed over at five thousand meters, dropping twenty 160-kg bombs. They claimed a hit on a large transport and described the enemy's flak as "*violentissima.*" In fact, their bombs missed, and the barrage slightly damaged three of the aircraft. Four S.79s of 41° *Gruppo Siluranti* aborted their mission because, having been ordered to attack a battleship, their torpedoes were set to run at too great a depth.[31]

At 2000 as the sun sank, *U 77* missed just astern with a salvo of torpedoes fired at the destroyer *Pakenham* on the screen's starboard side. The entire screen turned and laced the sea with depth charges, but the submarine escaped. Then at 2020 a Beaufighter reported that enemy motor torpedo boats were approaching from the northwest. It had spotted the German 3rd S-boat Flotilla: *S 54, 55, 56, 58, 59,* and *60.* They had departed Derna late that afternoon and sighted the enemy at dusk.

Between 2050 and 2110 sixteen Ju 88s from II./LG 1 made their second strike of the day. *Birmingham* reported one plane diving on her, but the bombs fell well clear. Another unit, 12./LG 1, was ordered to attack but missed the enemy in the dark. Throughout the day dogfights cost the British five Beaufighters and the Germans two Bf 109s. Antiaircraft fire accounted for two Ju 88s, and two more crashed returning to base. Not including the action against *Tetcott,* the British claimed that they inflicted four certain casualties on the enemy and four "damaged probably crashed."[32]

In addition to the loss of *Bhutan* and damage to *Potaro, Paladin,* and *Bulkoil,* it had been a trying day in a way that Pugsley expressed well. "In the heat of a sweltering Mediterranean summer day, the sweating guns' crews were dazed and exhausted by the jarring blast of their guns, firing barrages in rapid fire. The blistered gun barrels, shimmering in their own heat haze, told a tale of ammunition being used up at an alarming rate."[33]

As night fell Admiral Vian ordered the convoy to change formation. The fleet destroyers took station ahead of the merchant ships in an antisubmarine screen while cruisers and more destroyers followed astern and single destroyers hovered ten thousand yards out on the four quarters. Ever careful when it came to the expenditure of antiaircraft ammunition, Vian surveyed supplies and judged that the fleet had used too much beating back the day's air attacks.

Despite the darkness eleven Ju 88s shadowed the convoy in shifts, dropping flares and an occasional bomb. *Birmingham* reported detonations in her vicinity at 2147, 2314, 2328, and 2350. The British, concerned that gunfire might provide a point of aim, did not engage these aircraft. The flares turned the sea yellow and silhouetted the vessels in their harsh light. The crews found them unnerving while the German S-boat captains, who were lurking on the edge of contact, were frustrated. As Admiral Vian noted, "as the enemy was using flares in profusion, the area was well illuminated and . . . the Fleet proved an unattractive proposition to the Boats, who made no attack." In fact, *Airedale*, on the convoy's port quarter, engaged four S-boats, claiming damage to one, while *Aldenham,* on the starboard quarter, traded machine-gun fire with another that approached from astern. Her captain reported, "the Hun was apparently taken by surprise and was heard to yell as tracer ammunition struck him." The boat's return fire killed one of *Aldenham's* crew and wounded two.[34]

THE ITALIAN SORTIE

At 1845 a reconnaissance plane from Malta, undeterred by the squadron's escort of two CR.42s and two MC.200s, sighted Iachino's squadron clearing the Gulf of Taranto. It radioed a report giving course and composition correctly but misidentified the battleships as *Cavour* class vessels, not the vastly more powerful *Littorios*. Malta followed this up with an overflight of Taranto, which at 2000 reported that the two modern battleships, two heavy and two light cruisers, and eleven destroyers had sailed. Rome intercepted the 1845 dispatch and had it decoded by 2235, five minutes after Harwood himself received the message. Vian had picked it up at 2220, and at 2315 he signaled Harwood asking whether he should turn back considering that the Italian battle fleet was on course to intercept the convoy in less than eight hours and that with clear conditions and a light southeasterly breeze forecast for the next day he could not expect "to hold off such a force from early morning to dusk."[35]

The fact that Vian made such a signal in the first place is curious and suggests that he was testing his new commander in chief. After all, an Italian sortie was expected, and Vian had formulated detailed plans for such an eventuality. As in the March operation he intended to divide the escort into two large components—a striking force and a close escort to protect the convoy. The close escort included *Coventry*, the ten Hunts, the minesweepers, and the corvettes. The striking force would consist of, depending upon conditions and how much forewarning there was, two or three groups and eight or nine divisions. If contact occurred, the convoy would turn south while the striking force moved out in divisions to repel the attackers. Vian intended to cover the convoy with smoke for as long as practicable and to force the Italians to keep their distance by threatening torpedo attacks. This was largely a repeat of the March plan, but instead of a gale blowing into the enemy's face, the Italians would enjoy the weather gage and clear conditions. Vian was aware that he might need to fight for an extended period, so the torpedo-bearing units were restricted to salvos of "about 25% of outfits, unless a really good opportunity to fire should be presented." Vian also intended for all warships in a group to concentrate fire on one target, making the fullest use of radar ranges. As range closed, divisions instead of groups would concentrate. He hoped to obtain decisive results against two enemy targets as quickly as possible. Vian's plan was reasonable and his force was strong in torpedo-armed warships. However, it was also exactly what Iachino expected. The Italian admiral was anxious to make contact as early as possible and to fight from long range with the benefit of aerial spotters overhead.[36]

Harwood had all of his pieces in play, and his intention was "to evade the enemy surface force by turning the convoy back . . . while our air striking forces and submarines delivered their attack."[37] The complication was that the Italian sortie had come earlier than he anticipated. In fact, Supermarina's Admiral Sansonetti had timed his fleet's intervention brilliantly. The battleships would be crossing the submarine picket line only an hour before they intercepted the convoy, and the air strikes would likewise occur near dawn. Thus, Harwood's problem was that Vian was farther west than the margin of safety allowed. Accordingly, the commander in chief signaled Vian that the convoy was to continue for another two hours and then reverse course to the east along the same track pending further orders.

At 0145 Vian instructed his units to turn as ordered. This was a tricky evolution for the large formation to execute at night with enemy motor torpedo boats nipping at its heels and bombs falling randomly from overhead. Unsurprisingly, the convoy did not maintain a steady course, and Admiral Tennant's *Newcastle*, followed by the light cruiser *Arethusa* with the destroyers *Zulu*,

Sikh, Hasty, and *Hotspur* screening, needed to turn out twice rather than once, falling back several miles as a result. Zigzagging at sixteen knots the admiral had trouble arranging his escort and lost track of *Zulu.* Meanwhile, the commander of the 3rd S-Boat Flotilla, Lieutenant Siegfried Wuppermann, frustrated by the flares, decided to attack the escort rather than the convoy itself and maneuvered *S 56* ahead of *Newcastle* into a large gap between *Zulu* and *Hasty. Newcastle's* lookouts reported the boat's wake, but the cruiser delayed illuminating thinking it might be *Zulu.* When the wake faded, a searchlight snapped on and revealed the S-boat "lying practically stopped."[38] Immediately, *S 56* launched two torpedoes from only five hundred yards. With the tracks frighteningly visible, *Newcastle* applied starboard wheel and rang up full speed. She evaded one weapon, but at 0351 the other torpedo blasted a thirty-foot hole in the cruiser's hull, disabled the forward turret, and damaged the machinery and structure. Fortunately, there were no casualties.

Hasty engaged with her port Oerlikon as the S-boat shot by fifteen hundred yards off the destroyer's bow and then chased for a half hour through thick and "very effective white smoke" before losing her quarry. Her captain noted, "I am certain that I hit the 'E' Boat and presumably damaged it." However, this was not the case. *Hasty* rejoined *Newcastle* at 0440.[39]

Meanwhile, Tennant ordered *Arethusa* to join the convoy and the destroyers to screen his damaged flagship, but *Zulu* did not receive the order and accompanied *Arethusa.* After inspecting damage and shoring up bulkheads, the admiral determined *Newcastle* could still make twenty-four knots, and so he turned to catch up to the convoy.

At 0516, while zigzagging at twenty knots, *Newcastle* spotted and turned away from colored lights off her port beam. Ten minutes later lookouts reported a torpedo track on the port bow, stretching from the port quarter with a second track parallel and nearer to the ship. The cruiser applied full starboard wheel and avoided the closer track, which was "clearly defined with a wide oily appearance." However, *Hasty,* which was in the process of taking station ahead of *Newcastle* after her "E" Boat chase, turned too late and caught the second weapon forward on the port side. There was a massive explosion that blew away the destroyer's bow from "A" gun forward and wrecked the bridge. As *Newcastle* passed Tennant personally hailed the destroyer by megaphone to say that he would send assistance. There was no answer, and he had the impression that "all had been killed on the bridge and on the fore part of the ship." In fact the torpedo killed thirteen men. *Hotspur* came up and evacuated the stricken ship's crew and finished her with a torpedo. The British never saw *S 55*, which delivered the blow, and blamed a submarine for the sinking.[40]

ATTACKS ON THE ITALIAN FLEET

As MW11 headed east Iachino's fleet pressed south. At 2303 the Italians responded to the sighting report that had been decoded a half hour before by coming to course 140 degrees and then back to 180 degrees two hours later, hoping this jog would confuse any enemy aircraft searching along their projected track. Indeed at midnight Malta had launched a strike of four torpedo-armed Wellingtons from 38 Squadron. Two hours later *Legionario's* radar reported an air contact. This was a reconnaissance plane that at 0224 reported one battleship, two cruisers, and four destroyers, course 190 degrees, speed twenty knots. Around 0300 *Legionario* scoped more aircraft passing ahead of the battle force from east to west. These were the Wellingtons. Shortly after, the drone of aircraft engines sounded ominously over the water. Iachino ordered smoke at 0325. *Littorio* led *Vittorio Veneto* with three destroyers off either beam and a pair flanking *Littorio's* bow. At 0339 a flare burned brightly to port and then, a few minutes later, another. The Italians steered 40 degrees to starboard away from the lights.

As the British continued illuminating, Iachino began shifting course 30 degrees every five minutes and thickened the massive curtain of smoke. Finally the Wellingtons released a dozen flares in an attempt to overwhelm the artificial fog, but these just made an "imposing and picturesque light show on the thick smoke screen." Only one Wellington launched torpedoes, and both missed. The attack was over by 0400, and by 0415 Iachino was back on course for "Point Alpha" where the Italians expected to intercept the convoy.[41]

At 0525, Admiral Harwood considered that "the risk of further approach to bomb alley [outweighed] the risk of interception by surface forces."[42] He thus radioed Vian to turn the convoy back toward Malta on a west-by-northwest course. The Italian battleships were approaching the submarine picket line, and three critical air attacks were scheduled, which Harwood believed would be enough to repel the enemy. The first, a dawn strike by nine Beauforts of 217 Squadron Coastal Command, which had arrived in Malta on 10 June in transit to Ceylon, had already lifted off. Beauforts based at a field east of Tobruk and USAAF B-24s from Suez would follow.

Unfortunately for Harwood's plans, 217 Squadron was not a veteran unit. Only one of the formation's pilots had ever dropped a torpedo in combat, and few had experience in night operations. Thus, after takeoff, four of the squadron's nine planes missed the rendezvous and proceeded independently. This led to the attack being delivered in three uncoordinated waves.

At 0604 a lookout aboard *Littorio* spotted an aircraft off the starboard bow. The Italians were expecting German fighters and believed it was friendly. In fact, it was the first of the 217th's planes to find the enemy. The Beaufort approached Gruppo Garibaldi from ahead and then flew up along the starboard side. The cruisers were in a line of file steaming at twenty knots with *Garibaldi* in the lead followed by *Aosta, Gorizia,* and *Trento* with two destroyers on each side. Admiral De Courten reported that his ships were silhouetted against the clear eastern horizon and caught by surprise—especially by how fast the attack developed. The solitary plane turned toward *Trento* (the last ship in the line). Facing little flak it pressed in to two hundred meters, and its torpedo stuck home. The blast caught the attention of the group of five aircraft thirty-five miles away. Hugging the sea, these Beauforts rapidly bore in from both sides "with determination and skill." However they faced intense fire and dropped their torpedoes from a thousand meters. The cruisers maneuvered violently, swinging to face the tracks bow on, except *Gorizia*, which presented her stern by circling northeast.[43]

As Admiral Iachino watched from *Littorio's* bridge, he noted *Trento* dropping out of formation with a column of intensely black smoke ascending from her forward funnel. Then three more Beauforts—the other stragglers that missed the rendezvous—appeared. Flying low and fast, they headed for the battleships. The formation opened fire with all weapons—even the 120-mm destroyer guns, which did not have the elevation or fire control to serve as antiaircraft weapons. This barrage was far more formidable than the one faced by the aircraft that had attacked the cruisers. Iachino wrote, "evidently the quick maneuvering of the battleships disoriented the attackers, causing them to scatter." One plane dropped at 4,500 meters and another from 1,500 meters. The third drew away and then swung back and dropped at *Vittorio Veneto* at 0651 from 2,500 meters. It then passed between the two battleships. The Italians observed several antiaircraft shells hit and were impressed by the plane's unperturbed progress. They believed they had shot down two planes while the pilots reported they had torpedoed one cruiser and two battleships. In fact, one plane was lightly damaged and one other made a crash landing upon its return to Malta.[44]

This attack was the battle fleet's first experience with the Beaufort, and the Italian sailors considered it a formidable weapon—much faster than their old adversaries, the Swordfish and Albacore, and more resistant to their anti-aircraft weapons.

As the fleet reformed, Iachino detached *Pigafetta* and *Saetta* to screen *Trento*. He wrote, "With a saddened heart, I watched [*Trento*] drop gradually farther and farther way while the column of black smoke continued to rise densely toward the sky, clearly indicating a boiler room fire. However, *Trento*'s hull seemed to float almost normally, just slightly down by the bow, suggesting that the damage was not irreparable."[45]

The Italian commander and his captains did not realize that by avoiding the aerial torpedoes, they had confounded another foe. Harwood's submarines, following the operational plan, had begun heading southwest to act as a moving screen for the convoy. However, after hearing that the Italian fleet was at sea, Harwood ordered the submarines back to their original station. They were just arriving at this point when three of the 10th Flotilla's boats spotted the enemy force. *P 31* was too distant to attack; *P 34* broke off her approach at 0622 and dove deep when the cruisers began abruptly zigzagging. *P 35* reached position against *Littorio* and was about to launch when the battleship swerved to avoid the Beaufort attack. At 0646, the submarine fired four torpedoes toward *Vittorio Veneto*'s port quarter from five thousand yards. Although she reported one hit, in fact all weapons missed.

When the submarines surfaced a tower of smoke marked *Trento*'s distress, and they headed toward this beacon. The cruiser's crew struggled with the blaze and did not control it for several hours. *Pigafetta* had just passed a towline when *P 35* arrived. At 1010 the submarine shot two torpedoes at the immobile ship from four thousand yards. One exploded near turret two and detonated the bow magazine causing *Trento* to sink rapidly. When she sailed from Taranto the cruiser's crew numbered 1,151 men, but the destroyers rescued only 602.[46]

Following the air attack Iachino concentrated on locating the convoy. He calculated that it should be close if it had followed a direct course toward Malta at its reported speed of fourteen knots, and he was anxious to establish contact so he would have plenty of daylight to settle the issue. He ordered De Courten to launch an Ro.43 spotter to search the immediate vicinity. Then at 0700 a message from Supermarina indicated that German S-boats had reported the convoy at 0230 at a position farther east than Iachino anticipated. He concluded that either this report was inaccurate or the British had slowed down for some reason.[47]

Based on Iachino's expectations and disappointment, there is little doubt that Harwood was correct in ordering the convoy to reverse course when he did. The rapidity of the Italian sortie had upset British timing. It caught the submarines out of position and forced them to rush to make contact; it forced air attacks farther south and west than planned and made the convoy slow its progress. Harwood clearly had not anticipated an energetic response by the enemy fleet. It is worth noting that he had no direct experience fighting the Italians, and so the Royal Navy's institutional mindset regarding Italian military competence may have influenced his assumptions.

IACHINO'S PROGRESS SOUTH

At 0655 Vian responded to Harwood's 0525 signal ordering a course reversal. As MW11's fifty vessels described semi-circles on the placid morning waters of the eastern Mediterranean, Harwood anxiously awaited news in his command post after a very long night that had followed several long days. He had received no word about the dawn attack from Malta while the scheduled RAF and the USAAF strikes were still two hours from target. At 0705 he jumped back on the airwaves and instructed Vian "to avoid contact until aircraft have attacked, which should be by 10.30. If air attacks fail, every effort must be made to get convoy through to Malta by adopting offensive attitude. Should this fail, and convoy be cornered, it is to be sacrificed, and you are to extricate your forces, proceeding to the eastward or westward." The purpose of this communication is difficult to discern. Harwood later stated he wanted to avoid the loss of the entire force should it be cornered, but Vian's orders already covered this eventuality. Instead, it suggests that Harwood found the stress of passively awaiting events difficult.[48]

Nine B-24 Liberators, seven USAAF and two RAF, took off from Fayid Field near Suez at 0430. This was the first U.S. army air force contribution to the Mediterranean war, and the British pinned high hopes on these capable aircraft with their modern bombsights. Next, at 0625, a dozen Beauforts of 39th Squadron lifted off from Sidi Barrani just behind the front lines after the capture of Bir Amud, their normal base.[49]

At 0828 a British reconnaissance aircraft signaled that two battleships, three cruisers, and nine destroyers were 150 miles from the convoy and steering straight toward it at eighteen knots. Supermarina had this message decoded within thirty-seven minutes.[50] Harwood also received it relatively quickly, and shortly thereafter he ordered Vian to reverse course to the east southeast, again pending results from the air attacks. Of all Harwood's orders that morning, this one seems most questionable, especially considering his instructions issued ninety minutes before for Vian to assume an offensive attitude should the air attacks fail. Although communications were slow, he knew that both air strikes were about an hour from target while the Italians were still several hours from interception. In that context Harwood's actions seemed indecisive and it could not have enhanced Vian's uncertain confidence in his commander in chief. Nonetheless, at 0940 the convoy described another semi-circle and began heading away from Malta.

A crucial aspect of the mid-June operation was the delays experienced by British radio traffic. In this regard Supermarina was more efficient then Harwood's improvised command center and team. The Italian naval headquarters was accustomed to exercising control over forces at sea and, after some teething problems in the war's first year, considered its system effective. Moreover, Admiral Sansonetti had nearly a year's experience as operational head of Supermarina, and he had a practiced and competent staff.

Admiral Iachino, rapidly approaching Point Alpha, was also struggling to construct a picture of the situation. Iachino had a history of missed opportunities. Faulty reconnaissance and bad assessments by Supermarina had prevented him from intercepting Force H after it bombarded Genoa in February 1941. The next month at Matapan, he had failed to profit from a situation where he had a British cruiser squadron under his battleship's guns and ended up losing an entire cruiser division because of reconnaissance breakdowns and bad assumptions. In September 1941 during Operation Halberd he turned away from a slightly inferior British fleet because of poor reconnaissance and excessive caution. At First Sirte in December 1941 and Second Sirte in March 1942 he intercepted inferior British forces too late in the day to obtain decisive results. Now, however, Iachino had his chance—his last chance, in fact—to erase more than a year of frustration and to silence a growing chorus of young officers who considered him unfit to command. It seemed that conditions were perfect: the weather was good, the day had just begun, he was closing his quarry, and he enjoyed massive superiority. He still worried about his past nemeses, however, namely inadequate reconnaissance and enemy air power.

Trusting his assets more than those of the Regia Aeronautica or Luftwaffe, he ordered *Gorizia* to launch an observation plane, but it crashed on takeoff. Then, at 0700, Supermarina updated its 0625 communiqué with another sighting report filed by the German S-boats at 0351. This left Iachino "somewhat perplexed" because it put the convoy slightly west of its last reported position.[51] Ten minutes later a German aircraft confirmed the S-boat sighting report. Iachino accepted this because it was current and made in daylight. He turned the fleet slightly east to course 140 degrees. He calculated he was 180 miles from the convoy and that if the British continued to sail west, as he assumed they would, he could make contact well before noon. However, to be absolutely sure, he ordered more observation planes aloft.

At 0847 Iachino received another German aerial report. From this the admiral learned that at 0730 the convoy was heading on course 330 at fourteen knots just 140 miles to the southeast. The admiral wrote, "I was especially pleased to see my doubts about the direction of the convoy's course resolved; apparently it had never intended to reverse course, or if it had, it was only temporary and was now on course for Malta."[52] These happy ruminations were interrupted shortly after 0900, however, by an emergency signal from *Gorizia*: two large aircraft flying fast and low were heading to attack *Littorio*. The battleship's 90-mm guns opened up, but just seconds later a lookout spotted planes approaching at high altitude. Four Messerschmitt Bf 110s had also joined the Italian fleet, but they took no notice of the aerial menace, and the Italians could not communicate with them because the codes had been changed the day before and the Luftwaffe had not provided the new ones.

The planes sighted at high altitude were the American B-24 Liberators. The Italians had been fixated on the familiar danger presented by torpedo-bombers and completely missed the threat fourteen thousand feet overhead. Iachino wrote, "We barely had time to look up when we saw around us several large columns of water rise up from either side of the bow."[53] Bombs rained down around *Littorio* and *Vittorio Veneto,* and one hit the base of *Littorio*'s forward turret, killing one man and wounding twelve. The turret's operation was unimpaired, but the impact shook the catapult, destroyed the floatplane resting atop it, and damaged two others. There was also minor splinter damage. Bombs fell so close to *Vittorio Veneto* that their splashes drenched her decks.

From their lofty altitude, the B-24s watched a forest of geysers envelop their targets and concluded they had smashed the Italian battleships—they claimed a half dozen hits on each. Next the bombers observed the Beauforts begin their attack. Finally, when the German escorts attacked following their mission, they claimed they downed one Bf 110. It seemed a brilliant début for the Americans in the Mediterranean war.

The 39th Squadron's raid, on the other hand, suffered misfortune en route. A dozen Beauforts, led by a Maryland, took off at dawn. They were operating at the extreme limit of their range and would continue to Malta after the attack. There was supposed to be an escort, but the local RAF command diverted the allocated fighters to a ground attack mission instead. This proved unfortunate when five Bf 109s flying to cover an attack on the convoy surprised the Beauforts and shot down two of them. Two others had to jettison their torpedoes in evasive maneuvers, and three used so much fuel in the action they had to abort. One of these crashed behind Axis lines. Only five Beauforts continued the mission.[54]

At 0940 the Maryland located the Italian squadron and fired a flare to guide the remaining Beauforts to their target. The torpedo-bombers approached the head of the *Littorio* column in two groups. Their intention was to attack from both sides, but the battleships threw up an intense flak barrage and then made a 180-degree turn so the groups attacked sequentially from the same side. Gunfire struck two of the three aircraft in the first group, and they launched torpedoes at about four thousand meters. The other group pressed on and dropped at two thousand meters from astern. The Italians combed the oncoming wakes. One passed between two vessels and then harmlessly exploded. The Beauforts continued on and arrived at Malta safely. They reported one hit on a battleship, and the B-24s witnessed one cruiser and one destroyer being hit. Admiral Iachino wrote, "We were annoyed by [the Beauforts'] apparent invulnerability but we were more annoyed by the inaction of the German fighters that had done nothing to suppress the attack or chase the enemy following the attack."[55]

AXIS AIR STRIKES

From 0655 to 0930 Convoy MW11 steered west undisturbed but worried about the prospect of action, which, failing news of the air attacks, Vian believed to be impending within several hours. In light of her damage, he offered to send *Newcastle* to Alexandria with two Hunts, but Tennant "refused to part company."[56] Then at 0925 Vian received Harwood's response to the 0828 sighting report ordering him to reverse course to the southeast. At 0940, even as the British airstrikes were under way, Vian ordered the convoy to come about for the third time.

In the operations room where Harwood was struggling to exercise command, however, a shroud of silence descended for two critical hours. In his report, Air Vice-Marshal Leonard Slatter wrote, "During the whole of the morning the Commander-in-Chief, Mediterranean, was greatly hampered in making a decision as to whether to turn the convoy toward Malta, as no results of our air attacks on the enemy had been received, and it was not known whether Malta had attacked or not." He further recommended that "Striking forces and shadowers . . . should report at once any results observed from attacks. This is of the greatest value to the Commander-in-Chief, and was not done in this operation." At 0830 and 0944 there were reports that a cruiser had been damaged and was retiring. Not until 1115, however, did Harwood finally hear from the Malta-based 217 Squadron, which claimed hits on both battleships and a cruiser. The admiral accepted this apparently wonderful news at face value— it seemed to vindicate his plan, its major assumptions, and every order given up to that point. At 1151 he signaled Vian to resume course for Malta. However, he explained his order by including the results claimed by 217 Squadron and he repeated his 0705 oxymoron to avoid action, to adopt an offensive attitude, and to sacrifice the convoy if necessary.[57]

After shrugging off the 0945 air attack Iachino resumed his south-by-southeast heading and started to actively seek the convoy's whereabouts. At 1013 Rhodes forwarded an 0805 German sighting that seemed to put the enemy too far east. The admiral had more confidence in his own floatplanes. At 1017 *Gorizia*'s Ro.43 signaled briefly that it had sighted a ship and then went off the air. To the Italian admiral it seemed "that the enemy was close and that tactical contact was imminent."[58]

At 1150 twenty Ju 87s from St.G.3 approached the convoy. They formed up twenty miles astern and attacked in three groups. Three bombers near-missed *Euryalus*. Six bombed *Birmingham* sailing ahead of the merchantmen, and the shock from a near miss disabled the large cruiser's number one turret while splinters knocked out the HA/LA fire control director. This left Vian with just one small 6-inch and four 5.25-inch antiaircraft cruisers to counter two 15-inch battleships, one 8-inch, and two 6-inch cruisers should a surface action develop.

Shortly after noon Harwood's enthusiasm was rattled by a report that, as of 0944, the enemy fleet was continuing south at eighteen knots. At 1245 he expressed his frustration and doubt when he radioed Vian. "I must leave decision to you whether to comply with my 0705/15, or whether to again retire with hope of carrying out a night destroyer attack, if enemy stands on." He sent this message under the impression that Vian had received and acted upon his 1151 signal. However, this was not the case. Vian did not get Harwood's order to turn toward Malta until 1345, nearly two hours after it was dispatched. Shortly thereafter he received a report from aircraft "T" shadowing the Italian fleet that the Italians were about a hundred miles astern and pressing on. He concluded that his commander lacked a complete picture of the situation and remained on course to Alexandria. His report ironically explained, "My heavy striking force, the Fourth Cruiser Squadron, being somewhat under the weather, I held on to the eastward awaiting the Commander-in-Chief's reactions to Aircraft T's report." He received Harwood's 1245 at 1420 and took this as an affirmation that he was handling the situation correctly.[59]

As the British thrashed about south of Crete, Iachino pressed onward at twenty knots. The Admiral was frustrated with the quantity and quality of information he was receiving even though he catapulted more spotters at 1047 and 1210. Then at 1240 *Aviere* reported smoke on the horizon. The fleet increased speed to twenty-four knots. The tension increased when, at 1247, *Camicia Nera* from Gruppo Garibaldi signaled "Large enemy naval force on the horizon." Convinced that he had at long last run down the convoy, Iachino reported the contact to Supermarina, ordered battle stations, and came to twenty-eight knots. Meanwhile at 1215 Supermarina sent a signal, received at 1245, ordering Iachino to withdraw if he did not have definite news of the enemy. This crossed Iachino's communication and was quickly canceled. However, Iachino continued to harbor doubts because his spotters were reporting empty seas. Finally, the smoke was identified as belonging to a crashed Italian reconnaissance plane.[60]

At 1335 the British spotter NVYT reported two battleships, three cruisers, and nine destroyers heading on course 120 degrees (east by southeast) at twenty-five knots. Supermarina had the decrypt by 1406 (before Harwood) and noted that the British had placed the Italian force sixty miles too far west.[61]

At 1410 Iachino advised Supermarina that his floatplanes had explored a hundred miles along his course and had not encountered the enemy. This convinced him that the British had turned back toward Alexandria, a conviction reinforced by a 1440 message from Aerosquadra V in Libya that the convoy was twenty miles east of its 1145 position and heading toward Egypt. At 1500 the *Littorio* swung in a large circle to a north-by-northwest heading and reduced speed to twenty knots. Iachino had closed to approximately one hundred miles of the enemy, but if the convoy continued to withdraw, there was insufficient time left to run it down before dark. The admiral was disappointed but wrote "there was nothing else but to retrace our steps." He drew consolation, however, in that the most important result—stopping the convoy—had been obtained. Moreover, a small possibility of action lingered: at 1543 Supermarina radioed that "if you are not able to engage enemy by 1600 head toward Navarino. Stop. Action will possibly be taken tomorrow if allowed by range."[62]

At 1516 aircraft NVYT reported Iachino's turn.

At 1535, when the convoy was fifty-five miles south southwest of Gavdos Island, or approximately a hundred miles east of the westernmost point it had reached at 0145 that morning, thirty Ju 87s of II./St.G.3 escorted by Bf 109s attacked from astern. A dozen Stukas mobbed *Airedale* on the starboard quarter. Four aircraft peeled off and dived, one after the other, as the destroyer came to full speed and tried to fend off the attackers with a barrage from her pompoms, port Oerlikon, and rapid-firing 4-inch battery. However, she could not maneuver effectively "owing to the close proximity of other ships." Two bombs near-missed to port and one to starboard. Two direct hits aft followed. These ignited a fierce fire, and then a magazine exploded. The commanding officer's report was a sobering testimony to the blast's horrific impact: "There was no part of the ship remaining abaft the searchlight platform. The forward end of the after super-structure was curled back over the searchlight super-structure and the ship's side abreast this position was also folded back toward the bow. The upper deck amidships was badly buckled."[63]

Airedale began to settle, and the crew abandoned ship. *Aldenham* and *Hurworth* eventually rescued 133 men, and then *Aldenham* torpedoed the wreck while *Hurworth* shelled it for good measure.

As *Airedale* underwent her travail, nine dive bombers swarmed *Centurion;* bombs exploding close alongside caused flooding in the old dreadnought. Other aircraft attacked the convoy, but without results. British gunners claimed four planes, but in fact antiaircraft fire downed one.[64]

At 1605 aircraft NVYT's report that Iachino had turned north reached Harwood after only a fifty-minute delay. At 1625 he signaled Vian. "Now is golden opportunity to get convoy to Malta. Have Hunts, *Coventry,* minesweepers, and corvettes enough fuel and ammunition for one-way trip? If so I would like to turn convoy now, cruisers and destroyers parting company after dark and returning to Alexandria."[65]

At 1755, before Vian had received this message, six German bombers struck followed by a solitary plane at 1810. Then, at 1815, eight Cant Z.1007bis of the 35° Stormo arrived over the convoy and dropped fifty-four 100-kg HE bombs from high level. They claimed hits on four units and snapped photographs of a destroyer apparently on fire. In fact, they landed one bomb fifty feet to starboard and another three feet to port of the Australian destroyer *Nestor.* "The shock to the ship was very severe . . . the bridge, mast and funnel [area] flexing violently, throwing personnel to the deck . . . The main damage however was to the hull, which was extensively distorted and holed on the port side." No. 1 Boiler Room flooded with the consequent total loss of steam and electric power. Down by the head and listing to port, the destroyer drifted to a stop as the convoy passed her by. *Birmingham* and a freighter were also straddled in this attack, which the British characterized as "extremely accurate."[66]

At 1818, as the Cants disappeared, the first of nine Ju 88s swooped in. They claimed that they overwhelmed a cruiser with six bombs and scored two other hits on a large ship; in fact, they near-missed *Arethusa,* which lost her radar to splinter damage, and *Centurion,* which suffered flooding in two boiler rooms. Eleven S.79 torpedo-bombers from Cyrenaica's 131° and 133° gruppos and four from the Aegean's 204° Squadriglia arrived as this attack was under way. British fighters harassed the S.79s as they jockeyed to make their runs. The bombers finally dropped at 1850 from each quarter at ranges the British stated to be about four thousand yards. All torpedoes missed. The escorting fighters tallied their score as three S.79s and two Ju 88s. In fact, a P-40 of the 250th Squadron downed one S.79. For their part the S.79s claimed they sank one destroyer, damaged two cruisers, and shot down three enemy fighters.[67]

At 1838, responding to reports that the Australian destroyer's damage was not irreparable, and even as S.79s maneuvered along the convoy's margins, *Javelin* took *Nestor* under tow using a 4.5-inch wire cable. Vian sent *Eridge, Beaufort,* and *Hurworth* to stiffen the cripple's antiaircraft screen. *Nestor's* captain reported that the little group experienced three high-level and one torpedo attack after 1900, while under tow at four knots, and that they shot down two of the attackers.[68]

Eighteen Ju 88s delivered the day's last series of attacks between 2108 and 2200. To the British it seemed the German aircraft loitered astern waiting for favorable light conditions before attacking the convoy from each quarter. When they finally struck, bombs splashed all around the merchant ships and escort but hit nothing. Overall, the Germans sent 130 Ju 88s and Ju 87s against Vigorous, but only eighty-four found the enemy. They asserted that they sank one disguised ship (*Centurion*), one cruiser, and one destroyer and damaged four cruisers, two destroyers, and five merchantmen. They also claimed credit for downing twenty-one British aircraft, all at the cost of a Ju 88 and a Ju 87.[69]

At 1825 Harwood, still waiting to hear that Vian had seized the "golden opportunity," sent another signal improving on his plan: Vian was to send only the four fastest merchantmen to Malta and beef up the escort with *Arethusa* and two of the fleet destroyers.

At 1842 Vian responded to Harwood's 1625 signal. The commander in chief had issued a qualified order, and Vian did not hesitate to seize the out it gave him. He radioed back that the Hunts were down to 30 percent of their ammunition supply—insufficient for a renewed run for Malta—and maintained his easterly course awaiting Harwood's response. Vian's signal took nearly two hours to reach Harwood. At 2053 the commander in chief accepted the failure of his first major operation and signaled: "Return to Alexandria with your whole force."[70]

An hour after Iachino turned north, German fighters shot down the reconnaissance aircraft shadowing him, and the British lost track of his position. Malta dispatched a replacement, but fighters intercepted it as well. The picket line submarines attempted to reach an attack position but failed. Iachino passed just to the east of the 1st Flotilla. *Porpoise* was closest, and although her captain learned as early as 1535 that the Italians were headed back his way, a German fighter drove him under at 1935. At 2000 an aircraft forced *Thrasher* also to dive, and her captain only caught a distant periscope glimpse of passing battleships.

Malta dispatched a third patrol plane (FS8Q), and at 2255 it reported two battleships, two cruisers, and four destroyers steaming north by northwest at twenty knots. Five Wellingtons of Squadron 38 were already airborne, and they located the Italians around midnight. Supermarina had decrypted the 2255 sighting at 2325. Iachino had also intercepted the British reports and anticipated trouble. At 2250 the admiral changed course to 250 degrees. Then at 2330 after *Legionario*'s radar picked up the British bombers, Iachino came to 210 and then 160 degrees, a heading of south by southeast. Despite these evasive efforts seven flares appeared in the sky eight thousand meters to starboard at 0036 on 16 June. The Italians responded with clouds of smoke and altered course to the east. However, the flares revealed gaps in the protective coverage. Iachino attributed this to the atmospheric conditions, and on *Littorio*'s flag bridge one of his officers muttered that he felt naked in the harsh orange light.[71]

All five of the Wellingtons dropped their torpedoes. Four missed, but one plane had pressed forward to a thousand meters before launching. The *Littorio* immediately steered to present her stem to the oncoming weapon. "There passed a minute that seemed to last an eternity, and then we heard the distinctive rumble of the explosion against *Littorio*'s hull on the starboard bow." The ship oscillated with a slow rolling motion. She shipped a thousand tons of water and took on a list, but this was quickly corrected with counterflooding, and damage control sealed off the affected area. Iachino reported, "It was worth noting that the consequence of this attack was considered relatively small." *Littorio* returned to a north-by-northwest heading and continued at twenty knots for Taranto. The Italians made port at 1700 on 16 June. *Littorio* spent three months in dock repairing the damage.[72]

Vian's return to Alexandria was also costly. He decided to "dispense with the usual evasive courses and steer as far North as would clear all known U-Boats. This would result in the Fleet being outside fighter protection during the following morning—but I considered U and E-Boats during the night a greater threat." Vian's assessment of the threat proved accurate. At 0127 on 16 June *U 205* penetrated the convoy's screen and fired a salvo of torpedoes at the light cruiser *Hermione*, which was stationed on the starboard quarter. One detonated to starboard amidships. There was "a shattering explosion, accompanied by flash, and the whole ship was violently shaken." The machinery compartments rapidly flooded, and within a minute *Hermione* was listing 22 degrees to starboard. She hung there for about thirty seconds, and then the list began to slowly increase. Counterflooding had little chance against such drastic damage, and at 35 degrees the captain ordered abandon ship. Within two minutes the cruiser capsized to starboard while still under way. *Aldenham*, *Exmoor*, and *Beaufort* rescued 440 men, but 88 were lost. *U 205* had left Salamis on 11 June and returned to La Spezia on 23 June; this was the only success German submarines achieved during the operation.[73]

The destroyer *Nestor* also proved impossible to save. Towed by *Javelin* and escorted by *Eridge* and *Beaufort,* the four ships formed a mini-convoy that fell progressively astern of the main force. Although *Nestor* yawed badly under tow, she was making fourteen knots when, at 2259, the line parted and was lost. It took ninety minutes to pass a new tow, shackling a 4.5-inch cable to a 2.5-inch cable at *Nestor*'s end, but this broke at 0435 on the 16th while still 230 miles west of Alexandria. This left only 3.5-inch cables available aboard the Hunts. In the breaking dawn, the escort believed it spotted German S-boats. *Nestor*'s captain decided that continuing the tow would invite the loss of the entire force, so at 0700 he ordered his ship scuttled. Once this was accomplished, the other three destroyers sped east and caught up to the main convoy at 1550 on the 16th.

The day of the 16th passed without further attack, although the destroyers responded to several submarine contacts during the early afternoon off the Egyptian coast. Incremental flooding forced *Centurion* to reduce speed and undertake emergency repairs. The corvettes *Delphinium* and *Snapdragon* stood by, and later, when she got under way, Vian turned the entire fleet 180 degrees so they could catch up.

That evening Vian arrived at Alexandria. In response to a submarine alert, the screening destroyers dropped depth charges from the entry to the swept channel. *Centurion,* drawing forty-two feet of water, could not clear the bar and anchored in the roads. *City of Lincoln, City of Pretoria, City of Edinburgh, Rembrandt,* and *Potaro* entered port along with the bulk of the escort. *Pakenham, Griffin, Inconstant,* and *Fortune* shepherded *Bulkoil* and *Ajax* to Port Said.

ANALYSIS

In the operation the British lost a cruiser, *Hermione;* three destroyers, *Hasty, Nestor,* and *Airedale;* and two merchant ships, *Aagtekerk* and *Bhutan.* Three cruisers, *Centurion,* a corvette, and two merchant ships suffered significant damage. The Italians lost a heavy cruiser, *Trento,* and had a battleship moderately damaged. The battle to stop convoy MW11 was a victory for the Italian fleet despite the fact that its warships never engaged the convoy. Instead, the threat of a confrontation—backed of course by the force and the will to carry it out—defeated the largest Malta convoy of the war.

In most English-language histories of the Mediterranean war, Operation Vigorous is considered "an imperial balls-up." It is briefly narrated, and much of the analysis regards whom to blame. For example, Correlli Barnett writes, "Yet the cinching factor in the defeat lay in the C-in-C's dithering which led him to order Vian to turn his convoy no fewer than six times." However, Barnett also quotes a letter from Admiral Vian written in 1954 to answer the question whether the convoy would have got through if Cunningham had been in command. Vian wrote "no flag officer ever thought of not going through with a direct operation order from Andrew; but he would never issue one not capable of achievement with the forces allocated." Vian seems to be implying that Cunningham would never have agreed to the operation with the forces available. But Cunningham himself wondered (also in 1954) why Harwood did not order Vian to press on when first queried at 2315 on 14 June. The other conclusion suggested by Vian's statement is that Harwood lacked the tools to get the job done. After the battle Harwood complained that "Events proved with painful clarity that our air striking force had nothing like the weight required to stop a fast and powerful enemy force, and in no way compensated for our lack of heavy ships."[74]

In fact, Vigorous was a repeat of several Malta operations that had been conducted without battleship support. However, the December 1941 and the January, February, and March 1942 convoys had benefited from the shorter days and the fact that the Italian fleet did not sail or intercepted the British late in the day or under atrocious weather conditions. Thus the Italian response, not the force deployed, was the greatest difference between the winter convoys and the June operation. In fact, Vigorous was an impossible proposition from the start unless the Italian fleet failed to act or proved very brittle, as Harwood anticipated.[75]

The other factor, which Harwood surprisingly made little complaint about, was the speed at which signals were received and acted upon. The all-important report that the Italian battleships were at sea was sent to Malta at 1845/14. It did not get to Harwood for nearly three hours. His instructions to Vian took up to ninety minutes to reach the admiral. The news that the Italian fleet was still coming even after all the fulsome claims of success by the airmen was two and a half hours in arriving. The official British history notes that "The conduct of the whole operation had been hampered by meager information, and some important signals had taken a long time to get through."[76]

Another factor that affected the operation was the quantity and quality of Harwood's signals. His attempt to manage the operation from ashore without the communications, intelligence, or staff to do the job properly proved unwise. In retrospect, Harwood would have been better served had he sent Vian to sea with the job clearly defined and then silently awaited events. However, to list the things the British commanders did or did not do that caused the operation to fail is to ignore one half of the picture—what the Italians did right. Supermarina provided intelligence and a minimum of direction. It made sure that Iachino was under way not too soon and not too late. The fleet skillfully met four air attacks and evaded the line of submarines twice. Ultimately, this defeated Convoy MW11, not British mistakes.

6

OPERATION HARPOON

It is regretted that owing to the fact that Ithuriel was so busily employed, no accurate records or estimation of numbers can be given.

Lieutenant Commander D. H. Maitland-Makgill-Crichton, HMS Ithuriel

THE WESTERN CONVOY operation, Harpoon, followed the template established by operations Substance and Halberd. Aircraft carriers would provide fighter cover over the transports during the passage from Gibraltar past the Axis air bases on Sardinia and Sicily. The convoy would reach the entrance to the Sicilian narrows at dusk. There the escort's heavy ships would turn back and leave the transports protected by cruisers and destroyers. Daylight would find the convoy through the narrows and off Pantelleria, poised to make the final run to Malta under the cover of the island's fighter squadrons.

PLANS

Vice Admiral Alban T. B. Curteis, the Home Fleet's second in command, began planning Operation Harpoon on 23 May. He and a small staff completed drafting the orders on 2 June and met with the captains assigned to the operation on 4 June. The British planners estimated Italian naval strength and deployments as being one 15-inch and three 12.6-inch battleships at Taranto along with two 8-inch and three 6-inch cruisers and fifteen destroyers. They believed that Naples had one light cruiser and seven destroyers, Cagliari two light cruisers, Messina three destroyers, and Palermo four destroyers. They estimated German air strength at fifty-four bombers and thirty-nine fighters at Sicily and Sardinia and Italian air forces as having fifteen bombers, thirty-five torpedo-bombers, and thirty fighters at Sardinia and fifty bombers, twenty torpedo-bombers, and ninety fighters at Sicily. The assessment considered that one-third of the aircraft would be unserviceable, leaving thirty-six German and seventy-six Italian bombers available to attack the convoy. The planners believed that three degrees east longitude was the farthest enemy torpedo-bombers could strike and 105 miles was the extreme range of enemy fighters.[1] The principal assumption, however, was that the Italians would respond to the operation as they had in the past. Thus, practices that served before were used again with little innovation—in fact, Curteis judged the risk of a surface encounter so negligible that the largest ship he assigned to accompany the convoy after the heavy escort turned back was an old antiaircraft cruiser, and he gave this force to an acting captain who had no experience of independent command.

Admiral Curteis was an experienced sea officer. He made captain in 1926 and rear admiral in August 1938. He commanded the 2nd Cruiser Squadron from May 1940 to May 1941 and participated in the French campaign and the hunt for *Bismarck*. In June 1941 he was made second in command of the Home Fleet. He served under Admiral Somerville in Operation Halberd in September 1941 and commanded the squadron of two battleships and two cruisers dispatched to head off Admiral Iachino after an Italian torpedo-bomber damaged Somerville's flagship, *Nelson*. Curteis was promoted to vice admiral on 31 December 1941, and in March 1942 he led the heavy cover force for convoy PQ-12 against which *Tirpitz* had sortied. Thus, he had twice come close to leading battleships into action against enemy capital ships, but chance had denied him the opportunity to reach this professional milestone.

The Harpoon convoy formed up at the Clyde and sailed as Force T (escort) and convoy WS19Z on 4 June with the transports *Troilus* (convoy commodore), *Burdwan*, *Chant* (ex–*Hulda Maersk*), *Orari*, and *Tanimbar*. The escort consisted of the light cruisers *Kenya* (flag of Vice Admiral Curteis) and *Liverpool* and the 17th Destroyer Flotilla with *Onslow*, *Bedouin*, *Icarus*, *Marne*, *Matchless*, *Escapade*, *Blankney*, *Middleton*, *Badsworth*, and the Polish Hunt class destroyer *Kujawiak*. *Orari* was representative of the convoy's merchant vessels. She was armed with a 4-inch gun, a 12-pounder, one 40-mm, a pair of 20-mms, and various machine guns and UP rocket-bombs. She had a naval liaison officer, five naval signalmen, and a short-range radio. Twenty-two DEMS personnel manned the guns. She carried a mixed (and volatile) cargo which included large quantities of ammunition, coal, and gasoline and two thousand tons of light diesel.[2]

The convoy enjoyed good weather through the Bay of Biscay and navigated the Straits of Gibraltar during the night of 11–12 June. The British attempted to frustrate Axis intelligence agents operating near Gibraltar and took care that the convoy and escort kept out of sight during daylight. For example, on 10 June *Kenya, Bedouin,* and *Kujawiak* waited until dark before dashing to port in advance of the transports to refuel. The value of these precautions, however, was small. As early as 4 June Italian naval intelligence advised Supermarina that a Tangiers newspaper had printed a notice that an "American tanker of 10,000 tons" had arrived in Gibraltar, and this sparked a special scrutiny of the situation. The next day agents reported that several steamers loaded with supplies had arrived and would try to reach Malta.[3]

At 0300 on 12 June "Group 2" slipped their moorings at Gibraltar and sailed to join the convoy. This force included the battleship *Malaya;* the carriers *Eagle* and *Argus;* the antiaircraft cruisers *Charybdis* and *Cairo;* the destroyers *Wishart, Westcott, Wrestler, Vidette, Antelope, Ithuriel,* and *Partridge;* the fleet minesweepers *Hebe, Speedy, Rye,* and *Hythe;* the motor launches *ML 121, 134, 168, 459,* and *462;* and the American tanker *Kentucky.* The minesweepers and motor launches were destined for Malta to supplement the base's minesweeping capabilities. The fast minelayer *Welshman,* veteran of many solo Malta runs, was temporarily attached to the escort while the tanker *Brown Ranger,* escorted by the corvettes *Geranium* and *Coltsfoot,* proceeded separately to refuel the short-ranged destroyers during the second day while still beyond range of Sardinian-based bombers. The Home Fleet contingent and Group 2 rendezvoused at 0800 on 12 June and headed east together. The plan called for each of the transports to tow a motor launch, but, as was the case with the Vigorous convoy, the towing gear proved unable to cope with the strains imposed by the relatively high convoy speeds and kept parting. Eventually, the attempt was abandoned, and the boats proceeded under their own power.

News of Group 2's sailing arrived at Supermarina within hours. An appreciation issued later that day noted that Force H [*sic*] had left Gibraltar and that at midnight "an unknown convoy of eleven units including escort entered the strait from the west and did not put into Gibraltar." From this, and the continuing arrival of air units at Malta, Regia Marina staff concluded that "taking advantage of the new moon, the decreased [Axis] air activity and strong aerial reinforcement of Malta, [the enemy] wants to pass an important supply convoy [to Malta]." Operations aimed against North Africa, Corsica, Sardinia, and even into the Gulf of Genoa were considered possible, but unlikely. The navy dispatched three submarines into the Western Mediterranean to join

Table 6.1. Operation Harpoon Escort

Name	Commander	Type	Tons Std.	Main Guns	Secondary	Speed
Force W	V Adm. A. T. B. Curteis					
Malaya	Capt. J. W. Waller	BB	34,000	8 × 15in	12 × 6in	23
Eagle	Capt. E. G. Rushbrooke	CV	22,600	9 × 6in	20 a/c	24
Argus	Capt. G. T. Philip	CVL	14,000	4 × 4in	20 a/c	20
Kenya	Capt. A. S. Russell	CL	8,600	12 × 6in	6 × 21in TT	33
Liverpool	Capt. W. R. Slayter	CL	9,400	12 × 6in	6 × 21in TT	32
Charybdis	Capt. L. D. Mackintosh	CL	5,600	8 × 4.5in	6 × 21in TT	32
17th DD Flot						
Onslow (F)	Capt. H. T. Armstrong	DD	1,610	4 × 4.7in	4 × 21in TT	36
Icarus	L Cdr. C. D. Maud	DD	1,370	4 × 4.7in	5 × 21in TT	36
Escapade	L Cdr. E. N. Currey	DD	1,405	4 × 4.7in	4 × 21in TT	36
13th DD Flot						
Wishart (F)	Cdr. H. G. Scott	DD	1,140	3 × 4.7in	6 × 21in TT	34
Westcott	Cdr. I. H. Bockett-Pugh	DD	1,100	4 × 4in		25
Wrestler	Lt. R. W. Lacon	DD	1,100	3 × 4in		25
Vidette	L Cdr. E. N. Walmsley	DD	1,090	3 × 4in		25
Antelope	L Cdr. E. N. Sinclair	DD	1,350	3 × 4.7in	3 × 21in TT	35
Force X						
Cairo	Act. Capt. C. C. Hardy	CLA		8 × 4in		
11th DD Flot						
Bedouin (F)	Cdr. B. G. Scurfield	DD	1,850	6 × 4.7in	4 × 21in TT	36
Marne	L Cdr. H. N. Richardson	DD	1,920	6 × 4.7in	4 × 21in TT	36
Matchless	L Cdr. J. Mowlam	DD	1,920	6 × 4.7in	4 × 21in TT	36

Ithuriel	L Cdr. D. Maitland-Makgill-Crichton	DD	1,360	4 × 4.7in	4 × 21in TT	35
Partridge	L Cdr. W. A. Hawkins	DD	1,610	5 × 4in	4 × 21in TT	36
12th DD Flot						
Blankney (F)	L Cdr. P. F. Powlett	DE	1,050	6 × 4in		29
Middleton	L Cdr. D. C. Kinloch	DE	1,050	6 × 4in		29
Badsworth	Lt. G. T. Gray	DE	1,050	6 × 4in		29
Kujawiak (PO)	Cdr. L. Lichodziejewski	DE	1,050	6 × 4in		29
Minesweepers						
Speedy (F)	L Cdr. A. E. Doran	MS	800	1 × 4in		17
Hebe	L Cdr. G. Mowatt	MS	800	1 × 4in		17
Rye	Lt. J. A. Pearson	MS	605	1 × 3in		16.5
Hythe	L Cdr. L. B. Miller	MS	605	1 × 3in		16.5
Force Y						
Geranium	L Cdr. A. Foxall	DC	1,170	1 × 4in		16.5
Coltsfoot	Lt. W. K. Rous	DC	1,170	1 × 4in		16.5
Brown Ranger	Master D. B. Ralph	AO	6,700	1 × 4in		13
Special Service						
Welshman	Capt. W. H. Friedberger	CM	2,650	6 × 4in		40

Table 6.2. Operation Harpoon Convoy

Vessel	GRT	Nationality	Fate	Speed
Troilus	7,422	British		14.5
Burdwan	6,069	British	Sunk air/surf	14
Chant	5,601	US/Danish	Sunk air	14.5
Orari	10,350	British	Damaged mine	16
Tanimbar	8,169	Dutch	Sunk air	14.5
Kentucky	9,263	US	Sunk air/surf	16

the six already there. *Zaffiro, Velella, Emo,* and *Bronzo* patrolled in the vicinity of Oran between Cape Falcon and Cape Ferrat. *Otaria, Uarsciek, Giada,* and *Acciaio* guarded the waters between Cape Ferrat and Cape Bougaroni, and *Alagi* positioned herself off Cape Blanc. Supermarina also arranged for intensive reconnaissance on the day of the 13th and alerted the fleet for a possible move to Naples.[4]

These prompt reactions reflected the hard lessons Operations Substance and Halberd had taught Supermarina. In the case of Substance, naval staff had assumed that the British were conducting an operation to fly off fighters to Malta. Reconnaissance was inadequate, with the first sighting of the enemy not coming until the convoy was nearly halfway to the Sicilian narrows and the second when it was off Bone. By that time it was too late for the battle fleet to intervene. In Operation Halberd the fleet sortied well in time to intercept the convoy, but the British had an unusually strong escort of three modern battleships, and excessive caution, poor tactical reconnaissance, and a lack of coordination with the air force frustrated the navy's efforts.

With Operation Harpoon Supermarina considered all possible contingencies and implemented a vigorous program of aerial reconnaissance to obtain the information needed to make correct decisions. Also, coordination between the air force and navy, and with the Germans, was improved by promptly conferring at the highest levels and sharing information.

REFUELING THE FLEET

On 12 June the convoy made steady easterly progress at twelve to thirteen knots. As one of the merchant captains recorded, "The whole force looked ... able to cope with anything."[5] The only incident Admiral Curteis re-

Table 6.3. Refueling Operations 13 June 1942

Ship	Left Screen	Fueled From	Rejoined Screen	Time Expended
Badsworth	0430	*Brown Ranger*	1010	5 hr. 40 min.
Blankney	0430	Could not find tanker	0930	n/a
Blankney	0958	*Brown Ranger*	1410	6 hr. 10 min.
Middleton	0958	*Brown Ranger*	1420	6 hr. 20 min.
Kujawiak	1115	*Liverpool* parted line	1215	n/a
Marne	1150	*Brown Ranger*	1620	6 hr. 30 min.
Bedouin	1205	*Liverpool*	1425	2 hr. 20 min.
Matchless	1347	*Brown Ranger*	1720	3 hr. 30 min.
Ithuriel	1420	*Liverpool*	2300	n/a
Kujawiak	1500	*Brown Ranger*	1745	2 hr. 45 min.
Partridge	1600	*Brown Ranger*	1830	2 hr. 30 min.
Wishart	1715	*Brown Ranger*	2010	2 hr. 55 min.
Vidette	1748	*Liverpool*	2300	5 hr. 20 min.
Wrestler	1805	*Brown Ranger*	2040	2 hr. 35 min.
Westcott	2025	*Brown Ranger*	0615 14th	n/a
Antelope	2025	*Brown Ranger*	0615 14th	n/a
Cairo	Not given	*Brown Ranger*	a.m. 14th	n/a

corded was an encounter with a Spanish freighter. In fact, a German aircraft spotted the convoy southwest of the Balearic island of Ibiza that evening.

On 13 June Axis aircraft picked up the convoy early and submitted reports throughout the day. *Eagle* dispatched fighters against these snoopers at 0810, 1206, 1405, 1720, and 1930. A Hurricane bagged a Ju 88D at 1405. At 1720 the carrier reported, "5 shadowers were in sight of the fleet within half an hour. They were driven away by fighters but not engaged owing to various reasons, the chief of which was lack of speed." At 1930, however, the combat air patrol shot down a Cant Z.1007bis of the 212° Squadriglia.[6]

At ninety minutes before dawn on the 13th, Curteis started detaching the screen's destroyers to refuel from *Brown Ranger*. However, the first ships sent could not find her and later complained the tanker was twenty-five miles out of position. Oiling finally commenced after 1000 and was not completed until dawn the next day. The tanker serviced *Cairo* and eleven destroyers while *Liverpool* topped off three destroyers.

Onslow, Icarus, and *Escapade* did not refuel. The times required to fuel ships—in three cases, escorts were more than six hours from their duties—

signified problems with the process, and reports mention continuous breaking of the tanker's gear.

As the thirsty destroyers topped their bunkers, Supermarina considered
its options. By midday on 13 June it was clear that the British had a dual operation under way and that the battle fleet would be better employed against the
eastern convoy. The western force was assessed as consisting of a battleship,
two aircraft carriers, at least five cruisers, fifteen destroyers, and at least six
transports and a tanker. Based on past practice, Riccardi and Sansonetti anticipated that the convoy would arrive at the entrance to the Sicilian narrows
at sunset on 14 June. At that point the carriers and battleship and their screens
would turn back while the convoy and a reduced escort would transit the narrows hugging the Tunisian coast. Dawn on the 15th would find the convoy
off Pantelleria and under the protection of Malta's recently augmented fighter
forces.

Supermarina prepared a multilayer response based upon this assessment.
Submarines would attack the enemy as far west as possible. Air attacks would
reduce the convoy's strength as it approached Sardinia, focusing on the carriers and the escorts that would accompany it on the last passage between Pantelleria and Malta. MAS boats would strike at night as the convoy threaded the
mine barriers in the Sicilian narrows. Finally, at dawn, a force of light surface
units suited for action in narrow and mined waters would intercept the survivors. The 7th Division at Cagliari, two light cruisers and three destroyers under the command of Division Admiral Alberto Da Zara, was available for this
mission. Da Zara, who had just turned fifty-four, had skippered MAS boats as
a lieutenant in the First World War. In the 1930s he had served as captain of the
cruiser *Montecuccoli* and later the *Aosta* during the Spanish Civil War. Da Zara
was promoted to rear admiral in 1939. When Italy declared war he led the 4th
Division's "*Di Giussano*" group; however, he served mostly ashore, commanding the Venice arsenal and the antisubmarine inspectorate. He took over the
7th Division in March 1942 and flew his flag in the cruiser *Eugenio di Savoia*.

To intercept the convoy off Pantelleria at dawn on the 15th, the 7th Division needed to get under way by the afternoon of the 13th. In fact, it sailed for
Palermo at 1720, and at 2200 Admiral Riccardi advised Comando Supremo,
Superaereo, and the German naval command that the 7th Division would engage at dawn on the 15th.[7]

That evening a reconnaissance aircraft from Malta reported that enemy
cruisers and destroyers had departed Cagliari. Admiral Curteis received this

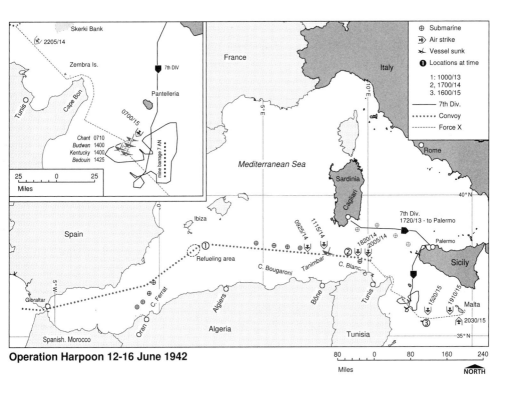

Operation Harpoon 12-16 June 1942

report at 2245. Supermarina intercepted a contact report from aircraft 8BVQ at 0310 reporting Da Zara's division north of Sicily's western tip heading east at twenty-two knots. The Italians also intercepted an order for two bombers to use flares and assumed this prefigured an attack on the cruisers.[8] Despite these ominous warnings, however, the 7th Division arrived safely at Palermo at 0700 on 14 June.

INITIAL CONTACTS

The submarine *Uarsciek* launched the first attack against the convoy at 0252 on 14 June. Based on the sound of detonation after a 135-second run, the boat claimed one definite hit. Apparently it was a premature, because *Eagle's* report noted two loud underwater explosions at 0255. Next an Italian seaplane sighted the convoy at dawn on 14 June fifty miles north of Cape Bougaroni. Two fighters attacked the snooper and forced it to ditch before it could report. However, the submarine *Giada* had the enemy in sight and at 0605 dispatched a brace of torpedoes against *Eagle*. Three detonations followed, and the submarine claimed success. *Eagle's* log noted a loud underwater explosion at 0614.[9] Shortly before this, *Escapade* reported a submarine and opened fire, but her target proved to be *Westcott* rejoining the convoy after screening *Cairo* during the cruiser's refueling.

Italian aircraft made another sighting at 0745 ninety miles southwest of Cape Teulada. The convoy was approaching the intervention zone of *Aeronautica della Sardegna* (Air Sardinia). In response to the developing situation, the Regia Aeronautica had energetically reinforced the island. With 175 operational bombers and fighters, it awaited the enemy with a force far larger than the British expected.

The navy was also marshaling reinforcements. Admiral Sansonetti rang Admiral Da Zara shortly after his arrival in Palermo. The deputy chief of staff summarized the situation and instructed Da Zara to be five to ten miles southeast of Pantelleria at dawn on the 15th "to strike the decisive blow." He told Da Zara that the large destroyer *Premuda* would shortly be arriving in Trapani and would be added to his force. Da Zara asked for the heavy cruiser *Bolzano* then at La Spezia and argued that if she was ready to sail she could arrive in time, but Sansonetti said this was not possible. Da Zara later wrote that he believed that such a fast and heavily armed vessel could have provided him with decisive force.[10]

THE MORNING ATTACKS

A major concern of General Giuseppe Santoro, the air force deputy chief of staff, was the enemy carrier fighters. In an attempt to reduce their number by damaging a flight deck before Air Sardinia unleashed its big effort, he dispatched an early, surprise strike consisting of eight CR.42s of the 24° Gruppo armed with 100-kg wing bombs and guided by a pair of unarmed S.79s. Because the CR.42s were attacking at the extreme limit of their range, they were manned by volunteers who were prepared to either continue to Algeria or ditch.[11]

At this time the convoy was steering east in two columns. *Kenya* led the northern (port) column followed by *Troilus, Orari,* and *Chant* while *Liverpool* preceded the southern column followed by *Burdwan, Kentucky,* and *Tanimbar.* Fifteen destroyers and four fleet minesweepers protectively circled six to seven thousand yards from the transports while *Malaya* followed between the two columns and *Welshman* trailed her. The carriers maneuvered independently to the north. *Charybdis* and *Vidette* screened *Argus* while *Cairo* and *Wishart* protected *Eagle*. *Wishart* had just replaced *Wrestler*, which split a boiler tube and could not steam fast enough to stay with the carrier. The sea was calm and winds light from the northwest. Visibility was extreme, and there was no cloud cover.

The CR.42s appeared overhead at 0925. *Malaya's* radar gave nearly a half hour's warning, but the raid still achieved tactical surprise. The bi-wing fighters split into two sections and dived on *Argus* from out of the sun off the starboard bow. The Italians claimed two hits on the extreme rear of the carrier's flight deck, but in fact one bomb near-missed *Charybdis* and another fell fifty yards off the carrier's bow.[12] Fulmars chased the intruders as they sped off and splashed a pair of CR.42s and one of the S.79s. Two CR.42s landed in Algeria. The other S.79 returned to Sardinia with one crewmember dead and the others wounded. The surviving CR.42s claimed they shot down two Fulmars.

Superaereo immediately evaluated the reports from this first strike and decided it had accomplished its goal. Santoro thus unleashed Sardinia's entire operational air strength. Between 1110 and 1125 eighteen S.79s of the 46° Stormo, fourteen S.84 torpedo-bombers of the 36° Stormo, and eighteen Cant Z.1007bis tri-engined bombers of the 9° Stormo delivered a series of strikes. Twenty MC.200s and nineteen CR.42s of the 16° and 24° gruppos escorted the attackers.[13]

The torpedo-bombers led in two formations of sixteen aircraft each. The first flew beyond the range of the northern destroyer screen and circled behind *Welshman*. As they were reaching their attack position the other section, consisting mainly of S.84s, lined up against *Kenya's* column. For many of the airmen this was their first action, and it was literally a baptism of fire. Flying low and slow they endured a storm of antiaircraft fire as they crossed the line of destroyers before dropping their weapons from roughly four thousand yards at 1112. The British admiral ordered a 45-degree turn toward the enemy just as the weapons hit the water, and all torpedoes missed.

As Admiral Curteis' column successfully maneuvered around the attack, the first group swung into position against the southern column. Descending from five hundred down to one hundred feet the tri-motored bombers pressed through the bursting antiaircraft fire and dropped their torpedoes beginning at 1116 from about two thousand yards. Steaming at twenty-one knots *Liverpool* was tardy in turning to meet the attack. Two torpedoes crossed the cruiser's bow and streaked down the ship's port side, and another missed under the stern. As one of the Savoias, riddled by the cruiser's flak and burning fiercely, passed low over the forecastle and crashed into the sea three hundred yards off, the fourth torpedo blasted *Liverpool*. It ripped a rectangular hole twenty-four feet long and nineteen feet deep in engine room B on the cruiser's starboard side, killing fifteen men and wounding twenty-two. The steering gear jammed, and flooding forced the ship four feet down by the stern with a 2-degree list. A torpedo also broke the back of the Dutch transport *Tanimbar* at the column's rear. Several British captains commented that the torpedo-bombers exhibited "outstanding bravery" and that their attack was "unexpectedly impressive."[14]

Almost simultaneously with the first wave of torpedo-bombers, the Cants attacked in two sections from out of the sun. One released from an elevation of four thousand meters, and most of their bombs fell around the carriers. *Eagle* reported a detonation several hundred yards off her starboard beam. At 1126 the other section hit the foundering *Tanimbar,* hurrying the steamer on her way down. Twenty-three of the transport's passengers and crewmen died, but sixty-five were rescued. Other bombs missed *Argus* by three hundred yards.

British fighters mixed it up with the Italian escorts. *Eagle* had six Hurricanes and two Fulmars on patrol while *Argus* had flown off two Fulmars. *Wrestler* witnessed one Fulmar splash a torpedo-bomber and then saw it jumped by three Italian fighters. The British aircraft went into a spin and then leveled out at a hundred feet. At that point an overeager gunner manning the destroyer's starboard 20-mm gun opened fire, "regrettably hitting with the first burst." The Fulmar crashed, but *Wrestler* rescued one survivor.[15] At 1201 three torpedo-bombers that had not been able to launch during the mass attack a half hour earlier approached *Kenya*'s column flying low and dropped their torpedoes at long range before retiring north.

During this strike, the British lost three aircraft, including the Fulmar finished off by *Wrestler*. MC.200s bagged a second Fulmar and a Hurricane. In return FAA fighters accounted for two MC.200s and an S.79 while the ship's antiaircraft weapons downed six S.84s and one S.79. An Italian seaplane rescued one set of crewmen after seven hours in the water, but the rest perished.[16]

In a meeting held at 1400 that day, General Santoro gave the cheerful news to Admiral Riccardi and the German liaison that the preliminary results indicated six ships hit: *Argus,* the battleship, a cruiser, and three transports. An unknown vessel was seen down by the bow. In the first two strikes Air Sardinia suffered heavily, losing three S.79s, six S.84s, four CR.42s, and a pair of MC.200s in dogfights. The fighters claimed eight British units.[17]

THE AFTERNOON ATTACKS

At 1145, barely making headway, *Liverpool* turned toward Gibraltar. At 1215, once the skies were clear of enemy aircraft, *Antelope* approached and passed a tow. After the cruiser jettisoned various items, such as its aircraft, starboard torpedoes, boats, derricks, and davits, speed improved to nine knots. Admiral Curteis ordered *Westcott* to escort *Antelope* and the crippled cruiser back to Gibraltar. As the destroyer passed the site of *Tanimbar's* demise, her captain noted, "Passed burning wreckage of Merchant ship; boats, scattered wood and [illegible] were aflame; no sign of life amid the floating merchandise. The body of a child of about 4 years old was seen floating vertically, head just submerged supported by a life jacket."[18]

This division of two elderly destroyers and a crippled cruiser proved a more tempting target for Air Sardinia than the main convoy. At 1531 five CR.42s led by a Cant Z.506 dive-bombed *Liverpool*. The first two were already descending before lookouts spotted them. "One or two bombs fell unpleasantly close to the starboard side and threw up a column of water which subsided on the Air Defence Position." The shaking increased the ship's list from 8 to 10 degrees, and she settled farther down by the stern.[19] At 1800 eight Cant Z.1007bis attacked from high altitude. *Antelope* had time to slip the tow and allow the cruiser to maneuver independently, and the bombs missed by a thousand yards. Ahead of *Liverpool,* however, a stick near-missed off *Westcott's* starboard quarter, and splinters killed three men and wounded eight. Eight minutes later seven fighter-escorted S.79s approached and attacked singly. The first two were shot down after launching their torpedoes, and the last five dropped from greater ranges, which allowed the cruiser to take avoiding action, although she could only be maneuvered with difficulty at a speed of four knots.

At 2015 five Cants attacked from high altitude, but their bombs fell wide. At 2225 three S.79s approached and dropped torpedoes from a distance, all of which *Liverpool* easily avoided. On the 15th at 1420 three more S.79s attacked, again from long range and again without result. This was the last strike against the *Liverpool* group. On 16 June a tug from Gibraltar relieved *Antelope,* and the crippled cruiser made Gibraltar on the evening of the 17th after a 650-mile tow.

Given her speed and the number of attacks she endured, *Liverpool* was fortunate to survive.

As Air Sardinia persecuted the cruiser, the convoy peacefully steamed east for several hours. This gave *Eagle* a chance to strike below damaged Hurricanes and range fresh aircraft on deck. Air Sicily, in conjunction with German units, was scheduled to attack as the convoy approached 10 degrees east. Units from several bases were involved and, like Sardinia, Air Sicily had arranged for the various groups to take off "with clockwork punctuality" because it wanted the attack to be delivered simultaneously by different types of aircraft in an effort to overwhelm the defense. The escort included Re.2001s and MC.202s, both types being more capable and modern than the MC.200s that equipped Sardinia's best squadrons. A scarcity of aerial torpedoes, however, only allowed one all-out strike. Sardinia had used all but twelve of its supply in the morning strike and vainly expended the rest against *Liverpool*.[20]

During the afternoon Admiral Da Zara met with one of his destroyer commanders, Captain Ignazio Castrogiovanni. It was the first time the two had worked together, and Da Zara shared his ideas about their upcoming mission. He also consulted further with Supermarina. The admiral was concerned about missing the British force during the night, but Sansonetti reassured him that aircraft would keep the convoy illuminated with flares. He also worried about coming under air attack during his nocturnal transit around Sicily's western end and south into the Sicilian narrows—heavily mined waters with an evil reputation in the Italian navy as the graveyard of several destroyers and torpedo boats. On that point Sansonetti remarked that while the 7th Division might be brightly lit, "more flares over you means fewer over Iachino." Da Zara considered this cold comfort as the 7th Division, with seven destroyers in attendance, sailed from Palermo at 1900 to carry out its mission. Nonetheless, Sansonetti was right: Malta lacked the resources to deal with every threat.[21]

The Sicilian-based units began their attacks at 1820 when twelve Ju 88s of KGr 606 swung in from the west and descended in a series of dive-bombing runs from ten thousand feet. The strike was not detected until the first planes were over the carriers. Four bombs landed 150 yards ahead of *Eagle*. A very near miss off *Argus*'s starboard bow shook the carrier severely and drenched personnel with water but left hull and machinery undamaged. Two Hurricanes were aloft, and *Eagle* launched two more during the strike. They claimed that their counterattack forced four of the Ju 88s to jettison their bombs early. In turn the Germans shot down one of *Argus*'s Fulmars and reported that they crippled a merchantman.[22]

At 2000 *Welshman* struck out on a high-speed run for Malta, and *Kujawiak* assumed the lead of the port column. Five minutes later, with the convoy fifteen miles off Cape Blanc, enemy aircraft appeared to the northeast. Radar gave nearly an hour's warning that a large strike was inbound, and *Eagle* flew off four extra Hurricanes to orbit ten miles away in the direction of the approaching attack. Nonetheless, four destroyers were out of position investigating submarine contacts or dropping depth charges as the air attack developed.

Fourteen S.79s of the 132° Gruppo arrived first. As they began to deploy, Hurricanes intercepted and shot down one of the tri-motor bombers. Then the escort, seventeen Re.2001s of the 2° Gruppo and seven MC.202s from the 51° Stormo, confronted the carrier fighters. As the torpedo-bombers proceeded to work their way around the convoy's stern to attack from the starboard side, the Italian air force history noted that "the superiority of the Re.2001 and the MC.202 with respect to the British naval aircraft allowed our fighters to maintain supremacy of the skies during the entire action." The British slant on the air battle was that the Hurricanes quickly expended their inadequate supply of ammunition, forcing them to act as "spectators while this formation was parading round the Force out of gun range." Admiral Curteis later reported "our fighters met considerable fighter opposition and were therefore unable to assist in breaking up the attacks."[23]

As the torpedo-bombers made their large loop, the level bombers, five S.79s, nine S.84s, and four Cant Z.1007bis, approached from the starboard bow shortly after 2000 and flew down the length of the columns through violent antiaircraft fire to drop their ordnance. Although the crews reported hits, in fact their bombs missed. The defending fighters were otherwise occupied, and all bombers returned safely to base. Simultaneously with the high-level attack, seventeen Italian Ju 87s of 102° Gruppo, escorted by nineteen MC.202s of 155° Gruppo, attacked the convoy's port side screen. They dove in from seven thousand to one thousand feet and near-missed the destroyers *Icarus* and *Wrestler*. One captain reported that they completely distracted the screen's attention from the torpedo aircraft. *Wrestler*'s commander wrote, "Fortunately they all came in from the bow and I was able to turn on to each attacker, using full speed and helm. This lesson, which one learnt in Norway and France, stood me in good stead and none of the four near misses (within 50 yards) did any underwater damage." One bomb exploded so close it drenched everyone on the bridge. The dive bombers claimed they hit a cruiser and merchantman. Operating at the extreme limit of their range, one of the Ju 87s ran out of fuel and had to ditch at sea, but a German floatplane rescued the crew.[24]

Meanwhile, the torpedo-bombers and Admiral Curtis jockeyed for position. As the aircraft tried to line up for a favorable approach angle, the admiral ordered successive turns to maintain a bow-on heading to the line of attack. *Argus,* two miles out on the convoy's starboard quarter, assessed this attack to be "paradoxically much more efficiently and vigorously performed than the relatively more successful though more expensive torpedo-bomber attack in the morning." Although three planes dropped their torpedoes just three hundred yards from the small carrier, the target angles were poor, and *Argus* maneuvered so that they passed down the port side, one just missing astern. The rest of the torpedoes likewise failed to connect. By 2025 the attack was over.[25]

British fighters downed one S.79, and flak accounted for another. One Hurricane was lost to an S.79's defensive fire and another crash-landed while *Hebe* shot down a Fulmar by mistake. *Onslow's* Captain Armstrong in his report commented, "the air attacks . . . were unexpectedly impressive. The high level bombers kept good and close formation and were undeterred by H.A. fire. The torpedo-bombers also pressed their attacks well home."[26]

As the aircraft returned and reports were collated, Air Sicily claimed one cruiser and one transport sunk and a battleship, carrier, two cruisers, three other warships, and one transport damaged. The Germans said they damaged two transports.[27]

There was also a submarine scare during this attack. The submarine *Alagi* spotted ships at 1845. She approached and witnessed the air attack. At 2030 the Italian boat scoped *Malaya* fifteen thousand meters away and approached to attack. Meanwhile, near the convoy's head the destroyer *Middleton* sighted a periscope during the dive-bombing attack and dropped one depth charge. *Onslow* later reported: "She then hauled down her black pendant. As no further information could be extracted from her, and she could not be induced to drop more depth charges, *Onslow* hauled round to the position and dropped a full pattern."[28]

At the same time (2030) *Hebe* and *Kujawiak* were attacking contacts south of the convoy. Later, *Malaya* reported a periscope near the convoy's rear, and at 2055 the aptly named *Speedy* rushed up and dropped depth charges. Her cap-

tain reported, "Five charges were dropped and exploded, and about five seconds later two further explosions were heard. . . . This was followed by large air
bubbles and immediately afterwards the submarine broke surface, lying over
on its side with a list of at least 80; probably more than 90 degrees. The colour
appeared to be dark green. It remained on the surface for about five seconds,
after which it sank and further large air bubbles were seen to come to the surface to the right of the position in which the submarine sank, and there were
slight traces of oil."[29] However, notwithstanding these convincing details, there
was no submarine in the area, and Admiralty staff correctly disallowed the
claim.

During *Alagi's* approach, she spotted a carrier conducting flight operations headed straight toward her, and at 2210 the submarine launched two torpedoes at this target. She signaled her sighting at 2305.

On the evening of 14 June Supermarina deployed a section of torpedo
boats to patrol west of Trapani in case the British tried to transit the northern
part of the strait as in the past two operations. Headquarters also dispatched
three squadrons of MAS boats to assume ambush positions in the Straits of
Sicily. However, rough waters forced them to abort their mission.

FORCE X SEPARATES

At 2110 Beaufighters from Malta arrived over the convoy to help the
depleted and tired carrier air groups. Twenty minutes later, still sixty miles
northwest of Cape Bon, Force W turned back. *Icarus, Escapade,* and *Vidette*
joined *Charybdis* and the two carriers while *Onslow* and *Wrestler* screened *Malaya,* and *Wishart* took care of *Kenya.* The balance of the convoy, Force X under
the command of (Acting) Captain Cecil C. Hardy in the antiaircraft cruiser
Cairo with five fleet destroyers, four Hunt destroyers, four minesweepers, and
the convoy's five surviving merchantmen, continued east under a darken-
ing sky.

Captain Hardy had commanded the sloop *Falmouth* in the East Indies station from 1937 to January 1941 and had been awarded a DSO for "good service
in sinking the Italian submarine [*Galvani*]." He spent a year in the Admiralty's
Training and Staff Duties Division before being given *Cairo* in January 1942
with the rank of acting captain. Considering his past service, the command of a
light cruiser, much less of an entire force including a convoy and two destroyer

divisions, was a large jump in responsibility. Moreover, his orders were difficult, almost contradictory. They called for him to "bear in mind the conflicting requirements of the safe arrival of the convoy and the need for economy of fuel and to a lesser extent of ammunition so that no extra ship need enter Malta."[30]

The merchant ships led by *Troilus* formed a single line on a course for Zembra Island. The escorts, led by *Bedouin* and the fleet units of the 11th Flotilla, screened the line of transports. At 2205 nine Ju 88s attacked from out of the darkness with the British ships silhouetted in the afterglow of sunset. They dropped their ordnance from about a thousand meters, but no bombs hit. Three planes failed to return to base. Beaufighters shot down one while antiaircraft fire accounted for another.

At 2315, less than two hours into his return passage, Admiral Curteis received a signal from Vice Admiral Ralph Leatham at Malta. This stated that two enemy cruisers and four destroyers had departed Palermo at 2125. Curteis considered the report's implications and decided not to reinforce Force X with one of his cruisers. He gave several reasons, but the biggest was "I did not consider the Italian Force . . . would go into the area in which the convoy would be by the following dawn as I have always understood the Italians avoid this area owing to the danger of air attack from Malta." And even if they did, "Judging from past encounters with the Italians, the convoy escort was large enough to deter them from doing any harm to the convoy."[31] Thus, displaying the same complacent mindset that infused Harwood's planning, Curteis continued steaming west back toward Gibraltar.

As the convoy steamed close along the African shore, the darkness seemed to offer little sanctuary. Lookouts reported parachute flares to the northeast and assumed their location was being marked for attack. Then, while rounding Cape Bon, the destroyer *Blankney* reported signals that had the appearance of tracer bullets fired into the sky. At 0212 units of the 11th Flotilla engaged an object seen in the darkness to starboard. *Ithuriel's* captain wrote, "the enemy was seen to be a destroyer, and hits were scored upon her." *Marne* reported that she was taking return fire and that shells were splashing ahead of the ship. However, "a suspicion already crystallized in my mind and I ceased fire just before the signal was received from *Bedouin* to do so." In fact the enemy vessel was the wreck of *Havock*. This destroyer had put into Malta for repairs after being heavily damaged by *Littorio* on 22 March in the Second Battle of Sirte. However, she sustained further damage on 3 April in an air raid, and two days later

Havock set out for Gibraltar to complete her repairs. She ran aground near Kelebia Lighthouse shortly after midnight on 6 April. At 0317 that same morning the Italian submarine *Aradam* torpedoed the wreck. The next afternoon the crew abandoned ship and detonated the aft magazine. French authorities subsequently interned *Havock*'s crew.[32]

As the British proceeded, Da Zara's division was on course to intercept. His mission began poorly. First, *Premuda*, an ex-Yugoslavian destroyer that had been taken over by the Regia Marina in 1941 and was larger and more heavily armed than any Italian destroyers, reported that there had been insufficient fuel available for her to top her bunkers. Next, the squadron was hardly under way when the destroyers *Zeno* and *Gioberti* reported mechanical problems. Da Zara ordered them to return to port. In the case of *Gioberti* this was particularly distressing because she had just finished a long refit. Da Zara wrote that if a speed of twenty-two knots forced two of his destroyers to drop out, what would happen when they were operating at battle speeds? He was not concerned about fighting without destroyers, only that one or two disabled destroyers might force him to adopt a defensive posture once battle had been joined. More worries arrived when Supermarina forwarded the report from a reconnaissance aircraft that a heavy cruiser was steering east north of Cape Bon. Headquarters included with this information instructions for the admiral to avoid superior forces. Nonetheless, Da Zara resolved that he would fight any number of ships with equal armament and up to a single cruiser with 8-inch guns. "The decision was not heroic, but rational and conscious. After Punta Stilo, the Gulf of Genoa, Sirte, and Second Sirte, the Italian navy needed a 'surface success.'" Da Zara considered that he had the means and opportunity to achieve that success.[33]

As the Italians proceeded, no more mishaps occurred. There was no drone of aircraft engines overhead nor the sudden brightness of aerial flares. The weather and visibility were "extremely favorable." "The night was superb and right before our bow the constellation of Scorpio shined." The admiral's chief of staff remarked that the 7th Division would be fighting under the banner of Antares, and concerns waned as the late spring night passed.[34]

For the British likewise the passing of the night watches seemed to calm the jitters originally inspired by the onset of darkness. After shooting at *Havock,* the convoy continued on course. Dawn was expected to bring a continuous escort of Beaufighters. So far, the British had good reason to be satisfied with the operation's progress. If past experience was any guide, the most dangerous part of the voyage was over. Only one transport had been lost, and just one cruiser had sustained major damage.

FORCE W'S RETURN

Before continuing on to the clash between Force X and the 7th Division, it is convenient to relate Force W's return to Gibraltar.

Despite Admiral Curteis' concerns that Force W would still be within "easy striking distance" of the Italian air force at dawn on the 15th, the first alarm did not come until 1100, when *Charybdis* dropped depth charges after her lookouts reported a submarine ahead of *Kenya*. At 1315 on 15 June three torpedo-bombers approached from the force's port beam and dropped their weapons from four miles. There were two Hurricanes in the air before the attack developed, and two more were flown off. They claimed that they splashed one of the attackers.

At 1504 one S.79 approached in line with a Swordfish that was flying anti-submarine patrol. It got the flotilla's attention when it "broke formation" and dropped a torpedo from six thousand yards. Two patrolling Fulmars chased the bomber for twenty miles, getting in one short burst of fire but doing no damage.

At 0800 on 16 June *Argus* and *Malaya* screened by *Escapade, Wishart, Wrestler,* and *Vidette* continued on to Gibraltar while *Eagle, Kenya,* and *Charybdis* with *Onslow* and *Icarus* turned back to support the returning units from Force X. At 1715 *Eagle* and the two destroyers likewise turned for Gibraltar. At 2017 on 17 June Force X's survivors joined *Kenya* and *Charybdis,* and together they proceeded to Gibraltar.

7

THE BATTLE OF PANTELLERIA

It was an exciting month for my young warriors who drained
to the bottom the intoxicating cup of success.

Division Admiral Alberto Da Zara

AT 0620 THE EASTERN sky was beginning to brighten. A light northwest breeze rippled the surface of the sea. Force X bore twenty-five miles southwest of Pantelleria, steaming toward Malta at a steady twelve knots. The merchant ships sailed in two columns with *Cairo* leading. The destroyers screened
the formation—the 11th Flotilla with *Bedouin* (Commander B. G. Scurfield),
Partridge, Ithuriel, Marne, and *Matchless* was to starboard, while the 12th Flotilla's *Blankney* (Lieutenant Commander P. F. Powlett), *Badsworth, Middleton,* and *Kujawiak* sailed to port. The minesweepers *Speedy* (Lieutenant Commander A. E. Doran), *Hythe, Hebe, Rye,* and the six motor launches brought up
the rear. At 0620 *Cairo* received a radio report that at 0600 a Beaufighter, one
of five that had departed Malta before dawn to cover Force X, had spotted two
enemy cruisers and four destroyers fifteen miles off the convoy's port beam.
Cairo had fighter direction facilities, but they did not work in this instance as
the pilot reported to Malta and Malta forwarded the information to Hardy,
thus delaying the British captain's receipt of this vital news.

The Italian formation, led by the 10th Destroyer Squadron, followed by
the cruisers and the 14th Squadron, had Pantelleria abeam to starboard and
was steaming due south at twenty-four knots. An hour before, it had deployed
from night cruising to battle formation, expecting to confront the enemy at
first light. But just to be sure the cruisers each launched an RO.43 floatplane

at 0620. As the planes soared off their catapults it seemed a perfect launch. However, a Beaufighter splashed *Eugenio's* aircraft at 0710 while *Montecuccoli's* damaged its radio on takeoff and, although it faithfully followed the convoy, it could not report.

On both fleets binoculars studied the horizon. At 0627 *Matchless* reported two cruisers and three destroyers fifteen miles to the northeast. At 0630 *Cairo* confirmed, and at the same time *Oriani*, leading the Italian formation, signaled smoke and the uncertain shape of many ships on the darker western horizon. Admiral Da Zara was pleased to make contact but considered the odds unfavorable. He estimated that the enemy had three cruisers and eight destroyers including, perhaps, the heavy cruiser Supermarina had warned about that night. The Italian admiral immediately rang up twenty-eight knots. A north–south mine barrage, 7 AN, ran ten miles east of his position. This barrage, which dated from 11 June 1940, consisted of 393 P 200 mines; because of an unusually strong current running the night they were laid, many mines had activated their hydrostatic anchors prematurely. This resulted in the mines lying too close to the surface. Over the years storm effects had caused many to break free and drift, and the Regia Marina considered the area west of the field hazardous because it was subject to these floating menaces.

At 0638 Da Zara increased speed to thirty-two knots. Because of the barrage that prevented him from maneuvering east, he decided to pull ahead of the convoy and attack it from the south, driving the enemy across the mines. At the same time the 14th Squadron's Captain Castrogiovanni came on the high-frequency voice radio to report that *Malocello's* best speed was twenty-eight knots and his squadron was dropping behind. Da Zara radioed back instructing Castrogiovanni to attack the convoy independently. The destroyer captain turned his two ships to a west-by-northwest heading shortly thereafter while the rest of the Italian force pressed south.

Upon being confronted by the enemy Captain Hardy later reported that he immediately ordered *Bedouin* to act independently while he held the Hunts and *Cairo* back to make smoke. "My immediate intention was to gain time and to fight a delaying action in the hope that an air striking force could be sent from Malta." Apparently he was unaware that Malta's air assets were already committed to attacking Admiral Iachino's fleet threatening the Vigorous convoy. Only four FAA Albacores and two Beauforts with crews even more inexperienced than those already committed were available, and it would be four hours before this scant force would answer Hardy's call.[1]

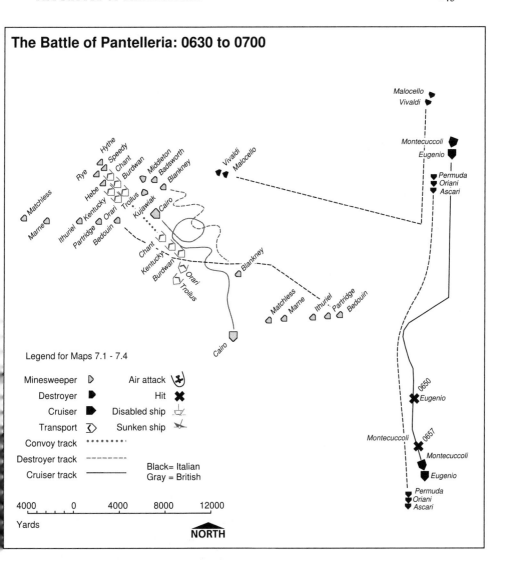

The Battle of Pantelleria: 0630 to 0700

Legend for Maps 7.1 - 7.4

Minesweeper	◁	Air attack	⚓
Destroyer	◀	Hit	✖
Cruiser	◀	Disabled ship	⚓
Transport	◇	Sunken ship	⚓
Convoy track	••••••••		
Destroyer track	--------		
Cruiser track	————	Black= Italian	
		Gray = British	

4000   0   4000   8000   12000

Yards

NORTH

OPEN FIRE

At 0639 the Italian cruisers lofted a broadside toward *Cairo* from nineteen thousand meters. The 6/53-in (152-mm) Ansaldo 1926 weapons that constituted the cruisers' main battery fired a 100-pound (45.3-kg) projectile to a
maximum range of 24,720 yards (22,600 meters) and had a theoretical firing
cycle of twelve seconds. The lead destroyers of the 10th Squadron were armed

with four 4.7/50 (120mm) O.T.O. 1931 guns that fired a 51.8-pound (23.5-kg) shell to 19,900 yards (18,200 meters) with a firing cycle of ten seconds. The guns on the 14th Squadron's destroyers were Ansaldo 1926 models that had a higher elevation and could range to 21,430 yards (19,600 meters). *Premuda*, the ex–Yugoslavian destroyer leader *Dubrovnik*, had four 5.51/56-inch (140-mm) guns that fired an 87.7-pound shell to a range of 25,590 yards (23,400 meters).[2]

The Italian gunners found the range quickly. *Eugenio* straddled *Cairo* on her second salvo while *Ascari* and *Oriani* engaged the 11th Flotilla and *Premuda* targeted the convoy. The motor launch *ML 135* reported that small caliber shells straddled at this time while the convoy commodore wrote that the "Italians opened fire at extreme range and salvoes almost immediately fell close to the convoy." *Kujawiak's* war diary noted, "The first salvo was very precise. H.M.S. *Cairo* was straddled. Some of the shells fell alongside *Kujawiak*."[3]

In his memoirs Admiral Da Zara wondered why the British failed to maneuver or return fire during the first critical minutes and supposed he had obtained complete surprise. British reports suggest that this was partially true. *Marne*, the fourth destroyer on the unengaged side, only received an enemy report at 0638 from *Blankney*, the lead destroyer on the engaged side. *Partridge* did not detect the Italians until 0640. In other words, they were not aware of the enemy until twenty minutes after *Cairo* received a radio report of an Italian force bearing down and ten minutes after Hardy's ship had visually sighted the enemy. *Matchless* reported that at 0640 *Bedouin* hoisted the signal to come to eighteen knots and head toward the enemy. All this time the convoy maintained its original course. Hardy wrote that he ordered the convoy to steer for "territorial waters" at 0645 (fifteen minutes after visual contact) and then to come to course 240 degrees at 0650. The convoy commodore wrote that after the convoy began receiving fire "*Cairo* and destroyers made a smoke screen and the convoy was turned so as to retire keeping the smoke screen between them and the enemy. I then received a signal from *Cairo* to make for territorial waters." In sequencing these events, it is useful to remember that the relatively slow transports were under fire and that blowing smoke obscured the visual signals they relied upon.[4]

At 0645 *Marne* answered *Eugenio's* fire from a range she reported as 18,600 yards. The Italian admiral expressed amazement that he had discharged a hundred and fifty rounds before the enemy replied, but he did not realize that he was only facing destroyer-sized weapons. In fact, Da Zara carefully observed these initial salvoes, anxious to see whether the height of the geysers indicated

Table 7.1. Italian Forces at Battle of Pantelleria

Name	Commander	Type	Tons Std.	Main Guns	Secondary	Speed
VII Division	Div Adm. Alberto Da Zara					
Eugenio di Savoia	Capt. Arturo Solari	CL	8,750	8 × 6 in	6 × 3.9 in 6 × 21 in TT	33
Montecuccoli	Capt. Franco Zannoni	CL	8,875	8 × 6 in	6 × 3.9 in 6 × 21 in TT	33
10th DD Sqdn	Capt. Riccardo Pontremoli					
Ascari	Capt. Pontremoli	DD	1,850	4 × 4.7 in	6 × 21 in TT	34
Oriani	Cdr. Teodorico Capone	DD	1,750	4 × 4.7 in	6 × 21 in TT	33
Premuda	Cdr. Vittorio Prato	DD	2,100	4 × 5.5 in	6 × 21 in TT	31
14th DD Sqdn	Capt. Ignazio Castrogiovanni					
Vivaldi	Capt. Castrogiovanni	DD	2,125	6 × 4.7 in	4 × 21 in TT	28
Malocello	Cdr. Mario Leoni	DD	2,125	6 × 4.7 in	4 × 21 in TT	28

8-inch shells. The Italian admiral said that the British fire was good and quickly straddled, and by the splashes he concluded he was facing 6-inch ships. There is generally a large difference between the column of water raised by a 4.7-inch and a 6-inch shell, so the Italian admiral's confusion should be clarified. *Matchless* and *Marne* were armed with the new QF Mark XI 4.7-inch gun that fired a modern, 62-pound projectile to a range of 21,240 yards compared to the 4.7-inch guns on the other destroyers, which fired a 50-pound shell to a range of 16,970 yards. The 4-inch QF Mark XVI guns arming *Cairo, Partridge,* and the Hunts fired a 35-pound shell to a theoretical maximum range of 19,850 yards. Differences in shell weight, muzzle velocity, design, and charge gave each weapon different characteristics and contributed to Da Zara's misimpressions. *Marne's* captain observing his own splashes described them as enormous.[5]

By 0645 *Bedouin* had accelerated to twenty-two knots. The flags flying at her masthead signaled: "Enemy in sight," "Steam for full speed," "Twenty-five knots," and "Form single line ahead." As *Bedouin* drew ahead of the convoy, *Partridge* and *Ithuriel* followed roughly seventeen hundred yards apart in a loose line of bearing. *Marne* and *Matchless,* steaming at thirty-two knots to catch up, trailed three thousand yards off *Ithuriel's* starboard quarter. For *Bedouin's* Commander Scurfield, it was a moment of realization. "This is what I had been training for twenty-two years, and in nearly three years of war these were the first enemy ships I had seen . . . it was to my mind merely a question of going bald-headed for the enemy and trying to do him as much harm as possible by gun and torpedo." His enthusiasm reflected the inexperience of Hardy's scratch force. *Partridge's* war had begun two months before when she formed part of USS *Wasp's* escort during the carrier's sortie to deliver Spitfires to Malta. *Ithuriel* had been in commission for four months and had a "fully diluted crew."[6] *Marne* and *Matchless* had six months' experience, mostly escorting convoys in the Arctic. They had little practice working together and none at surface combat. The Italian units, on the other hand, had faced the enemy repeatedly. *Ascari* was a veteran of the Action off Calabria of 9 July 1940, the Battle of Cape Spartivento on 27 November 1940, the Engagement off Gavdos on 28 March 1941, and the Second Battle of Sirte on 22 March 1942. The other destroyers had similar resumes, and within squadrons the ships, with the exception of *Premuda,* knew each other well.

While the 11th Flotilla steamed hell-bent toward the Italian cruisers, *Cairo* and the 12th Flotilla circled and laid smoke to mask the vulnerable transports.

The convoy began its wide turn to starboard to a southwest heading shortly before 0700, nearly forty minutes after contact.

Da Zara considered Scurfield's charge bold but reckless. At 0646 the Italian cruisers trained their guns on the leading destroyers and began snaking to confuse the enemy aim, steering west of south to block the convoy and avoid the mine barrage. Scurfield remembered, "Their spread was good—too good perhaps at that range—and the shooting seemed to be unpleasantly accurate." Within a minute *Bedouin*, now steaming at twenty-five knots, answered from eighteen thousand yards followed by *Partridge*. *Ascari* and *Oriani* continued to engage the charging destroyers, but once the cruisers switched targets, they had difficulty observing the fall of their shot, which was necessary for accurate shooting. Up through 0709 *Ascari* expended ninety rounds while *Oriani* fired sixty. They claimed two hits on *Bedouin*.[7]

At 0650 *Cairo* opened fire. Captain Hardy claimed that this was "largely for moral effect as the enemy was never within effective range of the four-inch guns."[8] At the same time *Ithuriel* joined in against *Montecuccoli* from 14,700 yards. The Italian warships suffered their first damage when a shell struck *Eugenio* near the waterline in the vicinity of the sick bay and killed two men. *Marne* delivered this blow—impressive shooting at extremely long range for the 4.7-inch mount. *Premuda's* dangerous guns, meanwhile, had shifted target from the convoy to *Ithuriel* showing that Scurfield's charge had relieved pressure on the merchant ships.

THE 14TH SQUADRON'S ATTACK

After Da Zara ordered Castrogiovanni to attack independently, the destroyer captain approached the enemy directly, sailing west by northwest. His two vessels shelled the convoy until the growing wall of black, gray, and white smoke being spewed by *Cairo* and the 12th Flotilla completely fouled their aim. *Vivaldi* reported, "As we closed the enemy, followed by *Malocello* four English destroyers turned to intercept us opening a heavy fire." From the British perspective, *Blankney* led *Middleton, Badsworth,* and *Kujawiak* south and sighted *Vivaldi* and *Malocello* bearing 30 degrees from their heading. "12th Division . . . opened fire at extreme range on the northern pair of destroyers, which seemed to be working round the convoy." To the south *Matchless* and *Marne* also engaged. *Matchless* reported: "At [0654], two enemy destroyers who had lagged behind their cruisers came in range of *Matchless* and fire was opened on the rearmost ship. *Marne* opened fire at about the same time on the leading ship." The British destroyer reported the range as about eighteen thousand yards, but it was certainly much less. "Target was repeatedly crossed with zig-zag salvoes. Within a few minutes the enemy made smoke and retired at high speed." In fact, at 0700, Castrogiovanni ordered a turn to port, and from an estimated range of 5,800 meters each destroyer launched two torpedoes toward the convoy. *Vivaldi* targeted *Chant* and *Malocello* a destroyer, most likely a minesweeper, although *Kujawiak* reported dodging a torpedo. This was ten minutes after Hardy had ordered the convoy to steer 240 degrees, but the Italian destroyers observed their targets still following an easterly course. At 0705, five minutes after launch, *Chant* suddenly exploded. The Italian destroyers observed flames and a column of black smoke ascending above the smoke screen and naturally assumed their attack was the cause.[9]

Da Zara also believed *Vivaldi*'s torpedo sank *Chant* and called Castrogiovanni's maneuver "brilliant and decisive." The model W270f 21-inch torpedo used had a speed of thirty-eight knots, or 1,283 yards a minute. Thus, it had a run to target of approximately five minutes, and so the timing of *Chant*'s destruction was consistent with *Vivaldi*'s claim within a reasonable tolerance for error. However, the literature of the battle with one recent exception does not consider the possibility that an Italian destroyer may have been responsible for *Chant*'s demise.[10]

Most histories credit German Ju 87s with this kill. This comes from Captain Hardy's report that states *Chant* was sunk by "an air attack on the convoy at about 0710, which is believed to have been made by 8 Ju 87s. *Chant* had received three direct hits and *Kentucky* had been near missed. One enemy plane had been brought down by ships' gunfire." There are several problems with this account. Hardy did not observe the attack, and although the reports filed by other ships that were in a better position to observe speak of aircraft attacks at around this time, they disagree as to details. The captain of *ML 135* stated "at approx. 0700/15 merchant ship *Chant* was attacked and hit by bombs." The convoy commodore's report said, "at 0640 an air attack developed and M.V. *Chant* was hit and subsequently sank, there were near misses on the remainder of the convoy and the U.S. Oiler *Kentucky* was disabled." The 3rd ML Flotilla's commander reported that "an air attack commenced about 0700 by J.U.88s and S.S. *Chant* was hit and sank in a few minutes. . . . One plane was seen to crash." The Royal Navy liaison officer aboard *Kentucky* wrote, "During the morning, enemy planes were frequently overhead, and about 0800 *Kentucky* was disabled by a stick of bombs that fell 10–15 yards away on the starboard quarter." *Kujawiak* observed, "one burning plane fell onto the tanker and set it on fire." *Speedy* stated, "At 0705 the Convoy was attacked by Ju 88's and one Merchantman, S. S. *Chant,* received a direct hit and sank in about 10 minutes. *Speedy* shot down plane responsible." *Blankney* "observed German aircraft attack convoy." The master of the merchant ship alongside *Chant* wrote, "The *Chant,* on our starboard beam, was soon hit, listed badly and was well ablaze. She caused us some uncomfortable moments by careering over toward us. . . . She sank so rapidly that the water reached her "ammo" first. Her oil tanks burst as she went down leaving a terrific pall of fire and smoke that was visible for most of the day."[11]

The time range in these accounts for when the attack occurred is an hour and twenty minutes, and they disagree in their details. Hardy's report can be discounted because the only air unit equipped with Ju 87s on Sicily was the Italian 102° Gruppo, and it did not attack until six hours later. In fact, Air Sicily did not mount any strikes during the morning. It had expended all but four of its torpedoes, and the bombers were having problems refueling and rearming because the specialized personnel and most of the necessary materials were located on the island's western fields. Moreover, the Regia Aeronautica did not want to intervene during a naval action because of the risk of bombing friendly units.[12]

With respect to German units the records also contain ambiguities. The official Italian history states that two groups of Ju 88s attacked the convoy that morning. "According to the O.B.S. 'Summary' four aircraft carried out an attack from [0643 to 0730], sinking a steamer; another seven attacked from [0706 to 0722] hitting three steamers and a tanker. One Ju 88 was lost." German aircraft sighted the 7th Division at 0653 (and came under fire from the Italians) and were then chased by Beaufighters. After escaping the British fighters one Ju 88 bombed *Kentucky* at 0722. Another dropped its ordnance on *Vivaldi* at 0730 and missed. The two Ro.43s catapulted from the Italian cruisers were also in the vicinity, and one was shot down at 0710.[13]

It is a fact that shells being fired from long range were splashing into and around the convoy at this time. There were aircraft overhead. Smoke covered the scene, and visibility was variable. The preponderance of the evidence suggests that a Ju 88 bombed and sank *Chant,* but it does not exclude the possibility of an Italian destroyer torpedo: the transport's sudden and extreme list and rapid sinking indicated damage below the waterline such as a torpedo would inflict.

By 0656 *Bedouin* was 12,500 yards off *Montecuccoli*'s starboard quarter. *Partridge* and *Ithuriel* followed their flotilla leader, staggered to starboard. While *Eugenio*'s main battery concentrated against *Bedouin*, the cruiser's 3.9/47-inch O.T.O 1928 weapons began targeting *Partridge,* and *Montecuccoli*'s secondary battery opened up against *Ithuriel.* These guns fired a 30.4-pound shell (13.8 kg) to a maximum range of 16,670 yards (15,240 meters). In the midst of this action *Eugenio*'s captain called Da Zara's attention to *Montecuccoli.* The cruiser appeared to be the central figure in a monumental fountain. "In rapid succession the tall columns of water from the enemy salvos rose up and not one was falling before others welled up from the sea's surface while a wave of white form broke at the cruiser's bow." A 4.7-inch shell from *Ithuriel* punched into *Montecuccoli*'s officers' quarters, wounding eight men. A splinter struck the cruiser's nameplate and sheered off the letter "o" in the ship's motto, *Centum oculi,* so that it read *Centum culi.* At 0659 *Montecuccoli* switched her main battery from *Cairo,* which was chasing salvoes on a roughly parallel course off the enemy's starboard quarter, to the destroyers. She also launched two torpedoes.[14]

As the range between the cruisers and the 11th Flotilla dropped, the cruisers began to register hits. At 0702 a 6-inch shell slammed into *Partridge*'s forward torpedo mount. Two torpedo air vessels burst, propelling the warheads overboard to port and expelling the bodies to starboard. The explosion blasted a hole in the deck amidships, and splinters cut the port engine's main steam pipe. Out of control, *Partridge* veered in a wide circle as *Ithuriel* raced past to starboard following *Bedouin. Bedouin,* however, was experiencing worse trouble. A 6-inch round landed on the ship's bow at 0701 and tore away twenty square feet of plating. Another shell hit at 0702 and ripped a large hole above the waterline; a third at 0704 exploded in No. 1 Boiler Room and fractured a steam pipe. A fourth at 0705 toppled the mast.

At 0705 *Premuda* observed an enemy cruiser turn away in flames and claimed a hit. Her target was *Cairo* but the cruiser was near-missed, not hit. The large destroyer's four gun broadsides and the size of her shells, which were nearly 90 percent of a cruiser's 6-inch rounds, caused British observers to incorrectly conclude that the cruisers were dividing their fire between *Cairo* and

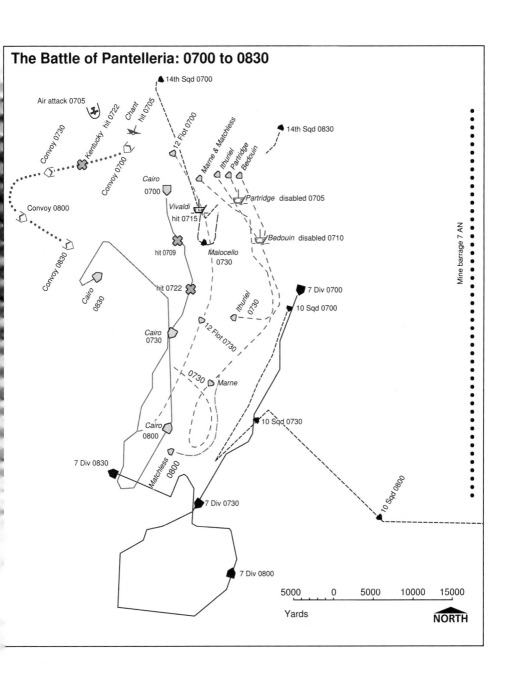

The Battle of Pantelleria: 0700 to 0830

14th Sqd 0700

Air attack 0705

Kentucky hit 0722

Chant hit 0705

Convoy 0730

Convoy 0700

14th Sqd 0830

12 Flot 0700

Marne & Matchless

Ithuriel

Partridge

Bedouin

Cairo 0700

Vivaldi hit 0715

Partridge disabled 0705

Convoy 0800

hit 0709

Malocello 0730

Bedouin disabled 0710

Convoy 0830

Cairo 0830

hit 0722

Ithuriel 0730

7 Div 0700

10 Sqd 0700

Cairo 0730

12 Flot 0730

Mine barrage 7 AN

0730 Marne

Cairo 0800

10 Sqd 0730

7 Div 0830

Matchless 0800

10 Sqd 0800

7 Div 0730

7 Div 0800

5000   0   5000   10000   15000

Yards

NORTH

the destroyers. At 0709 *Premuda's* gunners observed another hit, and this time they were right. *Cairo's* report stated: "The enemy's gunnery was good. . . . At this stage one hit by a six-inch projectile was made on *Cairo* but did little damage. [The 5.5-inch shell] landed on the fore superstructure."[15]

Meanwhile, *Eugenio* concentrated on *Bedouin*. At 0708 a fifth round struck the large Tribal-class destroyer's bridge, wrecking the director. A sixth round hit the radar hut a minute later. Captain Scurfield later recalled, "one of the first things to go was the mast, and with it the wireless. I knew the bridge had been hit. . . . most of the signalmen and 'rudolf' men on the flag-deck were either dead or wounded." At 0710 *Bedouin,* severely battered and rapidly losing way, began to turn to starboard. Hit number seven tore a gaping hole on the starboard side above the waterline, number eight ignited a large fire in the gearing room, and number nine plowed into a mess but failed to explode. Coming up hard *Ithuriel's* captain assumed Scurfield intended to launch torpedoes. Commander Scurfield later said the range was five thousand yards. Feeling that his ship "would not be able to go much farther," he ordered torpedoes fired. *Ithuriel* launched two as well. Her captain wrote, "This was I am afraid a bad error of judgment on my part as we were well outside [effective fire range] and our only chance to hit would have been if the enemy had altered toward after we had fired."[16]

Bedouin's agony continued. A tenth shell exploded by X gun and ignited the ready-use cordite. Number eleven penetrated the after cabin flat and holed the hull on the waterline. A twelfth blow disabled the starboard engine.

As this barrage was tearing *Bedouin* to pieces, *Matchless* approached *Partridge* intending to cover her with smoke, but the damaged destroyer "took a sheer to port and eventually completed a circle at speed out of control and H.M.S. *Matchless* had to leave her to port to avoid collision." *Marne* came up last and laid smoke as she sped past the flotilla leader.[17]

As the battle continued south *Cairo* maneuvered between the convoy and the enemy cruisers while *Ithuriel* now led the fleet destroyers. She tossed a few rounds toward *Vivaldi* fourteen thousand yards off her starboard quarter before reengaging the cruisers as she closed to eight thousand yards. Then she received Hardy's 0715 order for the fleet destroyers to close *Cairo*. Her captain wrote, "This I was not sorry to do as the ship was under very heavy and unpleasantly accurate fire."[18]

At 0705, as *Vivaldi* and *Malocello* headed southeast, they had little opportunity to celebrate what they believed was a successful torpedo attack. The 12th Flotilla was to their south while farther southeast the 11th Flotilla's larger destroyers were clearly in view and the two nearest, *Marne* and *Matchless,* had them under fire until 0710 when they switched their guns to Da Zara's cruisers. With the convoy cloaked by smoke (which the minesweepers and motor launches continued to refresh), Castrogiovanni's ships engaged the 12th Flotilla. *Malocello's* captain characterized the British fire as poor; nonetheless at 0715, as *Vivaldi* reported, "a shell exploded in the forward engine room; steam and oil pipes riddled by splinters. Other shell fragments ignited fire in adjacent main magazine." The source of this blow is uncertain—the timing suggests a 12th Flotilla vessel, but *Matchless* is another possibility. *Marne* observed smoke and fire on *Vivaldi's* bridge after a salvo from *Matchless* but timed this event at 0707. *Partridge* was also taking potshots at the two Italian destroyers throughout this period.[19]

Ahead of the cruisers *Ascari* and *Oriani* ceased fire at 0709. Da Zara watched the wakes of *Bedouin's* torpedoes pass astern on a sea "as smooth as glass." As *Ithuriel* withdrew and *Bedouin* and *Partridge* wrapped themselves in smoke, Da Zara judged that he had defeated the destroyer charge. However, he observed *Cairo* emerge from the smoke to the northwest shortly thereafter, and it seemed that two cruisers led by a large *Birmingham* class vessel with a battery of a dozen 6-inch guns were assuming the offensive role from the destroyers.[20]

The smoke was growing denser and visibility more problematic, although the gunnery of *Cairo* and the two Ms seemed rapid and effective to Da Zara. He wrote, "We ran on converging courses and the range diminished. At 0712 a magnificent salvo straddled perfectly." At the same time, however, *Eugenio's* lookouts reported an explosion on the bow of an enemy destroyer and observed her drop out of line. This was *Matchless,* under heavy fire but undamaged.[21]

At 0718 *Marne* shifted target to *Montecuccoli* and watched shells falling around the cruiser but, as her report complained, "it was impossible at that range with a squirming enemy making smoke to know if hits were being obtained." The gunners observed smoke between *Montecuccoli's* funnels and believed that they had struck a blow, but in fact *Montecuccoli* was next to inflict rather than receive damage when, at 0722, she straddled *Cairo.* One shell missed just astern and riddled the flagship with splinters. *Cairo* immediately sheered to starboard. Aboard *Eugenio* it seemed that broadsides had repeatedly struck the largest opponent. Da Zara remembered, "I could not burst out in a childish display of joy by throwing my hat into the air [but] the anti-aircraft lookouts stationed near the bridge applauded . . ."[22]

As Da Zara rejoiced in the belief that he had knocked a large British cruiser out of the battle, a Ju 88 dropped two bombs that "straddled [*Kentucky's*] poop" and drenched the deck with water. The concussion cracked the main generator steam feed pipe and filled the engine room with steam and ammonia. The crew had no parts to replace the pipe, and the chief engineer determined that, "lacking electricity, he could neither fill his boilers nor raise steam." Thus, there was no way to get the otherwise undamaged ship under way.[23]

VIVALDI

The news to the north was not so good for the Italians. By 0720 *Vivaldi* was aflame and dead in the water. Castrogiovanni ordered *Malocello* to withdraw, but instead she circled *Vivaldi* with smoke. The squadron commander had already sent a dramatic message to Da Zara that he would fight to the last and long live the king. At 0717 Da Zara ordered Pontremoli's 10th Squadron to Castrogiovanni's aid. Da Zara rationalized that if the destroyers were reunited into one group they "could also constitute a serious threat to the convoy."[24]

As *Malocello* stood by, *Vivaldi*'s crew struggled to control the fires and raise steam. Then *Blankney*'s flotilla, which was ten thousand yards south and steaming to close *Cairo*, emerged from a smoke bank. *Malocello* described this as an encounter with four destroyers led by a larger unit. She spread more smoke and "having received the order from *Vivaldi*, [we] attacked and approached to within 7,000 meters, launching against the enemy flotilla leader and shooting at another vessel." *Malocello* claimed her attack forced the foe to withdraw behind smoke. From the British perspective the flotilla commander assumed the Italian units were still trying to get at the convoy and decided to send *Badsworth* and *Kujawiak* to deal with them, but the Italian vessels disappeared in *Malocello*'s smoke before he could clear the signal flags, and so his flotilla proceeded south.[25]

Next the 14th Squadron ran into *Partridge*, which had corrected her steering problem and extinguished her fires. She reported that "two enemy destroyers which were still in sight and firing at 'Bedouin' were engaged, and withdrew to the South East. Smoke floats were dropped round *Bedouin*, and preparations made for taking her in tow." From the Italian perspective this event was more dramatic. "The enemy destroyers intensified their offensive, approaching to 4,500 meters: [*Vivaldi*] launched two torpedoes against the nearest one (that had on her bow the symbol "H68"), but they did not hit; meanwhile *Malocello* ducked into smoke, and continued to fire. Also the English destroyers launched two torpedoes that passed astern of our ships." *Partridge*'s number, G30, was apparently misread in the distance and smoke. The fact that the Italian report further noted that one of the enemy units appeared damaged and moved off at fifteen knots likewise suggests that *Partridge* was the opponent in this encounter.[26]

As the 10th Squadron steamed north to assist *Vivaldi*, a gap in the smoke suddenly revealed *Cairo* and several destroyers just 10,000 meters away. The gap closed before the Italian ships could open fire but Pontremoli considered it too risky to advance against a stronger force in such uncertain visibility. He also felt constrained by the mine barrage to his east and the risk of drifting mines, and so he decided to strike southeast toward the barrier's southern end. He would then sail due north east of 7 AN and meet Castrogiovanni above the barrier. This decision left *Vivaldi* unsupported for ninety minutes. Admiral Iachino later criticized this action in a letter to Admiral Da Zara: "It has already been noted that this squadron did not demonstrate initiative in the first round of combat when it lagged behind the cruisers and passively watched the enemy torpedo attack without intervening except with a few artillery volleys. No better was this squadron's behavior when at 0716 it was sent north to assist the *Vivaldi* group. . . . Mistaking them for a new enemy group . . . the squadron made its approach by heading southeast and then east of the mine barrier to get to the point in the north where *Vivaldi* waited for his assistance. Fortunately, the enemy had abandoned the attack against *Vivaldi*."[27]

The intense fire near *Vivaldi*'s engine room defied efforts to control it, but at 0746 the engineers generated enough steam to turn one turbine. This allowed the burning destroyer to start limping toward Pantelleria.

ACTION TO THE SOUTH

As the Italian destroyers fought their separate battles, Da Zara continued steaming southwest at high speed, weaving to complicate the enemy's fire control solutions as he sought to circle around the convoy. *Marne* and *Matchless* paralleled the Italian cruisers to the north at ranges as low as ten thousand yards, swapping salvos in an exchange described as "accurate, though neither succeeded in hitting." *Cairo* and *Ithuriel* proceeded about six thousand yards west of the "Ms," likewise pumping shells at *Eugenio*. At 0736 a salvo straddled *Cairo* and the British flagship swerved away making smoke. *Matchless*, which was pulling ahead of the other ships and running low on ammunition, slowed to twenty-five knots to let the formation catch up.[28]

By 0740 Da Zara was due south of *Cairo*. He wrote that "it was clearly the enemy's intention to force the passage east at all costs. I assumed therefore course 180 degrees in order to increase the range a little and avoid sudden destroyer attack." At 0745 the admiral decided to turn east in the direction he knew the enemy eventually had to go. "[My] purpose was to prevent the convoy from slipping past to the east by winding around its head and thus force it to reverse course once again."[29]

At the same time Hardy hauled around to port and ordered the destroyers to form up astern of *Cairo. Matchless* refreshed the smoke before taking station. The column, in order *Cairo, Marne, Matchless, Ithuriel, Blankney, Middleton, Badsworth,* and *Kujawiak,* then came about in succession to a course of 345 degrees.[30] As these events occurred to the south the convoy had begun broadly turning to port to resume course toward Malta. *Hebe* was standing by *Kentucky* preparing to take her under tow.

At 0754 Da Zara turned north once again, noting that "the enemy had adopted a clearly defensive tactic . . . and hiding behind a gigantic bank of artificial fog, he demonstrated the tragic 'consensual nature' of naval combat." After an hour of sustained gunfire, his magazines were running low of high explosive (HE) ammunition, which was most effective on the unarmored targets he faced. When *Matchless* emerged into view through the tendrils of fog at 0807 he switched to armor piercing (AP) rounds although it was unlikely they would encounter sufficient resistance to detonate their fuzes should they hit. Da Zara lamented that without destroyers, "all the chickens had come home to roost, I dared not break the smoke curtain with only my two cruisers." Instead he proceeded northwest, and between 0823 and 0837 the cruisers sporadically engaged "a small cruiser" (*Matchless*) that was extending the smoke. Ranges hovered around twenty thousand yards, and Da Zara characterized this portion of the action as "exasperating and inconclusive." At 0825 he radioed Air Sicily and asked for strikes against the enemy and news of their situation. He also noted the presence of enemy aircraft. Superaereo ordered Air Sicily into action, but to reduce the possibility of an unfortunate accident, it instructed the pilots to attack merchant vessels only. At 0930 four S.79s and nine S.84s of 4° Gruppo lifted off.[31]

Meanwhile at 0837 the 7th Division's renewed advance caused Hardy to order the convoy to reverse course back to the northwest while *Cairo* and the destroyers circled between the Italians and the convoy generating enormous quantities of smoke. At the same time Da Zara suddenly reversed course to the southeast. He thought that the convoy, which had been invisible since 0640, might be steering northeast to round the mine barrier's northern end.

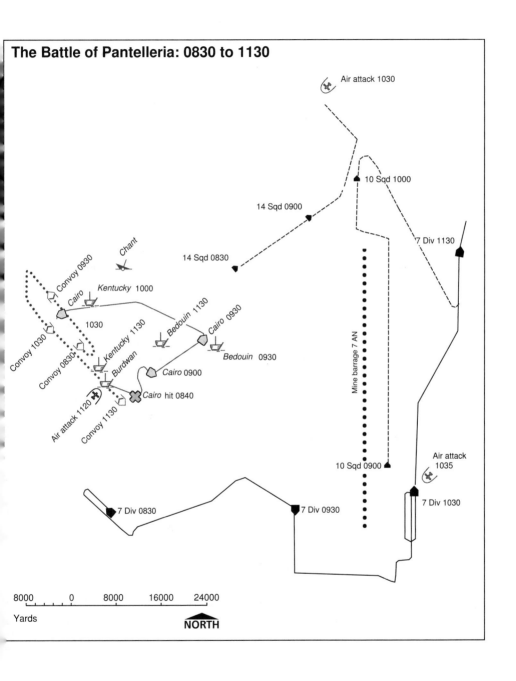

The Battle of Pantelleria: 0830 to 1130

Air attack 1030

10 Sqd 1000

14 Sqd 0900

7 Div 1130

14 Sqd 0830

Chant

Convoy 0930

Cairo

Kentucky 1000

Bedouin 1130

Cairo 0930

Convoy 1030

1030

Kentucky 1130

Convoy 0830

Burdwan

Bedouin 0930

Cairo 0900

Air attack 1120

Convoy 1130

Cairo hit 0840

Mine barrage 7 AN

Air attack 1035

10 Sqd 0900

7 Div 1030

7 Div 1030

7 Div 0830

7 Div 0930

8000   0   8000   16000   24000

Yards

NORTH

At 0840, as the ranges opened, a 6-inch AP round struck *Cairo* to starboard and penetrated an oil tank. The engine room began to flood, but the shell failed to detonate, and pumps kept pace with the water. At 0852 Da Zara came to port and began steering east northeast in a renewed effort to pinpoint the convoy's location. At 0900 Hardy ordered the 12th Flotilla to stand by the retreating convoy to improve the antiaircraft protection while he kept his cruiser and the three remaining fleet destroyers between the merchantmen and the enemy. To the east *Partridge* and *Bedouin* focused on survival. At 0900 *Bedouin*'s Commander Scurfield signaled *Partridge*'s Lieutenant Commander Hawkins that he was ready for a tow but as Hawkins reported, "owing to my port engine being out of action at the time, the tow was not passed until about 0940." Once they got under way Hawkins began towing *Bedouin* westward at a reported seven knots. He radioed Hardy that he intended to make for Gibraltar, but Hardy ordered him to join the convoy, "as I considered that this gave me the best chance of giving him protection." Hawkin's report of proceedings does not specify that he obeyed this order, only that *Partridge* maintained a westerly heading.[32]

At 0945 the 10th Squadron reached the top of the mine barrage and Pontremoli spotted *Malocello* and *Vivaldi* to the north. The squadrons united and made preparations to pass the tow to *Premuda* inasmuch as the large destroyer had the least fuel available. Da Zara, meanwhile, steered east northeast until 0910 when he turned southeast. The admiral finally decided to round the southern extremity of the 7 AN barrage and head north. He had already concluded that the British were seeking to round its northern extremity and that he could greet them there. Hardy was keeping Malta advised of his position and the enemy's relative bearing, course, and speed in signals generated at 0910 and 0932. Supermarina intercepted and decoded these messages at 1005 and 1015. Da Zara did not receive word that the convoy had turned south at 1010 which would have revealed that his assumption was incorrect.[33]

THE CONVOY CONTINUES

When Da Zara turned due south at 0930 his cruisers quickly disappeared from view, at which point Hardy came about to rejoin the transports. At 1010 the convoy, sailing in order *Troilus, Orari,* and *Burdwan,* altered course once again to 180 degrees. *Hebe* had *Kentucky* "comfortably" under tow. At 1020 the convoy's course became 130 degrees, and *Cairo* and the fleet destroyers assumed their stations five minutes later. However, because of *Kentucky*'s condition, the general speed was only six knots. At 1033 Hardy ordered *Ithuriel* to assist with the tow, hoping to increase *Kentucky*'s speed to ten knots, but he then "reconsidered," concluding he could not tie up a valuable destroyer while Italian warships remained a threat.[34]

Bombers from Malta appeared four hours after Hardy's request for help. At 1030 four Albacores of 830 Squadron made a low approach against *Premuda*, which was towing *Vivaldi*. Despite their target's slow speed and lack of maneuverability, all torpedoes missed. Five minutes later the two Beauforts attacked *Eugenio* and *Montecuccoli* as they were heading north and likewise missed. This strike was escorted by sixteen Spitfires and two Beaufighters. The RAF attack summary stated that "the Beauforts . . . set fire to a cruiser, and the second pilot, in an endeavour to make certain of his target, held his torpedo until within 300 yards of the vessel." The Albacores "scored two strikes on the second cruiser, causing a large explosion amidships. One large destroyer was also possibly hit."[35]

Sandwiched between these attacks came a strike by 4° Gruppo's nine S.84s armed with 160-kg antiship bombs. They reported a group of four merchant ships, three destroyers, and three smaller vessels. They dropped from three thousand meters and claimed hits on two of the merchant vessels, but in fact they bombed the *Vivaldi* group at 1037 and missed. The S.79s on the other hand reported spotting numerous warships, including two in flames, but no merchant vessels, and so returned to base. At 1000 three S.79s of the 279° Squadriglia took off in an offensive reconnaissance role.[36]

Four long-range Spitfires from Malta's 126th Squadron, fitted with detachable fuel tanks, appeared above the convoy at 1040. Their leader noted that on the way in they passed over the Italian cruisers and "Found ship burning and sinking." This may have been a reference to *Bedouin* or *Vivaldi,* but by that time each of these stricken vessels was in a group; fire and smoke from *Chant's* wreckage was another possibility. At 1040 the Spitfires shot down two of the S.84s that had just attacked the *Vivaldi* group. The fighters also accounted for a floatplane from the 144ª Squadriglia, which was tailing the convoy but had not yet radioed a report. Da Zara's frustration (he wrote in his memoirs that he would have given ten years of life for a plane to see beyond the smoke) was magnified by the poor tactical communication between Superaereo and Supermarina that continued to vex operations even as the war entered its third year.[37]

As the convoy slowly plodded eastward, eleven Ju 88s from II./LG 1, which had transferred to Catania that morning, arrived overhead as one shift of fighters had just returned to Malta and before the next arrived. They attacked in waves of four, three, and four aircraft between 1110 and 1122. Concussions from near misses jammed *Burdwan's* rudder hard-over, flooded the engine room, and killed three crewmen. Hardy directed *Badsworth* to take the merchantman under tow, but *Burdwan's* master had already ordered abandon ship. The German aircraft did not suffer any losses. Units of 12./LG 1, which had also transferred to Catania that morning, searched for but could not find the convoy.[38]

At 1120, a Beaufighter bounced the trio of S.79s that had sortied at 1000 and forced them to abort and land at Pantelleria. Two of these aircraft took off again at 1320. Four Spitfires of 601st Squadron arrived over the convoy at 1130.

The British were still 150 miles short of Malta, a long way at six knots, and even at that speed *Kentucky* was dropping astern. Reviewing the situation, Hardy wrote, "I decided to cut my losses and at 1142 ordered *Badsworth* and *Hebe* to scuttle *Burdwan* and *Kentucky* at the same time ordering the remaining merchant ships to proceed at their utmost speed." At 1200 *Rye* went alongside *Kentucky* to remove the crew while *Hebe* stood by to open fire. At the same time *Marne* observed *Partridge* with *Bedouin* in tow passing astern of the convoy heading west, corroborating *Partridge's* report that she never joined the convoy. *Kujawiak's* report also mentions that when the convoy passed the two destroyers were heading toward Gibraltar.[39]

As this transpired Da Zara ordered *Oriani* and *Ascari* to rejoin him, leaving *Premuda* and *Malocello* with *Vivaldi*. Although *Premuda* would have been the most powerful unit in a battle, she was low on fuel, and Da Zara thought it better that she shepherd *Vivaldi* to safety. The 10th Squadron joined the 7th Division at 1115. Da Zara arrived north of 7 AN at 1130. He radioed Air Sicily for news, but, receiving nothing, he started searching. In fact, as Da Zara sailed north, the convoy was thirty-two miles southwest of his position and steering southeast.

CONTACT REGAINED

Da Zara's northern excursion proved unproductive, and he turned west at 1207 and then southwest at 1220. By this time *Hebe* and *Badsworth* were dutifully pounding the abandoned *Kentucky* and *Burdwan* with 4-inch shells, igniting large beacon fires in the process. The two undamaged freighters and the rest of the escort were almost forty miles south by southwest of the Italians. At 1230 *Eugenio* sighted "a huge column of smoke" to the southwest. When the cruiser arrived in the vicinity nearly an hour later, she passed through an

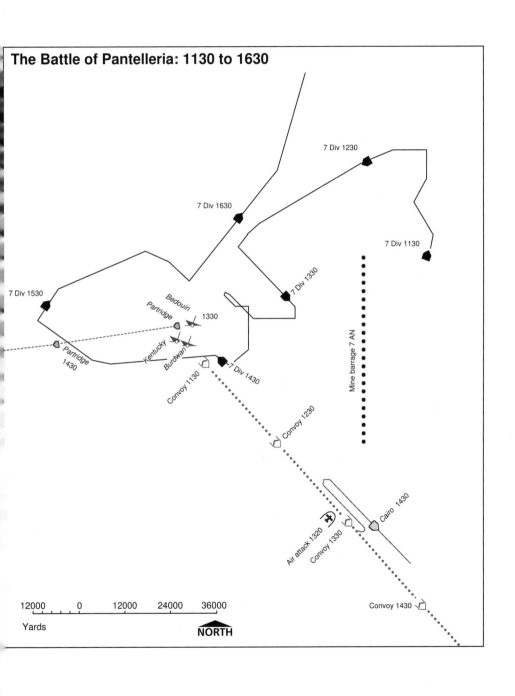

The Battle of Pantelleria: 1130 to 1630

7 Div 1230

7 Div 1630

7 Div 1130

7 Div 1330

7 Div 1530

Bedouin
Partridge
1330

Partridge
1430

Kentucky

Burdwan

7 Div 1430

Convoy 1130

Mine barrage 7 AN

Convoy 1230

Air attack 1320

Convoy 1330

Cairo 1430

Convoy 1430

| 12000 | 0 | 12000 | 24000 | 36000 |

Yards

NORTH

extensive debris field, leading Da Zara to conclude that a ship had been sunk some hours before and the crew already rescued. This was near *Chant's* final position. Two more large smoke plumes decorated the sky farther to the southwest. Da Zara called them a "fantastic spectacle," taking them as proof of his sortie's success.[40]

At 1255 *Hebe* saw vessels to the northeast and radioed *Cairo* that the enemy had reappeared. By this time *Kentucky* was "alight for most of her length and in a sinking condition." At 1316 the Italians spotted enemy warships standing by the burning vessels. The cruisers increased speed to thirty-two knots and at 1325 opened fire from twenty-one thousand meters against targets identified as two light units. *Hebe*, at the receiving end, was straddled; then one shell struck above the waterline, inflicting extensive splinter damage and igniting a fire, but it did not affect the minesweeper's speed. At twenty-three thousand yards this would have been the longest-range 6-inch hit obtained by either navy in the war. Da Zara ceased fire after four minutes because smoke expelled by *Rye* and *Hebe* made spotting impossible and he did not wish to waste ammunition. Also, the Italians credited the minesweepers with speeds far greater than they were capable of.[41]

At 1320 ten Ju 87s of 102° Gruppo escorted by twenty-five Mc.202s of 155° Gruppo attacked the convoy. Four Spitfires from 601 Squadron were overhead, and four more from 126 Squadron joined during the action. In the ensuing dogfight the Macchis shot down two Spitfires (they claimed four) while the Spitfires accounted for one Ju 87 and severely damaged two others. The Italian dive bombers (misidentified by the British as German while the Mc.202s were all called Messerschmitts) claimed a hit on one auxiliary cruiser and the destruction of two merchant ships, but in fact, they hit nothing.[42]

At 1341, twelve minutes after the Italians had ceased fire, Captain Hardy hauled around with *Cairo, Marne, Matchless,* and *Ithuriel* to support *Rye* and *Hebe*. Da Zara never noticed, as the British ships remained below the horizon. Instead the Italian admiral had identified two important targets as "Jervis" type destroyers, which were in fact *Partridge* and *Bedouin*. At 1335 he ordered *Ascari* and *Oriani* to finish off the cripples while *Eugenio* engaged *Bedouin* from 19,500 yards and *Montecuccoli* concentrated on *Partridge* from 21,300 yards. At 1357 *Oriani* and *Ascari* began shelling *Kentucky* from thirteen thousand yards, "provoking enormous fires."[43]

At 1400 Hardy reversed course once again after receiving a report that the Italians were sailing west. He reported that "having covered the *Badsworth,*

Hebe, and *Hythe* [*sic*], I decided I could no longer afford to steam away from the convoy which was then about fifteen miles distant." He made this decision even though the British vessels could hear gunfire to the northwest. *Kujawiak* noted that the cannonade was audible for more than an hour.[44]

Partridge, meanwhile, cast off her tow, circled *Bedouin* with smoke, and fled west. The destroyer was out of torpedoes, and her top speed was twenty knots. Six-inch salvos straddled until she "managed to hide behind smoke with the intention of returning to *Bedouin* as soon as possible."[45]

Da Zara ceased fire at 1410 as *Partridge* disappeared into her artificial fog. However, at 1420 *Montecuccoli* caught a glimpse of the fugitive destroyer and resumed her bombardment. Aboard *Bedouin* the chief engineer had just informed Commander Scurfield that he could finally light a boiler to give a speed of up to five knots when a torpedo-armed S.79, one of the pair that had departed Pantelleria at 1320, found the wallowing vessel and lined up for an attack. At 1425 the aircraft put a torpedo into the destroyer's engine room. There was a violent explosion, and *Bedouin* capsized to port, taking twenty-eight members of her crew down with her. In a parting shot her antiair gunners splashed the S.79. *Partridge* claimed she also engaged this aircraft, perhaps from a distance as it flew past. An Italian floatplane later rescued the crew.[46]

At 1433 Da Zara continued west, having sighted a mast on the horizon. At 1443, as they passed seven thousand yards away, *Oriani* torpedoed *Kentucky,* reporting that the weapon hit on the bow but deflagrated instead of exploding. At 1445 Da Zara brought *Partridge* under fire once again but had the impression the British ship was pulling away. By 1520 the Italian squadron was approaching the limits of its operational area beyond which Italian submarines were to assume that all surface ships were hostile. Five minutes later Ju 88s of KGr 606 bombed the Italian division from high altitude and, in what Da Zara described as a violent attack, bracketed *Ascari.* Then at 1530 Da Zara received orders from Supermarina that stated, "Except in particularly favorable circumstances, leave combat zone in time to pass Marettimo at 2200 and send serviceable destroyers to Naples. Stop. Action against the rest of the convoy will be conducted by air and submarines. Stop. 1305/15."[47]

Meanwhile German aircraft attacked the British (and Italians) beginning at 1520. German reports stated that seventeen Ju 88s from KGr 606 dropped 20,650 kg of bombs from 1520 to 1525 against nonspecified targets. This was the attack on Da Zara. Three more attacked a tanker at 1532 and signaled success while at 1535 another trio of Ju 88s reported hitting two merchant vessels, one already in a sinking state: in both cases *Kentucky* and *Burdwan*. On the British side *Partridge* recorded an air attack at the same time by four aircraft. Near misses caused the destroyer's rudder to jam hard to starboard. *Partridge* stopped to correct this defect and did not get under way again until 1645.[48]

When Hardy sortied west the convoy remained under the protection of only three Hunts, two minesweepers, and the motor launches. *Blankney's* captain was senior officer in command. At 1510 he steered the formation due east, the direct route for Malta, aiming to pass between Linosa and Lampedusa islands. At 1540 Hardy rejoined the convoy, followed by *Hebe, Rye,* and *Badsworth.*

At 1708 Da Zara's force experienced its last attack from three Albacores. Initially, the Italians mistook the aircraft for CR.42s, and *Montecuccoli* had to do some fancy maneuvering to comb the wakes of the torpedoes dropped against her. Re.2001 fighters shot down one of the attackers.

At 1730 *Welshman* rejoined the convoy south of Linosa to stiffen the escort. She had reached Malta that morning, landed her cargo, and departed again at 1300. Although *Welshman's* captain was senior to Hardy, he left Hardy in command to finish fighting his battle.

MINEFIELDS OFF MALTA

At 1910 ten Ju 88s of KGr 606 escorted by Bf 109s struck the convoy. Four 601 Squadron Spitfires opposed the Germans. *Marne* reported "heavy air attack by Ju 87s. Many near misses. Spitfires too low to intercept and not many attacks intercepted though enemy suffered afterwards." Two bombs near-missed *Matchless,* and "a splinter penetrated the ship's side forward above the main deck." *Troilus* and *Welshman* also experienced near misses. At 2030 eighteen Ju 88s of KGr 806 delivered the day's sixth and final air attack. They came out of the setting sun, but their best result was a stick of bombs that fell within thirty feet of *Orari.*[49]

Premuda towed *Vivaldi* into Pantelleria's tiny harbor, arriving there at 1530, and then proceeded to Trapani, entering port at 2200. The small Italian hospital ship *Meta* cruised the area after the battle and rescued 217 British personnel. A solitary Ju 88 attacked the fully illuminated vessel during her mission of mercy. Da Zara's cruisers and the other destroyers continued to Naples, docking at 1200 on 16 June. They had all guns elevated to their maximum in a signal of victory. Supermarina's initial assessment put the British losses as one cruiser sunk and one damaged, three destroyers sunk and several damaged, four freighters sunk or in flames, and one tanker in flames. This more than doubled the damage actually inflicted, but the results still justified celebration.[50]

Force X arrived off Malta at 2200 on 15 June. A major reason that minesweepers and motor launches had been included in the convoy's escort was to sweep the transports into port. The planners considered this necessary because the island's minesweeping resources had been decimated and Italian destroyers, MAS boats, and German S-boats had been strewing hundreds of mines around the island, particularly off Grand Harbour.

At 2006 Captain Hardy ordered *Speedy*'s Lieutenant Commander Doran, Senior Officer Minesweepers, to take his four fleet minesweepers and the motor launches ahead, in accordance with orders received from Vice Admiral Malta, and sweep the designated approach channel. Doran did so following what he believed were Vice Admiral Leatham's most recent instructions issued at 2325 on 14 June. *Hythe* led with *Speedy* and *Hebe* streaming sweeps on either quarter and *Rye* behind to cover gaps. Unfortunately, miscommunication and inadequate planning turned the convoy's bitterly won arrival into a debacle. *Speedy* was following instructions that gave the wrong entry point into the swept channel. Leatham broadcasted a correction at 2042/15 but *Speedy* was already a half hour down the wrong channel. Moreover, Leatham neglected to include Force X as an addressee in the correction, although Hardy was alert enough to pluck the message out of the air.

Leatham later provided the convoluted explanation that his signal of 2042/15 "assumed that the initial error [of 2325/14] had been corrected to all ships concerned and in consequence the signals which readjusted the navigational marks to meet the rapidly changing situation were not worded to put right a misunderstanding [of] which [the admiral] was not aware." Hardy reported that he passed along the updated information to Doran, but of course the minesweepers were already out of sight down the wrong channel. Moreover, all the planning for the operation had assumed that the escort would not enter the harbor and that the arrival would occur in daylight. There were no contingencies to cover the situation that the fleet found itself in: a night entry with the need for the escort to enter port and resupply.[51]

Hythe's sweep parted on an obstruction after only five minutes of streaming. However, the sweepers redeployed, and their equipment was functioning correctly when Lieutenant Commander Doran learned that the convoy was proceeding up a different channel. In fact, when *Cairo* arrived at the point marking the channel entrance, it was dark and the minesweepers were out of sight except for *Rye,* which "appeared to be steering somewhat to starboard of the proper course." Hardy had received reports that enemy MTBs were near the convoy. These were actually sightings of British MLs, but they made the captain think he had to act swiftly. He could see ahead of him beacons on *ML 126* and the drifter *Justified.* These marked a narrow channel that the mine-sweepers were supposed to expand, and so Hardy led Force X up this passage. *Cairo* led followed by the freighters, *Welshman* and finally *Ithuriel.* This central column was flanked by three destroyers on each beam. Hardy was extremely fortunate that he led *Cairo* up the narrow channel that had already been swept, but the two flanking columns were sailing through mined waters.[52]

At this point Doran learned of the mistake. The sweepers subsequently made "all speed with single Oropesa to head the Convoy at first bend at position 'Z' where channels joined. This failed and convoy got ahead of M/S's [sic] and entered harbour."[53] *Cairo* was streaming at fifteen knots, faster than the sweepers to begin with, and upon reaching Point Z, she did not wait for the minesweepers to appear. In fact, she had such a head of steam up that the drifter *Justified* had to avoid the oncoming cruiser, and in so doing was forced out of the channel, mined, and sunk.

At 0040 on 16 June *Badsworth* detonated a mine and came to a halt. *Ithuriel* altered to starboard to avoid the stricken ship, and *Kujawiak* followed in her wake. However, at 0053 as the Polish vessel was passing *Badsworth,* she likewise struck a mine and immediately listed to port. The inrush of water overwhelmed the pumps, and *Kujawiak* capsized at 0120. *Blankney* turned back to assist because "it seemed that there was no action being taken to stand by the casualties." The minesweepers arrived on the scene of this disaster and *Blankney*'s motor cutter, assisted by *Hebe* and *ML 134, 135,* and *459,* pulled the crew from the water.[54]

Cairo led the two surviving transports to the harbor's entrance channel, arriving there at 0125. *Troilus* and *Orari* then went ahead followed by *Cairo* and *Welshman.*

The convoy master aboard *Troilus* complained that the entrance to the harbor channel was difficult to identify owing to the large number of searchlights. Then at 0210, just behind him and only five hundred yards from the breakwater, *Orari* struck a small contact mine of the 200-kg "Vega" type that had been laid by Italian MAS boats operating out of Augusta. Fortunately, it exploded in the only hold that did not contain ammunition or fuel and, although "the ship listed heavily to port and started to settle by the stern," she managed to proceed up harbor to her mooring location. Flooding spoiled some of the cargo. At 0235 another Vega mine detonated on *Matchless's* starboard side between the two forward mounts. The explosion blasted a hole ten by seven feet in the hull and flooded a magazine and shell room; however, the destroyer remained on an even keel and entered harbor under her own power. *Blankney, Hebe,* and *Badsworth* all anchored to await dawn before proceeding. As *Blankney's* Lieutenant Commander Powlett wrote, "owing to the . . . fact that all navigational aids ashore were indistinguishable among the searchlights, aircraft homing beacons and smoke screen, I was by no means clear of my position—the only certain fact was that I was off the searched channel."[55]

The next morning while entering port *Hebe* hit a mine—probably a small German type—and suffered extensive damage forward. *Rye* bumped another head-on, but it did not explode.

The British official history commented, "After the day's happenings it was perhaps not surprising that misunderstandings should arise as to the precise channel [into Malta's Grand Harbor] to be swept and the order in which ships should arrive." "Misunderstanding" is a soft word to describe such a bad end to a costly venture. *Troilus* and *Orari* delivered 13,552 tons of cargo, subtracting the amount spoiled by *Orari's* mine damage. The bulk consisted of provisions such as canned foods, powdered milk and eggs, and solidified vegetables, flour, and sugar; they also carried coal, drummed fuel, antiaircraft ammunition, torpedoes, and spare parts. This was precious little considering the extent of Malta's needs, the scale of the two operations, and the losses suffered.[56]

RETURN TO GIBRALTAR

The captains of Force X did not rest after reaching Malta. First, they needed to see to the replenishment of their ammunition stores, which had been depleted in some cases to below 50 percent. Then, at 1000 Vice Admiral Leatham held a conference in his office. This was followed by another aboard *Cairo* at 1400. Finally, the outbound ships embarked passengers. In the case of *Marne* this totaled sixty people. Because of Malta's fuel shortages the destroyers did not refuel, and *Marne* arrived at Gibraltar with only 102 tons (18 percent) in her bunkers. *Ithuriel* had only 37 tons (8.5 percent).[57]

Welshman, Cairo, and the four operational destroyers, *Marne, Ithuriel, Blankney,* and *Middleton,* left Malta at 1900 that evening. At 2300 *Welshman* pushed ahead while the rest of Force X reverted to Captain Hardy's command

and continued at twenty-four knots, the highest speed the Hunts could maintain. Force X skirted the African coast and, upon rounding Cape Bon, passed a convoy of six French merchant ships escorted by the destroyer *Simoun*. At 0730 on the 17th lookouts sighted two aircraft in the distance, and for the rest of the day at least one unfriendly aircraft remained in view.

Axis aircraft made their first attack at 1235. Thereafter Captain Hardy reported nineteen attacks but his count includes seven sightings wherein no bombs were dropped. The last "attack," for example, at 1926 consisted of a single reconnaissance plane. Of the twelve actual air strikes the two largest, consisting of six Ju 88s, were made at 1305 and 1325. *Marne* characterized them as unsynchronized and as not being "pressed home." She was near-missed at 2042 by one "stick of large bombs." *Ithuriel*, on the other hand, reported that she "was subjected to a continual series of concentrated attacks and the rest of the day was such a struggle for existence that no accurate records could be kept." *Ithuriel's* survival was testimony to the difficulty of hitting a destroyer that was maneuvering at speed. Hardy wrote, "on numerous occasions sticks of bombs fell very close to *Ithuriel* and at times she was entirely enveloped in spray from which I was most relieved to see her emerge." Several sticks dropped close enough to cause the ship to whip, and splinters wounded a few men. One near miss to starboard near the after boiler room buckled the side plating and sprang an oil leak. Bombs also near-missed *Blankney* and caused minor damage.[58]

At 2017 Force X met Admiral Curteis with *Kenya* and *Charybdis* eighty miles northeast of Algiers, and the combined force returned to Gibraltar arriving at 1930 on 18 June, thus ending Operation Harpoon.

AS YE SOW SO SHALL YE REAP

The prospects for a significant British victory in the Mediterranean, so promising just one month before, had vanished. Prime Minister Churchill was in Washington D.C. where he had traveled expecting "to reach a final decision on the operations for 1942–43." He had timed the trip expecting that Mediterranean victories would allow him to stand shoulder to shoulder with the Americans, or perhaps slightly taller in the matter of setting strategic priorities. Instead, on 21 June the Minister of State dispatched a Most Immediate and Most Secret message that Tobruk had fallen. Churchill called this news "one of the heaviest blows I can recall during the war."[59] He was forced to immediately request from the Americans reinforcements of tanks, heavy bombing aircraft, or submarines.

Command and control problems were at the root of the mid-June failures, but there were other issues as well. Despite the rhetoric regarding the importance of supplying Malta, the quality of the effort fell short of the fine words. For example, aircraft carriers represented one of the Royal Navy's great advantages over the Italians. Even though the Royal Navy's best carriers were in the Indian Ocean for reasons discussed in Chapters 3 and 4, the Admiralty was confident that the fighters aboard the two old carriers being risked in the operation would give a significant advantage. However, *Eagle*'s Captain E. G. N. Rushbrooke's report highlighted several avoidable reasons why this did not prove to be the case. *Eagle* embarked sixteen Hurricanes and four Fulmars, and *Argus* had two Fulmars; of the sixteen Hurricane pilots only one was trained and experienced in carrier operations. The other fifteen had never seen combat. The planners sent *Eagle*'s very few fighters into combat with rookie pilots. Inadequate facilities on *Eagle* meant that only six aircraft could be maintained in the air at any one time. The Hurricanes were armed with only .303-caliber guns. As Rushbrooke commented, "a fighter without a cannon is quite ineffective against most modern shadowing enemy aircraft." He concluded, "In my opinion it is most surprising that very much more damage was not sustained by our ships in this operation. . . ."[60]

The disaster that befell Harpoon when it arrived at Malta and blundered into a minefield was another example of poor preparation. Vice Admiral Leatham submitted a report a month later to "elucidate the happenings in the searched channel . . . [because] it was obvious that things had not gone according to plan." To this one may ask, what plan? The pre-operation discussions held at Gibraltar did not go into sufficient detail for sweeping into Malta: *ML 459*, for example, knew nothing about it. And, while Malta's broadcast of incorrect information and its failure to include Force X among the addressees in the subsequent correction, submitted after the minesweepers were blindly sweeping the wrong channel, contributed to the disaster, the admiral's report focused on blaming Lieutenant Commander Doran and Captain Hardy and did not address the root problems or suggest procedures for preventing such foul-ups in the future.[61]

Regarding communications, the British relied upon visual signals rather than very-high-frequency voice radios, such as possessed by the Italians. On 14 June, the day of heavy air attacks, *Onslow*, leader of the 17th Destroyer Flotilla, received 140 "in" messages and generated 120 "out" messages. This was the equivalent of one every four minutes. This traffic overwhelmed the signals staff, which had been reduced from peacetime standards. The fact that "due to the large number of ships Fleet Wave Low Power (which was susceptible to interception and generally avoided for that reason) was of little value" showed that, like the Americans at the time, the British had inadequate procedures to ensure radio discipline and effective communications. As the commander of the 17th Flotilla lamented, "During the heat of the action it was often impossible to pass a signal by [visual means]."[62] There were several occasions during the battle when orders reportedly issued at a certain time were not followed or followed significantly later and when actions were intended but never carried out because of the difficulties of signaling.

Three years of accumulating losses and the stress of fighting a world war with a hemispheric fleet had forced the British to deploy scratch forces. An improvised formation forced to act in concert was not as effective as a seasoned flotilla. A case in point is the 11th Flotilla's charge straight into the superior guns of Da Zara's 7th (cruiser) Division. Captain A. L. Poland's handling of the 14th, or Captain St. J. A. Micklethwait's 22nd flotillas at the Second Battle of Sirte on 22 March provide examples of how cohesive units with experienced commanders better met a similar challenge.

Harpoon demonstrated, in fact, that the Regia Marina and Regia Aeronautica had evolved faster than their opponents. Reconnaissance was significantly improved, and air strikes were conducted in greater strength and with greater determination than at any time in the past. Air–sea cooperation was also better, although it still had a long way to go before it could be described as effective.

With respect to the surface engagement, Da Zara's choices have been scrutinized by all sides. Many British accounts assess the Battle of Pantelleria in terms of what the admiral did not accomplish. For example: "Tactically the Italian admiral had failed to act with the boldness to make the destruction of the convoy complete." Admiral Iachino also criticized Da Zara after the battle, stating that he operated at excessively high speed and was wrong to allow his cruisers and destroyers to become separated.[63]

It is true that the moment's tactical requirements seemed ill served by Captain Pontremoli's decision to support Captain Castrogiovanni's 14th Squadron by avoiding risk and circling the mine barrier. It is easy to question some of Da Zara's tactical decisions and assumptions, like his tendency to magnify his enemy's strength. His wrong guess that Hardy would make for the northern end of the barrier may have saved the British from total defeat because, although Da Zara did not do all the little things right, he did the biggest thing right: he persisted. He stayed around and kept coming back. As a consequence the convoy treaded water, and at 1130 it was little closer to Malta than it had been at 0630.

Indeed, criticisms that Da Zara lacked boldness, or fought at too high a speed, or mishandled his destroyers need to be balanced against wartime experiences and the situation that the Italian admiral faced. Supermarina tasked Da Zara with attacking an enemy force during the day in a region where he was subject to air attack (enemy and friendly) and hemmed in by minefields. Moreover, the enemy outnumbered him fourteen hulls to seven, and their guns fired a weight of shell totaling 23,340 pounds a minute compared to 20,000 for his ships. He believed that the enemy advantage was actually greater than this and he did not know that he had the heavier guns and thirty-six torpedo tubes as opposed to twenty-four for his opponent. The difficulties he overcame to obtain the results he did can be illustrated by comparing Pantelleria to other daytime strikes against convoys.

German warships attacked Allied convoys on three occasions in the Arctic. Twice, large German destroyers intercepted convoys protected by smaller British destroyers. They sank one merchant ship with a lucky long-range torpedo strike but could not penetrate the escort in either action. In the battle of the Barents Sea on 31 December 1942 German 11-inch and 8-inch gunned cruisers and six large destroyers were driven off by two British light cruisers and five small destroyers that skillfully used smoke and feinted torpedo attacks. They damaged only one freighter. In the Pacific, Allied cruiser-destroyer forces unsuccessfully attacked Japanese squadrons protecting convoys in the battles of Java Sea on 28 February 1942 and the Komandorski Islands on 27 March 1943, although in each case the escort was equal to or stronger than the attacking force. In the battle off Samar on 25 October 1944 four Japanese battleships and seven cruisers were defeated by smoke and torpedo attacks in a nearly six-hour action against American escort carriers protected by only two destroyers, four destroyer escorts, and scattered air attacks. In the Mediterranean, the British fleet declined to challenge Italian smoke screens in the action off Calabria in July 1940, and although Iachino was able to beat up the escort in the Second Battle of Sirte in March 1942, smoke and torpedo attacks successfully kept him away from the convoy.

These examples indicate the complexity of Da Zara's mission. During the Second World War surface warships achieved their best results against convoys at night. Da Zara, however, did better at less cost than any other surface force that attempted a similar mission during the day despite the complications presented by the minefield and the presence of enemy aircraft. Any evaluation of Da Zara's and Hardy's conduct of the Battle of Pantelleria must be considered in this context.

8

THE AUGUST CONVOY

The enemy will no doubt proclaim this as a great victory at sea, and so it would be but for the strategic significance of Malta in view of future plans.

Winston S. Churchill to Joseph Stalin, 14 August 1942

LONDON APPRECIATED the need for another Malta convoy even before Admiral Curteis sighted Gibraltar's rock. On 17 June, Churchill, on his way to Washington to meet with Roosevelt, wrote to the deputy prime minister, "I am relying upon you to treat the whole question of the relief of Malta as vitally urgent, and to keep at it with the Admiralty till a solution is reached." The same document revealed his continued hope of restoring the situation by means of a decisive naval victory. "Now that the Italians have shown a readiness to bring their battlefleet down to arrest a convoy . . . an opportunity of bringing them to battle might be found, which would have far-reaching effects." Meanwhile, the Admiralty appraisal concluded that the mid-June operations failed because the escorts were too weak. "Next time [the convoys] would have to be given priority over all other demands, for on the success or failure of [the next operation] . . . would hang the fate of Malta and hence in all probability of the Nile valley."[1]

The British situation on the ground continued to deteriorate. The 8th Army, which had retreated into Egypt on 13 June, left Tobruk strongly garrisoned with a division and three brigades. Nonetheless, Axis tanks penetrated the defenses on 21 June. Admiral Harwood immediately signaled the Admiralty, "Tobruk has fallen and situation deteriorated so much that there is a possibility of heavy air attack on Alexandria in near future, and in view of approaching full moon period I am sending all Eastern Fleet units south of the Canal to await events." The same day Malta's Governor Gort announced that rations were being cut to four ounces a day. On 29 July the New Statesman editorialized that the "military situation of the [Allies] is graver than at any time since 1940."[2]

On the Axis side the situation seemed correspondingly positive, although Malta remained a concern. Mussolini wrote to Hitler reiterating the importance of capturing the island and asking for the fuel oil needed to ensure the fleet's full participation in the planned operation. Moreover, air forces needed to be redeployed from Africa before the end of June for the invasion to proceed. Rommel, who was under orders to halt his advance on the Egyptian frontier, saw in the fall of Tobruk a grand opportunity to take Cairo—perhaps even Suez. Further encouraged by intercepted reports from the pessimistic American military attaché in Cairo, which said that the British would crack under one last blow, he wrote his own letter to Hitler requesting command of all troops and freedom to continue the offensive. This was agreeable to Hitler, who had long since abandoned the idea of invading Malta. On 23 June the Führer urged the Duce to authorize the African army's advance to the full destruction of the enemy's forces. Rommel already knew what the answer would be. In a 22 June meeting he invited his titular Italian superiors to lunch in Cairo. The next day the field marshal crossed the border, and by the end of June he had advanced to El Alamein, sixty miles short of Alexandria.[3] A British historian wrote,

> The end of June 1942 saw the entire Mediterranean strategy pursued by Britain since 1940 dead in the water. All the huge investment in shipping round the Cape, in the equipment, supplies . . . weaponry and military ration-strength poured into the Middle East in that shipping over the last two years, all the swaying Desert campaigns, had ended with a routed 8th Army preparing a last stand in defence of Egypt at El Alamein, only 60 miles west of Alexandria: with the Mediterranean Fleet's pre-war main base, Malta, neutralized; and with the Fleet itself having lost control of the Mediterranean, and even defeated outright in Operation Vigorous.[4]

However, at the high-water mark of the Axis advance, the pitiless reality of logistics intervened, and despite a strenuous effort to crack the British position in early July, Rommel was unable to advance beyond El Alamein.

On 27 July Comando Supremo indefinitely postponed the Malta invasion operation and focused on supplying the army in Africa by landing materiel as close to the front lines as possible. The recently introduced class of Italian motorized landing craft (motozattere) scheduled for the Malta invasion joined German MFPs in transporting supplies from Italy directly to Mersa Matruh.

The first such mosquito convoy arrived on 21 July followed by another three days later. The Regia Marina also conducted fifteen submarine supply missions during the month. The Mediterranean Fleet's abandonment of Alexandria for Haifa and Suez facilitated such operations although the British still tried to interdict this traffic. On 11 July four Hunts shelled Mersa Matruh and sank the German freighters *Sturla* (1,397 GRT) and *Brook* (1,225 GRT). On 19 July Admiral Vian with two cruisers and four fleet destroyers repeated the bombardment, damaging the cargo vessel *Città di Agrigento* (2,480 GRT), which bombers finished off that night. *Aldenham* and *Dulverton* had an inconclusive skirmish the same day with German S-boats operating from the small port. Nonetheless, four more barge convoys reached Mersa Matruh through 10 August. Chasing barges was also dangerous, as demonstrated by the fate of the Hunt-class destroyer *Eridge,* which fell victim to X MAS special attack craft on 29 August.

During July Italian convoys with some German units participating ran virtually unhindered to Africa. From 2 July to 4 July three transports escorted by three destroyers and five torpedo boats sailed from Taranto to Benghazi. British aircraft attacked with no results. From 8 July to 10 July five transports escorted by two destroyers (one German), two torpedo boats, and two German subchasers sailed from Suda Bay to Tobruk without loss. From 9 July to 11 July three transports escorted by four destroyers and four torpedo boats sailed from the Aegean to Benghazi without loss. From 20 July to 23 July one transport escorted by two destroyers and three torpedo boats sailed from Brindisi to Benghazi. From 20 July to 22 July one German transport escorted by a destroyer and three torpedo boats sailed from Suda Bay to Benghazi. On 25 July British aircraft attacked two transports escorted by two destroyers and two torpedo boats en route to Benghazi from Suda Bay and damaged the transport *Aventino* (3,974 GRT). On the 28th, British torpedo-bombers disabled the transport *Monviso* (5,322 GRT). In July materiel shipped to Africa from Italy and Greece totaled 97,332 tons, of which 91,491 tons (94 percent) arrived.[5]

GENESIS OF A CONVOY

On 24 July, after a week of tense meetings held in London, the American members of the Combined Chiefs of Staff, General George Marshall and Admiral Ernest King, finally agreed to abandon their plans for Operation Sledgehammer, a landing in northern France in September 1942, and to support an invasion of northwest Africa that fall. This agreement followed a five-month-long debate between the allies over grand strategy. In the end, Middle Eastern and Mediterranean events played a major role in forcing the Americans to accept British wishes in this matter—there were only 40,000 troops in the United Kingdom in July instead of the planned 100,000, in part because so much shipping was tied up transporting reinforcements to Suez. On 21 June, the same day the Combined Chiefs of Staff agreed to accelerate the delivery of U.S. troops to Britain, the fall of Tobruk required the Americans to agree to divert four hundred armored fighting vehicles to Egypt to help offset this disaster. This, along with the 8th Army's stand at the First Battle of El Alamein, which ended by 27 July, encouraged the British War Cabinet to reinforce the 8th Army, over the objections of the Chiefs of Staff Committee, for yet another offensive. From July to September 262 ships carried military cargos to the Indian Ocean compared to 98 in the April–June quarter. "This commitment of shipping could only be at the expense of imports into the United Kingdom, both of food and of the essentials for war production." Obviously the buildup of American forces in the United Kingdom also suffered.[6]

The Royal Navy's situation and the fact that the front was so close to Alexandria permitted just one Malta convoy operation from the west. This was named Pedestal. As usual, most of the units came from the Home Fleet. It was, in the eyes of its planners, "Harpoon over again on a larger scale," incorporating many of the lessons painfully learned in mid-June.[7]

The ships for Pedestal were gathered and received suitable alterations. As in the case of Harpoon, they were large and fast vessels, and some were veterans of past runs. The new drafts received enhanced antiaircraft outfits, damage control suites, and improved paravanes. For example, when *Empire Hope*, a seventeen-knot, 12,688-GRT refrigerated ship, was selected, she had one 4.7-inch gun mounted on her poopdeck. She received an additional eight 20-mm and four 40-mm guns in gun pits, Browning twin machine guns on each bridge wing, sixteen depth charges, and two aerial mine throwers.[8] The ships were loaded with mixed cargos to lessen the impact of anticipated losses. The Admiralty assigned an oceangoing tug to Pedestal in case another cruiser required a long tow back to Gibraltar, and vastly increased fighter support.

The American victory at Midway allowed the carrier *Indomitable* to redeploy from the Indian Ocean. In fact, having observed the power of carrier task forces employed by the U.S. and Japanese navies, the Admiralty collected *Victorious*, *Indomitable*, and *Eagle* for the operation. However, the ships had only their passage from Britain to work on joint operations and fighter direction. At the time Admiral Somerville observed, "In my opinion 3 weeks would be really all too short a time in which to develop the full offensive and defensive power of 3 carriers operating together. Many of us have had experience of operating a single carrier and some of us two carriers, but as the number of carriers increases, so does the complexity of the techniques which is required to obtain full results."[9]

The two carriers used in Harpoon had embarked eighteen fighters. For Pedestal there were seventy-two. *Victorious* had sixteen Fulmars, six Hurricanes, and fourteen Albacores; *Indomitable* had ten Marlets (F4Fs), twenty-four Hurricanes, and fourteen Albacores while *Eagle* carried sixteen Hurricanes. The Fulmars and Albacores were obsolete and the Hurricanes little better, but it was the best the Royal Navy could muster even after three years of war.

While preparations for Pedestal were under way the Royal Navy continued minor operations to maintain Malta's power of resistance. The fast minelayer *Welshman* made a solitary run to the island, leaving the Clyde after a boiler cleaning on 9 July. Her original cargo was 350 tons of powdered milk, edible oils, fats, and flour, ninety-eight tons of soap, and thirty tons of minesweeping equipment. During the passage through the Bay of Biscay, however, rough weather spoiled some of the deck cargo, "covering her minedeck with a viscous mixture of oil and milk."[10] After loading an additional cargo of ammunition, *Welshman* departed Gibraltar on 14 July accompanied by *Eagle,* two cruisers, and five destroyers. The next day *Eagle* flew off thirty-one Spitfires to replace wastage suffered by Malta's fighter forces while *Welshman* dashed for the island.[11] She survived attacks on 16 July from CR.42s, which got a near miss, from high-level S.79s, from eight Ju 88s, and from eight Ju 87s, which got another near miss. The submarine *Axum* also missed *Welshman* with a torpedo salvo. Three Italian destroyers sortied but could not find their quarry, and the minelayer arrived safely on the morning of 17 July.

After quickly unloading, *Welshman* left at dusk the next day. In deteriorating weather she slipped through a patrol line of six submarines off Cape Bon and sidestepped a torpedo boat squadron as well as a cruiser/destroyer force. Next, Ju 88s delivered an ineffective attack after a reconnaissance aircraft spotted her off Bougie on the morning of 19 July. Returning safely to Gibraltar *Welshman* passed *Eagle* and her consorts on their way to deliver more fighters to the island. The submarine *Dandolo* missed *Eagle* with a torpedo salvo, and the carrier dispatched twenty-eight Spitfires to Malta on 21 July. During July the submarine *Clyde* brought in 194 tons of supplies, including eighty-eight tons of aviation fuel. *Parthian* delivered forty-seven tons of ammunition, thirty-six tons of aviation fuel, and thirty-three tons of other stores. *Porpoise* and *Otus* also made supply runs from Alexandria. Aviation fuel constituted a large portion of these emergency cargos because consumption was running high and Governor Gort was concerned that there would be insufficient fuel to allow the fighters to protect the next convoy's arrival and unloading. Finally, the chiefs of staff decreed on 30 July that "strikes from Malta must be reduced to an absolute minimum" and that "transits, except for Beauforts, will cease."[12]

To offset the reduction of Malta's air striking power, five boats of Royal Navy's 10th Submarine Flotilla returned to the island: *P42* (*Unbroken*) on 21 July, *P44* (*United*) on 22 July, *P31* and *P34* on 30 July, and *Una* on 1 August. By 10 August the island's air strength included about a hundred Spitfires, thirty-six Beaufighters, thirty Beaufort torpedo-bombers, and a number of reconnaissance types.[13]

OPERATION PEDESTAL

Vice Admiral Alban Curteis, who led the last convoy, had been reassigned to the American and West Indies Station, and the Admiralty gave command of Operation Pedestal to Vice Admiral Edward N. Syfret. Syfret had replaced Admiral James Somerville as head of Force H and most recently had commanded the naval forces involved in the capture of Madagascar in May 1942. He led the covering force (Force Z) which, in addition to the three carriers, included two battleships, *Nelson* (flag) and *Rodney*, and three antiaircraft cruisers, *Sirius*, *Phoebe*, and *Charybdis*. A dozen destroyers screened Force Z. These included the Tribal class veterans *Eskimo*, *Tartar*, and *Somali*; the powerful L-class units *Laforey*, *Lightning*, and *Lookout*; the fleet units *Quentin* and *Ithuriel*; the Hunt *Zetland*, and three older and more lightly armed ships, *Wishart*, *Antelope*, and *Vansittart*. As in past operations, Force Z would cover the convoy up to the Skerki Banks where it would turn back.

Force X would escort the convoy through the Sicilian narrows to Malta and counter any Italian surface forces that intervened. It was commanded by the veteran Rear Admiral Harold M. Burrough. Burrough had led the 10th Cruiser Squadron since April 1940 and the close escort for the Halberd convoy in September 1941. Force X included Burrough's flag, the modern light cruiser

Nigeria, her sisters *Kenya* and *Manchester,* and the antiaircraft cruiser *Cairo,* still skippered by Captain Hardy. There were twelve destroyers including the fleet units *Ashanti, Intrepid, Icarus, Foresight,* and *Fury* and the Hunts *Derwent, Bramham, Bicester, Ledbury, Pathfinder, Penn,* and *Wilton.*

In a parallel operation the carrier *Furious* was to operate independently and dispatch a last-minute reinforcement of Spitfires to Malta. Eight old destroyers, *Keppel, Westcott, Venomous, Malcolm, Wolverine, Amazon, Wrestler,* and *Vidette,* were available to escort her or assist the other forces as required. Force R with four corvettes, *Jonquil, Spiria, Geranium,* and *Coltsfoot,* had the job of escorting the tug *Jaunty* and two tankers assigned to Pedestal, *Brown Ranger* and *Dingledale.* Four minesweepers operating from Malta, *Speedy, Hebe, Hythe,* and *Rye,* were to meet the convoy and sweep it into harbor to prevent a repetition of the disaster that marked Harpoon's arrival.

Pedestal was a massive commitment at this point in the war although the suspension of the Arctic convoys following the PQ 17 debacle freed many Home Fleet warships. Force Z departed the Clyde on 3 August, and in the early morning of 10 August the armada filed through the Straits of Gibraltar, cruising through clusters of Spanish fishing boats. Dense fog caused some disruption but did not screen the British from potentially unfriendly eyes. Besides the fishermen, an outbound French steamer passed up the middle between the convoy's two columns. For the two nights prior to the passage most of the escorts had shuffled into Gibraltar to refuel, and Axis agents reported their comings and goings.

After reforming into a four-column cruising formation, Pedestal headed east through calm seas as the various Axis headquarters evaluated reports such as "Informants report that from 0000 to 0200 hours on the night of the 10th there passed from the west into the straits about fifty ships of various tonnage among which there were numerous warships." Before midday on the 10th Supermarina concluded that fifty-seven British ships were heading toward Malta. For their part the British were receiving large quantities of Enigma intelligence, principally "regarding the high priority that the [German air force] gave to stopping [the] convoy, but little of immediate operational value to those defending it." For example, Allied intelligence estimates made on 9 August concluded in error that there were no German aircraft on Sardinia. There was no helpful signals intelligence from Italian sources.[14]

The Mediterranean Fleet, meanwhile, mounted a diversion. Three cruisers and ten destroyers accompanying three merchant ships sailed from Port

Said on the evening of 10 August. The next morning Rear Admiral Vian with two cruisers and five destroyers and one merchantman departed Haifa. The two flotillas united on the 11th and sailed west to the longitude of Alexandria, where, after dusk, the force dispersed and turned around. This effort was too little, too late, as the enemy was already focused on the much larger western force.

OPERATION ASCENDANT

In an operation run simultaneously with Pedestal, the British evacuated the units stranded in Malta after Operation Harpoon. The destroyers *Badsworth* and *Matchless* had patched up most of their damage suffered in the June battle and from incessant air raids during their two-month Malta layover. In Operation Ascendant they had to escort the transports *Orari* and *Troilus* back to Gibraltar. The merchant ships carried a cargo of scrap metal, empty ammunition cases, and worn-out gun barrels as well as prisoners and passengers. The ships got under way on 9 August, and after dark the crews painted Italian recognition colors, red and white stripes, on the forecastles. Nothing happened the first day at sea until shortly before midnight. Then the little convoy, proceeding in order *Matchless, Orari, Troilus,* and *Badsworth,* encountered an old adversary, the Italian destroyer *Malocello,* sowing mines in French territorial waters south of Cape Bon.

At 2200 *Malocello* sighted a shaded light to the south-southeast. Her skipper, Commander Pierfrancesco Tona, turned his vessel inshore and reduced speed to twelve knots. Gradually, the British column emerged into view, but Commander Tona assumed it was either a French or Italian force that his instructions had failed to mention. He decided—given his load of mines—to mind his own business and continue his mission. *MAS 552* and *553*, which were assisting *Malocello,* also spotted the convoy.[15]

Heading north to round Cape Bon, the British force passed the Italian destroyer; then at 2225 *Matchless,* under the command of Lieutenant Commander J. Mowlam, noticed the vessel forty degrees off his port quarter. *Matchless* sheered to starboard, fired two rounds that splashed four hundred yards behind target, and ordered the convoy to turn east away from the contact as *Malocello* replied with two salvos from her forward guns. The Italian also increased speed and came to port to open her arcs of fire. *Matchless'* searchlight briefly illuminated the Italian ship, and she fired star shells. From Mowlam's perspective, he saw a French minesweeper, and it seemed she gave an appropriate recognition signal. From the Italian point of view, the lights went out, and the strangers ceased fire and continued on their way. Neither captain was seeking a sea battle, so both continued their missions.

11 AUGUST

The 11th passed in peace for the Ascendant convoy as the attention of the Axis headquarters focused on the greater force approaching from the west. The first contact occurred at 0442 on 11 August when the Italian submarine *Uarsciek* launched a spread of three torpedoes against a target she identified as *Furious*. She heard two explosions after fifty seconds, and when she surfaced at 0927 she reported this as a success. The only British vessel to report this attack, however, was the corvette *Coltsfoot,* part of the screen for Force R, the tankers conducting refueling operations.[16]

Superaereo received its first report from a German aircraft at 1010: "Naval force composed of three carriers, three battleships, twenty cruisers and destroyers, twenty steamers, speed undetermined, route 90 degrees, position lat 38° 08' long 01° 56' E." Axis spotters continued to shadow the convoy despite efforts by the carrier fighters to keep them away.[17]

The Germans had been anticipating a Malta convoy, and as early as 5 August Kesselring reinforced Luftwaffe units on Sardinia and Sicily. However, the Field Marshal also considered possible an assault on Mersa Matruh or Crete. Supermarina believed a Malta convoy was almost a certainty, but given the number of enemy aircraft carriers involved it speculated that an attack on the Sardinian airbases might also be forthcoming.[18]

The Italians and Germans prepared separate responses, but at least the two air commands met to coordinate their attacks. These would begin as the convoy neared Sardinia and, as in the mid-June battles, seek to reduce the fighter and antiaircraft strength of the escort to give subsequent strikes a better chance of success. On the morning of 11 August Air Sardinia deployed 189 aircraft: 60 S.79 torpedo-bombers, 30 S.84s in the torpedo- and level bomber roles, 9 Cant Z.1007bis in the reconnaissance role, 8 CR.42 fighter-bombers, 22 MC.202, 30 Re.2001, 16 CR.42, and 14 G.50 fighters. It had sixty-seven torpedoes in inventory. Air Sicily had 103 planes including 14 S.79 and 6 S.84 torpedo-bombers,

25 S.84, S.79, and Br.20 level bombers, 11 reconnaissance S.79s and CR.25s, and as fighters 27 MC.202s and 20 CR.42s (in passage from Libya to Sicily). Sicily had thirty-six torpedoes.[19]

After consultation with Superaereo and Oberbefehlshaber Süd, the Regia Marina deployed twenty-two submarines and the Kriegsmarine two. Seven Italian and the German boats operated in the western Mediterranean north of Algiers. Ten Italian boats deployed between Fratelli Rocks and Skerki Banks, one west of Malta, one off Navarino, and three southwest of Crete. One German and several Italian motor torpedo boat squadrons waited east of Cape Bon to ambush the convoy as it transited the Sicilian narrows. Finally, Supermarina, using all fuel available, assembled a surface strike force of three heavy cruisers, three light cruisers, and eleven destroyers. They were to intervene south of Pantelleria at dawn on 13 August.

At 1230 on 11 August, when the convoy reached a position about eighty miles north of Algiers, or about 550 air miles from Malta, *Furious* began flying off her load of Spitfires to reinforce the island's air defenses. Meanwhile destroyers and cruisers separated to complete the torturous process of refueling from Force R's two tankers. Fueling had commenced at 1430 on 10 August and was still eight hours short of completion by the afternoon of the next day. The British continued to have difficulties conducting this important process, in part because of equipment failures.[20]

At 1315 the convoy was zigzagging at thirteen knots in four columns. Due to the refueling and *Furious'* activity, there were only thirteen warships in the screen when U 73 hit *Eagle,* on the convoy's starboard quarter, with four torpedoes. The old and hard-used carrier capsized and sank within eight minutes. One witness from *Phoebe* wrote, "[she] presented a terrible sight as she heeled over, turned bottom up and sank with horrible speed. Men and aircraft could be seen falling off her flight deck as she capsized."[21]

Some destroyers steamed to rescue *Eagle's* crew, and others, despite the hundreds of men in the water, dashed about scattering depth charges. In the end they saved 927 of the carrier's 1,160 men. *Furious* resumed flying off her Malta-bound Spitfires by 1350. Later that afternoon she turned back for Gibraltar screened by *Keppel, Venomous, Malcolm, Wrestler,* and *Wolverine.* The first two were loaded with *Eagle's* survivors. At 0100 on 12 August *Wolverine* picked up a radar contact and rammed and sank the Italian submarine *Dagabur.* The collision severely mangled the destroyer's bow and fractured her main steam pipe, but she was able to limp back to Gibraltar at six knots.

As the convoy resumed course the destroyers finished refueling and the screen was at full strength when, at 2056, twenty-six Ju 88s of KGr 54 and KGr 77 and three torpedo-armed He 111s appeared overhead. Hurricanes vectored in to intercept the attackers failed to make contact. Although the Germans claimed they hit a carrier and merchantman with bombs and torpedoed a cruiser, all the planes missed their targets while the British shot down four. This victory was diminished, however, when the Hurricanes returned after their fruitless sortie. Heavy flak greeted them, and several, landing through the barrage with empty tanks, crash-landed on *Victorious*.

On the night of 11–12 August bombers from Malta raided several Italian fields on Sardinia hoping to diminish the strength of the next day's raid. Ten Beaufighters roared over Elmas at last light and shot up the airfield, destroying an S.79 and damaging six other aircraft. At Decimomannu the raiders destroyed four S.79s, all loaded with torpedoes, and one Ca.164 ("*tipo turismo*") and damaged eight S.79s and three MC.202s.[22] The British planes also spotted Admiral Da Zara's 7th Division departing Cagliari. Italian intelligence intercepted and decoded the spotting report, and when an ASV Wellington attacked at 0130 on 12 August the forewarned Da Zara was able to evade its torpedo.

AIR STRIKES

August 12 was a long and difficult day for the convoy. By 0610 sixteen fighters were aloft in the dawning sky waiting for the first Axis move. *Kenya* reported that she avoided three submarine torpedoes at 0741, although there were no Axis boats in the area. In fact, imaginary submarine encounters filled the British reports. In a case of what the Italian official history describes as "an obsession with the underwater danger," at least four destroyers conducted depth charge attacks during the morning although all Italian submarines were east of La Galite and the convoy did not reach that point until afternoon.[23]

Nineteen Ju 88s attacked first that morning. The fighters confronted them twenty-five miles out. Although the British claimed they downed thirteen planes, eleven in air-to-air combat and two by flak, the actual count of six, one of which was downed by friendly fire on its return to base, was bad enough. One British fighter was lost, and the attack, a mix of high-level and shallow dive-bombing, was ineffective, although the Germans claimed hits on a cruiser and two transports.[24]

Air Sardinia's coordinated attack started at 1240 and lasted until 1330. It was intended to overwhelm the convoy's defenses with successive waves of high-level, low-level, and torpedo-bombers and secret weapons. First ten S.84s parachuted *motobomba* in the convoy's path. This novel weapon, being used for the first time at sea, was a self-propelled mine with a 260-kg warhead that slowly traveled in large circles.[25] Next eight CR.42s dove in to divert the fire of the destroyers from the torpedo attack that was supposed to follow right behind them. Fourteen MC.202s escorted these two groups.

The torpedo-bombers, thirty-three S.79s and ten S.84s escorted by twenty-six Re.2001s, had fallen behind, however, and then fighters intercepted the S.84s and disrupted their formation. Nonetheless, forty torpedo planes approached the convoy from both sides. The British reported that most launched from long range although several pressed in aiming for the battleships. The airmen claimed they sank two transports and a destroyer while hitting a battleship, three cruisers or destroyers, and two transports. In fact, turning judiciously, the convoy avoided all forty torpedoes. Next thirty-seven Ju 88s of KGr 54 and KGr 77 dived through the flak and the defending interceptors.[26] At 1300 a stick of bombs hit the transport *Deucalion* and brought her to a stop, heavily damaged. After some of the crew prematurely abandoned ship and the convoy had passed her by, she managed to get under way at ten knots and, attended by *Bramham*, headed for the coast hoping to make Malta independently.

Finally, the Regia Aeronautica deployed two more secret weapons: a remotely controlled S.79 loaded with a 630-pound armor-piercing bomb and two Re.2001s each armed with a 1,411-pound bomb adapted from 15-inch projectiles. A Cant Z.1007bis escorted by five G.50 fighters guided the attackers to their objective. The remotely controlled S.79 was supposed to crash a carrier after its pilot bailed out, but it did not respond to the controller aircraft, and ended up running out of fuel and plowing into an Algerian mountainside. However, the Re.2001s, which resembled Hurricanes, approached *Victorious* as if they intended to land and then peeled off, dropping on the carrier. One bomb hit the center of the flight deck but skittered over the side without exploding. The planes sped away before the carrier could open fire, leaving behind a slight bulge on their target's flight deck and a lot of excitement. From these massed strikes one S.79, two S.84s, and an Re.2001 failed to return, although the British claimed that their fighters shot down nine and their flak two of the attackers.[27]

As the convoy continued, submarine scares intensified. In the course of the operation Admiral Syfret ordered forty-eight emergency turns "in consequence of warnings of submarines given by the screen." By this time several contracts were real. At 1616 *Zetland* and *Pathfinder* detected an echo off the convoy's port bow, and, after the merchantmen had passed, *Ithuriel* assumed the hunt. Her depth charges brought *Cobalto* to the surface. *Ithuriel*'s captain rammed the distressed sub and sent her to the bottom, but the impact disabled the destroyer's sonar and crumpled her bow. Syfret remarked, "I thought the expensive method chosen . . . quite unnecessary. Moreover, I was disturbed at the resulting absence of *Ithuriel* from the screen when an air attack was impending." The escort also frustrated attacks by *Avorio* and *Dandolo*.[28]

At 1750 *Ithuriel* was steaming at twenty knots to catch up to the convoy, which had drawn ten miles ahead, when eight CR.42s escorted by nine Re.2001s dived on her. As in Operation Harpoon, the destroyer, mangled bow and all, proved adept at sidestepping bombs. She reported her attackers as four Ju 87s. The fighter-bombers claimed they damaged a merchant vessel while one of the escorts failed to return to base.

At 1835 the day's last large air attack arrived as the convoy reached a point eighteen miles northwest of Cani Rocks, and in contrast to earlier efforts, it proved devastating. It consisted of nine Italian Ju 87s of 102° Gruppo, twenty German Ju 87s of I./St.G 3, and fourteen S.79s of 132° Gruppo. Superaereo had intended to transfer eighteen Re.2001 fighters that had participated in the morning attack from Sardinia to Sicily to escort the dive bombers and a planned strike by forty high-level bombers, but after the exertions of the battle, the fighters could not be readied in time. This caused Air Sicily to cancel the high-level attack and transfer the 102° Gruppo to Pantelleria. Fighter support consisted of four Bf 109s covering the Germans and twenty-eight MC.202s screening the Italians. Twenty-two FAA fighters met the Axis force as it approached but could not break up the strike (they claimed they shot down seven enemy aircraft). The S.79s attacked on the convoy's starboard bow and beam. As the convoy turned to avoid the incoming torpedoes, the Italian Stukas near-missed *Rodney* with 500-kg bombs at the cost of two of their number. They claimed success against a battleship and four merchantmen. At the same time the Germans took on the carriers. "Appearing suddenly from up sun out of the smoky blue sky," a group attacked *Indomitable* from astern, and three bombs struck the carrier's flight deck. *Nelson*'s executive officer wrote, "all we saw of [*Indomi-*

table] for minutes was columns of spray. Finally, the maelstrom subsided, and there was '*Indom*', still there, but blazing both for'ard and aft of the island, with great columns of smoke pouring from her flight deck." Fifty men died, and the blasts wrecked the ship's flight deck and forward hanger. The Germans also claimed damage to a cruiser. Finally, an S.79's torpedo caught the destroyer *Foresight*. The explosion broke the warship's back and brought her "to a shuddering halt under a 'black cloud' as *Tartar* approached to stand by her." *Tartar* eventually took *Foresight* under tow, but the next day, with Axis reconnaissance aircraft overhead and reports of submarines in the area, *Tartar* scuttled the cripple.[29]

As the bombers withdrew, leaving the smoking carrier as a beacon of their success, Admiral Syfret ordered Force Z to reverse course and return to Gibraltar and for the convoy and Force X to continue east through the Sicilian narrows. *Indomitable*'s plight, and a boiler defect in *Rodney* caused by the attack, led Syfret to order the separation early. He wrote, "it seemed improbable that a further attack on Force X on any great scale would be forthcoming before dark, and having reached the Skerki Banks, it was hoped that the submarine menace was mostly over."[30] As Force X commenced its final run Admiral Burrough in *Nigeria* ordered the convoy to form two columns so it could steam through swept waters. He intended his flagship to lead the port file of seven transports with *Cairo* in the middle while *Kenya* led the starboard column of six transports stiffened by *Manchester* midway down the row. *Intrepid, Icarus,* and *Fury,* paravanes streaming for mines, led the way while *Pathfinder, Ledbury,* and *Bicester* guarded the starboard beam and *Ashanti, Penn,* and *Derwent* screened to port. *Winton* was to bring up the rear.

INTO THE NARROWS

Syfret's assessment of the submarine menace proved incorrect. *Axum* and *Dessiè* had, in fact, observed smoke from the burning carrier on the western horizon and waited in the narrow waters as a wealth of targets steamed toward them. At 1938 *Dessiè* fired four torpedoes from a distance of only two thousand yards, but all missed. *Axum,* her periscope unseen in the twilight waters, saw three ships overlap as *Nigeria* was speeding up to assume her position at the head of the port column and *Cairo* slowed. She launched four torpedoes at 1955. Sixty-three seconds later there was the sound of an explosion followed by a second and then a third blast. One weapon detonated against *Nigeria* to port, flooding the forward boiler-rooms. Power failed and the rudder jammed, causing the ship to circle to starboard as she slowed. Two torpedoes slammed into *Cairo* and blew away the antiaircraft cruiser's stern. Finally, a torpedo hit the tanker *Ohio*, ripped a twenty-foot-wide hole in her hull, and brought the large and valuable ship to a halt, on fire and with boilers extinguished.

This triple blow, the most successful single submarine attack of the war, caused massive confusion. Some ships proceeded, others circled back, and no orders were issued until Admiral Burrough transferred to *Ashanti* at 2015. *Nigeria* managed to reduce her list from 13 to 5 degrees and withdrew west, escorted by two destroyers. With stern low and bow riding high, Burrough ordered *Pathfinder* to sink *Cairo* after the survivors had been removed, but the destroyer's four torpedoes all malfunctioned. Depth charges did not affect the wallowing cruiser, and finally *Pathfinder* departed to catch up to the convoy, leaving *Derwent* to riddle the hulk with 4-inch shells. *Bicester* and *Wilton*, loaded with survivors, and *Derwent*, after she finally dispatched *Cairo*, accompanied *Nigeria* west.

At 2015 as the sun began setting, long-range Beaufighters appeared overhead. However, *Nigeria* and *Cairo* were the only ships with fighter direction facilities, and the planes drew fire from the escorts, causing them to turn away. The good news was that *Ohio* managed to control her fires and relight her boilers. Then, at 2035 as the light died in the west, thirty Ju 88s and seven He 111 torpedo-bombers struck. The lack of fighter cover and the convoy's disorganized state made this the day's deadliest raid. *Ashanti*, with Admiral Burrough embarked, was near-missed, causing a boiler to blow back and starting a serious fire. After passing *Ohio*, which sprayed the fire as the destroyer steamed alongside, Burrough ordered the tanker to proceed inshore and promised to dispatch an escort.

Meanwhile, an He 111 torpedoed *Brisbane Star*, blowing a hole through the vessel; despite flooding, she proceeded independently. Ju 88s near-missed *Empire Hope* repeatedly before a bomb detonated on board and brought her to a halt. At 2050 two more direct hits ignited her cargo of ammunition and aviation fuel, forcing the crew over the side. At 2102 a torpedo impacted *Clan Ferguson* with a massive explosion, and the ship began to settle amidst burning waters. About forty of her men eventually made it to Tunisia where they were interned; Italian seaplanes and an MAS boat rescued others. *Deucalion*, screened by *Bramham*, had been proceeding independently further inshore and behind the main convoy. At 2115 one of the He 111s torpedoed and sank her northwest of Cani Rocks. The Germans lost one Ju 88 in this attack. They claimed that they sank one merchantman and hit another ten as well as a cruiser.[31]

Amid this destruction and confusion *Port Chalmers*, with Commodore A. G. Venables, the convoy commodore, on board, began steering west. When *Melbourne Star* and *Dorset* signaled her for instructions, Venables told both to turn back. Along with *Almeria Lykes* they briefly followed *Port Chalmers*, but one of the escorts came up and signaled "course 120 degrees." With the exception of *Port Chalmers*, all turned once again for Malta.[32]

By 2112 the air attack was over and the minesweeping destroyers were just clearing Skerki Channel. *Kenya* and *Manchester* followed, and behind them steamed *Glenorchy* and *Wairangi*, the only two merchant ships to maintain position. Catching up were *Waimarama* and *Santa Elisa* while farther back *Melbourne Star*, *Dorset*, and *Almeria Lykes* were once again on course. *Pathfinder*, *Penn*, and *Ledbury* were strung out rounding up stragglers.

Just as the convoy was working to regain cohesion, the submarine *Alagi* sent a four-torpedo spread against *Kenya* as the cruiser crossed her sights. Lookouts spotted the tracks too late and one slammed into *Kenya's* bow, killing four men. The blast destroyed No. 6 Bulkhead and severely damaged the bow structure from keel to the upper deck. Nonetheless, the cruiser could still steam at convoy speeds and so maintained course.

By this time Syfret had learned that Burrough's flagship and *Cairo* were lost. Just ninety minutes before, at 1950, a reconnaissance plane had reported four cruisers and six destroyers on course to arrive off Pantelleria at dawn; mindful of Admiral Curteis' failure to reinforce Captain Hardy in the June operation, Syfret ordered the cruiser *Charybdis* and the destroyers *Somali* and *Eskimo* to reverse course and join Force X.[33] At 2115 they passed *Nigeria* and her escort of three Hunt destroyers (shortly to be reinforced by *Malcolm*). The fact that four of these valuable antiaircraft escorts were assigned to one damaged cruiser while nearly a dozen transports faced certain air attacks the next day suggests that the Royal Navy placed a higher priority on the cruiser's safety than the convoy's arrival.

Intrepid, *Icarus*, and *Fury*, paravanes streaming, rounded Cape Bon's rocky promontory shortly before midnight and began the twenty-mile jog south to Kelibia Point. From there the plan was to head straight for Malta. *Manchester* and *Kenya* followed closely while *Glenorchy*, *Almeria Lykes*, and *Wairangi* maintained pace with the warships. *Melbourne Star*, *Waimarama*, *Santa Elisa*, *Dorset*, and *Rochester Castle* were strung out astern with only *Pathfinder* in escort. Behind them *Ohio* had worked up to fifteen knots with the Hunt *Ledbury* in attendance. They passed *Empire Hope*'s burning wreck at 2348. Meanwhile at 0045 *Bramham*, loaded with *Deucalion* survivors, encountered Commodore Venables aboard *Port Chalmers* making his solitary way back to Gibraltar. Venables later reported that he was trying to save his ship "by leaving the convoy from the rear" and proceeding full speed westward. "Another destroyer overtook me and gave instructions to proceed to Malta—which was my intention as soon as circumstances appeared favourable."[34] In any case, after encountering *Bramham*, *Port Chalmers* reversed course. Shortly thereafter they came upon *Penn*, and the three ships proceeded together. Hugging the Tunisian shore, *Brisbane Star* sailed alone.

"E-BOATS"

Shortly after midnight the escorts made radar contacts with Italian and German motor torpedo boats. Supermarina had positioned thirteen MAS boats (*MAS 543, 548, 549,* and *563* of the 15th Squadron; *MAS 533, 553, 556, 560,* and *562* of the 18th Squadron; *MAS 552, 554, 557,* and *564* of the 20th Squadron); six of the brand-new and larger MS *motosiluranti* of the 2nd Squadron (*MS 16, 22, 23, 25, 26,* and *31*); and four German *schnellboote* of the 3rd Flotilla (*S 30, 36, 58,* and *59*). Murky visibility, manageable seas, and a dispersed convoy provided these small craft with ideal conditions.

At 0040 on 13 August two of the 18th Squadron's boats launched torpedoes toward the three minesweeping destroyers and then veered away under heavy fire. Twenty minutes later *S 59*, which was operating independently, reported hitting a tanker five miles north northeast of Cape Bon. She may have launched torpedoes against *Ohio* and missed.

At 0104 *MS 16* and *22*, which had been sheltering with engines off behind the wreck of *Havock*, ambushed the cruiser *Manchester* from very close range. *MS 16*'s first torpedo malfunctioned, but the second, fired three minutes later, exploded with an orange-red flash on the cruiser's starboard side near the after engine room. Thirteen men died in the blast, and the ship heeled and rapidly lost speed. *MS 22* scored with a second torpedo quickly thereafter. One member of the cruiser's black-gang recalled that "the first explosion plunged the engine-room into darkness and the second flung me from the platform on which I was standing. Only an uprush of water prevented me breaking my back on a fall to the engine-room floor."[35] The three transports following, *Almeria Lykes*,

Glenorchy, and *Waimarama,* maneuvered, one after the other, to avoid collisions and then continued on their separate ways.

At 0140 *Pathfinder* along with *Melbourne Star* and *Dorset* encountered *Manchester.* The destroyer stood by the cruiser and ordered the transports to keep
going. The cruiser's captain thought he could get his ship under way, so, after
taking off 158 nonessential personnel, *Pathfinder* continued east.

Ten minutes later and twenty miles south, *Intrepid, Icarus,* and *Fury* had
just passed Kelibia light where *MS 26* and *31* waited. A searchlight pinned *MS
26.* Under heavy fire, she roared off into the night to seek a new firing position.
MS 31, however, aimed two torpedoes at a destroyer and a transport looming
behind the destroyer from seven hundred meters. *Fury's* aft mounts fired at
the shifty target as the *motosiluranti* accelerated away. Both torpedoes struck
Glenorchy's hull, ripping it open to a flood of water. As the ship listed sharply to
port the crew, mindful of the vessel's dangerous cargo which included ammunition and aviation fuel, quickly abandoned ship. *MS 31* circled, and although
out of torpedoes, she maintained contact and radioed sighting reports to other
Italian boats.

At this time, Admiral Burrough aboard *Ashanti* was nearing the convoy's
head where he found plenty of action. At 0210 the leading destroyers brushed
by *MS 23* and *25.* The *motosiluranti* tried to attack a large transport following the
destroyers, but when they came under fire, *MS 25* disengaged and then swung
back to launch her torpedoes from long range and without result. *MS 23* reported that she was unable to get into firing position. Their two skippers were
later judged to have lacked aggressive spirit, but such a judgment could not be
levied against *MS 26.* She returned and roared up the convoy's starboard side.
While machine-gunning a merchant ship, the boat's captain saw a "cruiser" a
thousand meters to port bearing 50 degrees. He loosed his torpedoes at this
target and claimed a hit; but was again illuminated and forced to turn away
at speed. *Pathfinder* took off in pursuit. She reported, "we caught the E-boat
squarely in the beam of our big 44-inch searchlight, and every gun that would
bear, 4-inch, pom-poms and Oerlikons opened a rapid fire. Enveloped in shell
splashes, the E-boat shot ahead and swung round laying a smoke screen."[36]
MS 26 dropped depth charges in her wake, but the destroyer stuck to the chase
until the *motosilurante* entered a coastal minefield at 0245.

As *Pathfinder* drove off this threat, *Kenya* altered course to head toward
Malta, still 150 miles east. Shortly before 0300 Syfret's reinforcements, *Charybdis, Eskimo,* and *Somali,* caught up to *Ashanti.* At the same time *Manches-*

ter's captain decided he could not save his vessel and ordered the crew to abandon ship.

As the convoy proceeded it entered the 20th Squadron's zone. At 0310 *MAS 552* and *MAS 554* attacked what appeared to them to be a stopped transport escorted by a destroyer. Their target was *Wairangi*, and one torpedo struck the transport's port side. As the engine room flooded and the ship began to settle, the captain ordered abandon ship. At 0340 *MAS 554* reported that in a second attack she torpedoed and sank a large steamer—probably *Wairangi* again. However, even after the steamer's crew attempted to hasten her demise by opening water-tight doors, *Wairangi* continued to wallow above the waves while her men hovered nearby in their boats. Meanwhile *MS 31* had reached the southern limits of her assigned zone, so she turned north and, coming upon the *Port Chalmers* group, began to report their movements.

Between 0315 and 0330 MTBs torpedoed *Rochester Castle* and *Almeria Lykes*. The official Italian account credits *S 30* and *36* with *Rochester Castle* while most British accounts say that the two German boats accounted for *Almeria Lykes* and *MAS 564* probably accounted for *Rochester Castle* at 0329. The German war diary asserted that *S 30* sank *Almeria Lykes* and *Wairangi* while *S 36* accounted for *Santa Elisa* and *S 59 Glenorchy*. In any case, a torpedo hit *Almeria Lykes* forward in No. 1 Hold. As the engines stopped and the hold flooded, the crew abandoned ship. The British considered the American crew "somewhat anti-British" and in his report Admiral Syfret judged that the ship "could well have continued steaming to Malta." *Almeria Lykes* remained afloat, and the men were finally rescued by *Somali* and *Eskimo* when they returned the next morning searching for *Manchester* survivors.[37]

Rochester Castle reported being torpedoed at 0330 in No. 3 Hold a minute after engaging an enemy motor torpedo boat with her antiaircraft weapons. Despite the damage her engines remained on line, so she continued steaming at thirteen knots. Within forty-five minutes she had caught up to the rest of the convoy.

The last transport to run afoul of the Axis MTBs was *Santa Elisa*. *MAS 557* attacked her from astern shortly after 0430. The boat's torpedo missed, and she raced past the freighter with her 20-mm gun hammering away, killing four DEM gunners manning the ship's weapons. Then she circled around and at 0448 fired her second torpedo. This struck in No. 1 Hold, which was stowed with aviation fuel. The impact sparked a gigantic blast that shot flames into the sky and hurled several crewmembers overboard. The rest quickly abandoned ship. *MAS 564* had come up meanwhile, and at 0500 she launched her second torpedo against the same target and likewise claimed success. Finally, at 0508 *MAS 553* asserted that she attacked a tanker with two torpedoes and observed an explosion. This may have been *Santa Elisa* again. *Penn* rescued the ship's survivors about an hour later when she, *Bramham,* and *Port Chalmers* passed by. A Ju 88 finished off *Santa Elisa's* wreck at 0715.

This was the most successful motor torpedo boat action of the war, resulting in the destruction of a light cruiser and four freighters and damage to one freighter. It reflected what the Italian navy had expected to routinely achieve blockading the Sicilian narrows with their MAS boats. There were three reasons, however, why this action was not routine. First, the weather was perfect; second, the convoy was disorganized and the escort nowhere strong except at the formation's head; and third, the larger and more capable *motosiluranti* (not to mention German S-boats) were involved.

As in the mid-June operation, Supermarina had planned to intercept Force X at dawn with cruisers and destroyers. A surface attack would have capped Pedestal's cup of woe, but it never happened. Rear Admiral Parona's 3rd Division with the heavy cruisers *Gorizia, Bolzano,* and *Trieste* and Da Zara's 7th Division with the light cruisers *Eugenio di Savoia, Montecuccoli,* and *Attendolo* and eleven destroyers were steaming to intercept. However, shortly before midnight, six hours before contact, Mussolini recalled Parona. Various explanations are given. One is that Supermarina anticipated that the British air forces at Malta would make an all-out effort to stop the flotilla but the air force would only commit eighteen elderly CR.42s to protect the strike force. Or, there were only sufficient fighters to protect an air strike or the surface force, but not both. The Italian official history blames Kesselring, stating that he refused to grant German air cover because he did not believe that a division of Italian heavy cruisers could prevail over five British cruisers after what he considered to be the disappointing results off Pantelleria in the mid-June operation. British accounts explain that aircraft shadowing the strike force shined lights on the Italian warships and made plain-language signals that a massive bomber strike was inbound and these deceptions "alarmed" Supermarina.[38]

In fact, at 1825 the German air command advised Comando Supremo that while the two aircraft carriers had turned back, a battleship was proceeding east with the "clear intention of forcing the passage." The Germans considered that a landing on the African coast was likely, but Supermarina disagreed. Co-

mando Supremo referred the matter to Mussolini for a decision, advising him
that a Nelson-class battleship and a cruiser had joined the escort (the planes
actually spotted *Charybdis, Eskimo* and *Somali*). The Duce was advised that
Parona's force had no chance in clear weather, as forecast for the next day, against
a battleship's big guns and heavy armor, especially since an adequate air escort could not be provided. After an emotional debate Mussolini finally authorized the recall of Parona's cruisers.[39] This decision, based on poor information, proved doubly unfortunate for the Regia Marina the next morning when
the submarine *Unbroken* intercepted the Italian flotilla and fired a deadly salvo
that severely damaged *Attendolo* and *Bolzano*. The first had just completed repairs when USAAF bombers sunk her on 12 December 1942, and the other
never returned to service.

ON TO MALTA

At dawn Force X began its final run to Malta. Burrough commanded
from *Ashanti,* and he had with him the cruisers *Charybdis* and the damaged
Kenya, the destroyers *Somali, Eskimo, Intrepid, Icarus,* and *Fury,* and the transports *Rochester Castle, Waimarama,* and *Melbourne Star. Pathfinder, Bramham,*
and *Port Chalmers* were ten miles to the northwest while *Penn* was standing
by the stricken *Santa Elisa. Dorset* was off to the north but under orders to rejoin the convoy. *Ohio* and *Ledbury* were five miles astern. *Brisbane Star* was
still coming, having spent the night in the Gulf of Hammamet. At 0712, when
it seemed there would be no surface attack, Burrough ordered *Somali* and *Eskimo* to return and stand by *Manchester,* unaware that the cruiser had sunk at
0550 and most of the crew had struggled ashore on rafts and floats.

The convoy was supposed to be under the cover of long-range Beaufighters
by daylight, but attempts to jerry-rig a ship-to-air communication system on
Ashanti failed. Thus, the German Ju 88s from LG 1 that conducted the day's first
air attack between 0810 and 0842, when the convoy was about thirty miles south
southeast of Pantelleria, were not effectively intercepted. Twenty-six planes
had been dispatched, but only ten found their target. Three bombs landed on
Waimarama and detonated her deck cargo of aviation fuel and ammunition.
The ship literally disintegrated, losing eighty-seven men. Flaming debris show-
ered *Melbourne Star,* following astern. As she pressed on through the burning
waters, thirty-three of her men abandoned ship fearful that the flames would

ignite their own deck cargo of gasoline. As it was, paint blistered and lifeboats caught fire. The Germans lost one aircraft; they claimed hits on four steamers and one cruiser.[40]

After this strike, the stragglers caught up to the escorts. They proceeded in two columns. *Kenya* led the port column followed by *Rochester Castle* and later *Dorset*. *Charybdis* led *Melbourne Star, Ohio,* and *Port Chalmers* to form the starboard column.

The next air attack arrived at 0925 and consisted of eight Italian Ju 87s of 102° Gruppo escorted by eleven MC.202s. Admiral Burrough described the attack as of a "most determined nature." The Italian pilots considered the antiaircraft fire "violent." A 500-kg bomb near-missed *Ohio* off the port bow while one Ju 87, brought down by *Ashanti* and *Ohio*'s guns, crashed on the American tanker's poopdeck. At 0941 a bomb near-missed *Kenya*. The raid also damaged *Dorset* and *Port Chalmers*. Spitfires disputed the air over the convoy and shot down one bomber. In all, two Ju 87s did not return to base while the airmen claimed success against a tanker and a merchantman.[41]

At 1050 fifteen Ju 88s attacked from ahead. One, downed by antiaircraft fire, skittered across the sea's surface and smashed into *Ohio*'s hull. The concussion blew out the tanker's boiler fires. Sixteen Ju 87s of I./St.G 3 followed them. The dive bombers near-missed *Dorset* and brought her to a halt. "Water was pouring in from a gaping hole on the starboard side, and the generators were completely wrecked." *Rochester Castle* suffered engine failure after a series of near misses lifted her bow and caused flooding. However, her crew was able to restore power after ten minutes, and the ship continued with only six feet of freeboard. Two of the Stukas, one of the Ju 88s, and one of their escorting Bf 109s were lost while the German crews claimed that they hit a cruiser and four merchantmen, "of which one exploded and two sank."[42]

At 1120 five S.79s escorted by fourteen MC.202s made a torpedo attack. *Port Chalmers*'s starboard paravanes caught one torpedo. She managed to drop the gear and get free, but when the torpedo exploded against the seabed her captain described the uplift as tremendous. A Spitfire shot down one of the S.79s. The Italian airmen claimed they torpedoed one steamer.[43]

As the convoy continued *Penn* and *Ledbury* stood by *Ohio* while *Bramham* picked up *Dorset*'s crew, who had concluded the damage to their vessel was irreparable and had abandoned ship. By 1230 the convoy was in range of Malta's short-ranged Spitfires and, as Admiral Burrough reported, "thereafter was unmolested." Still concerned about *Manchester,* he detached *Ledbury* from *Ohio*'s assistance to see about the cruiser.[44]

Superaereo spent much of the remainder of the day chasing false contacts. At 1430 it dispatched three pairs of torpedo-armed S.79s to scout for the enemy or develop reported contacts. The first pair found a large, isolated steamer proceeding at slow speed in the Gulf of Hammamet. They attacked, but their torpedoes malfunctioned. The second pair found nothing, and the third pair disappeared. *Ledbury* reported an attack, and they may have fallen victim to her fire. At 1720 five Italian Ju 87s escorted by twenty-four MC.202s took off from Pantelleria searching for two steamers reported sixty miles southeast of the island, but they found nothing. Likewise, seven S.79s escorted by nineteen Re.2001s that lifted off at 1800 to look for a carrier reported north of Bizerte came up empty.[45]

At 1430 the Malta Escort Force—the minesweepers *Speedy, Rye, Hebe,* and *Hythe* and seven motor launches—joined the escort. At 1600 Force X, down to two cruisers and five destroyers, turned about to return to Gibraltar. In his report of proceedings *Ashanti*'s captain noted that "Course was shaped to pass 12 miles South of Linosa Island in order that enemy aircraft shadowing *Ohio* might be avoided." *Port Chalmers, Melbourne Star,* and *Rochester Castle,* "lying very low in the water," entered Grand Harbor at 1800. Fliegerkorps II had made a grand effort to finish off the cripples, sending twenty-nine Ju 88s, fourteen Ju 87s, and seven He 111s escorted by twenty Bf 109s from their Sicilian bases. However, only three of the Ju 88s and the Ju 87s managed to locate a target. A Ju 87 finally dispatched *Dorset*'s burning and abandoned wreck at 2015. *Ohio,* with *Penn* and *Rye* standing by, was hit again. *Rye* reported that "at 2024 twelve bombs fell within 20 yards of *Rye,* covering her with spray and splinters, but doing no effective damage." Despite the incessant attacks, *Ohio* remained afloat and was coaxed toward Malta under tow at four knots.[46]

More air attacks against the stragglers occurred on the 14th. At 1045 five Italian Ju 87s armed with 500-kg bombs and escorted by twenty MC.202s dived on the battered tanker. A bomb exploded in *Ohio*'s wake and gashed open her stern, but the ship still floated. Spitfires intervened and shot down the group commander and one of the other fighters. Finally on the morning of 15 August, down nearly forty feet and with a destroyer lashed to either side, the tanker reached her destination. One witness remembered, "The great ramparts and battlements of Malta, built against the siege by the Turks, were lined and black

with people. Thousand and thousands of cheering people." *Brisbane Star* likewise made port on the afternoon of 14 August after breaking free of the Tunisian shore at dusk on the 13th by convincing a French boarding party to let
her go.[47]

The main weight of the Axis air effort on 14 August was directed against
the ships of Force X, not the tanker *Ohio,* the more valuable (and easier) target.
This was in accordance with orders issued by OBS that "under no circumstances were they to attack damaged ships or those left behind." This order
was influenced by the way much of the force of the mid-June air attacks had
been dissipated by attacking *Liverpool* after she was damaged and out of the
action. Burrough's trials began before daylight when he reported an attack off
Cape Bon at 0130 on 14 August and claimed seeing an explosion "which was
believed to be an E-Boat blowing up." In fact, this was *MAS 556,* and she was
undamaged. At 0450 the submarine *Granito* near-missed *Kenya* while at 0912
a long series of air attacks commenced. These were delivered by twenty-six
Ju 88s, thirteen Ju 87s, fifteen S.84s, and twenty S.79s. *Kenya* sustained slight
damage from near-misses. "From 1000 to 1300 attacks were almost incessant
and included dive bombers, high level bombers, torpedo bombers and dropping of mines or circling torpedoes." Nonetheless, the warships made Gibraltar without further damage.[48]

ANALYSIS

The mid-August battle was the largest single convoy action fought in
the Mediterranean. The Axis forces, primarily Italian, won a tactical victory.
The combined use of air, surface, and submarine forces was extremely effective, especially considering the strength of the escort. The results measured in
terms of ships sunk showed that the Italians had finally obtained the skills and
weapons needed to make the cost of supplying Malta more than the British
could pay on an ongoing basis. The British could not routinely expend cruisers
and carriers and suffer losses of two-thirds of its merchantmen on such operations. Churchill described the results as a "magnificent crash through of supplies. "In fact the real mood was better captured by *Nelson's* executive officer.
On 16 August "all the commanding officers in the Fleet came on board for a
conference. Most of us felt depressed by the party. Operation 'M' for Murder
we call it." However, this victory came too late for Italy and it was too little.
The five ships that made port, the fifteen thousand tons of black and white

oil and the thirty-two thousand tons of general stores and ammunition they landed did not release Malta's population from their starvation rations (1,690 calories for adult male workers and 1,500 calories for women and children), but they were enough to keep the island going in hope of the next convoy. If the Italian cruiser divisions had attacked the convoy south of Pantelleria at dawn—especially considering that it was still scattered at that time—the Italians could have grasped the strategic victory they required. Instead, on 17 August as Rear Admiral Franco Maugeri, head of Italy's naval intelligence, recorded in his diary,

And Malta has resumed functioning despite all the losses we inflicted.[49]

9

TORCH TO THE END OF THE WAR

It was clear from the start that the landing of American forces in the Mediterranean was an event of great strategic significance, destined to modify and, in fact, to reverse the balance of military power in this sector, an event which was in Italian opinion if not decisive, certainly very important.

Benito Mussolini

EVEN AFTER OPERATION Pedestal there was still insufficient food to adequately feed Malta's population, but there was enough, supplemented by the harvest, to defer starvation. Shortages of fuel, ammunition, and torpedoes still limited the island's usefulness as a base against Axis traffic. A contemporary account related that "Owing to the necessity for conserving aircraft fuel, the bombing of land targets was almost nonexistent between the middle of June and the middle of November. All available fuel was needed for keeping fighters and reconnaissance aircraft flying and for attacks on shipping." In this context postponing the capture of Malta did not seem crucial to the Axis leaders. Hitler and Mussolini correctly believed that the war would be won or lost in Russia, and in August 1942 reports from the east were good. In an assessment made on 4 August Comando Supremo anticipated a separate peace with the Soviet Union that would oblige the western allies to accept terms with the Axis.[1]

FROM PEDESTAL TO TORCH

During the three months between Pedestal and Operation Torch, the 8 November 1942 invasion of French North Africa, the siege of Malta continued in full force. As early as mid-September the food situation was, once again, described to the chiefs of staff as "grave." The Royal Navy did what it could with submarines and blockade runners while submarines and aircraft, based mostly in Egypt or Palestine, strenuously chipped away at Axis maritime traffic. On 16 August *Furious* flew off thirty-two Spitfires to Malta, of which twenty-nine arrived, and on 30 October twenty-seven of twenty-nine Spitfires made it to the island. Submarines bringing supplies included *Clyde* on 30 August, 6 October, and 6 November; *P212* on 9 October; *P247* on 19 October; *Parthian* on 3 October and 2 November; *Porpoise* on 17 September, 7 October, and 6 November; *Rorqual* on 24 September and 22 October; and *Proteus* on 22 September. These boats brought "aviation spirit, special foodstuffs, diesel and lubricating oils and torpedoes." The blockade runner *Empire Patrol* (3,333 GRT ex-Italian *Rodi*) departed Alexandria on 1 November with gasoline and food, but had to turn back. Two small ships, *Ardeola* and *Tadorna,* loaded with flour, concentrated foodstuffs, and dried milk, tried to sneak in to Malta under the cover of Operation Torch, but French authorities seized them off Tunisia. The fast minelayer *Manxman* ran the island's blockade on 12 November with 350 tons of dried milk, cereals, and meat, and her sister *Welshman* arrived from Gibraltar on the 18th with a similar cargo. This record of sporadic sailings and arrivals demonstrated Malta's desperate isolation.[2]

With an Axis army positioned sixty miles west of Alexandria, Malta's impact on enemy traffic to North Africa has been presented as a major justification for the mid-June and August operations. The Allied ability to read certain Axis codes, especially Luftwaffe Enigma and the Italian C 38m, was, however, of greater consequence. Of the Axis ships sunk in transit to North Africa, signals intelligence was involved in nearly every case. Such intelligence provided "either the location in port or anchorage, or the timing or routing of the final voyage, in good time for the operational authorities to reconnoiter and attack."[3]

At the beginning of August, the 10th Submarine Flotilla had four boats just arrived at Malta and six more on patrol. Three boats of the 1st Flotilla, including one Greek, were at Haifa or Beirut, and six were on patrol, including another Greek unit. There were two boats at Gibraltar, two on their way to Malta loaded with supplies, and one under repair at Port Said. This was a major increase over July when only three boats were on patrol at the beginning of the month. Although activities associated with Operation Pedestal diverted several boats from the traffic war, submarines still made forty-six attacks using eighty-five torpedoes and accounted for seven merchant vessels displacing 40,041 tons. Malta-based boats sank one vessel, *Manfredo Camp-*

iero (5,463 GRT), and damaged *Rosolino Pilo* (8,362 GRT), which was later finished off with an aerial torpedo. Aircraft from Malta sank another three ships of 12,020 tons. Overall, Malta-based forces accounted for five of twelve ships sunk and 40 percent of the tonnage lost.[4]

After signals intelligence tipped off Rommel's impending attack against the El Alamein position, the chiefs of staff authorized Malta-based bombers to conduct unlimited operations during the final weeks of August. These strikes depleted the island's stock of aviation fuel and led to a steep reduction in subsequent flying operations and the termination of all transit flights through Malta. Submarines also sank a torpedo boat and damaged a heavy cruiser and a light cruiser during August. Signals intelligence had a role in nine of the sinkings (90 percent of the tonnage). The British lost the submarine *Thorn*.[5]

Axis shipments to Africa fell 20 percent in August compared to July to 77,542 tons, and of the amount shipped only 71 percent (54,655 tons) arrived, compared to July's 94 percent. Overall August was a successful month for the British although Malta's role in that success was limited. September, on the other hand, was disappointing from the British point of view. There were sixteen submarines on patrol on 1 September and twelve in port with two in Beirut, one in Port Said, four in Malta, and five in Gibraltar. Despite their numbers British and Greek boats made only thirty-four attacks, firing fifty-seven torpedoes, and sank six Axis merchant and auxiliary vessels displacing 12,196 tons. Aircraft sank four ships of 12,797 tons. Of the total tonnage sunk during the month, Malta-based forces accounted for four vessels, two by submarine and two by air, totaling 10,953 tons, or 45 percent of the tonnage sunk. The Axis dispatched 96,533 tons of materiel during September of which 77,226 tons, or 80 percent, arrived. Ultra played a role in seven sinkings that accounted for 88 percent of the tonnage sunk.[6]

On 14 September in a desperate effort to reduce Axis traffic, Admiral Harwood authorized a commando raid against Tobruk. One small column attacked overland while Royal Marines assaulted one side of the harbor and Highlanders the other. The operation relied upon "surprise and the belief . . . that the garrisons consisted of low-grade Italian troops." In fact, the garrison, which included a battalion of the San Marco Regiment, proved tougher than the attackers and the naval forces failed to land all the troops due to a lack of practice and proper equipment, poor navigation, and less-than-ideal weather. Casualties totaled over 740 men with most of the attackers captured. The British also lost the cruiser *Coventry,* the destroyers *Sikh* and *Zulu,* four MTBs, and two motor launches. A smaller raid against Benghazi likewise failed.[7]

Twenty submarines made war patrols during October of which twelve operated out of Malta. They made fifty-eight attacks firing 109 torpedoes and sank fifteen vessels (two in conjunction with aircraft) totaling 40,544 tons. Of this, Malta-based vessels accounted for nine vessels of 30,842 tons. Aircraft sank four ships of 18,273 tons with Malta squadrons accounting for one of 2,552 tons. Overall, Malta-based forces sank 57 percent of the total tonnage, their best showing during the period. Signals intelligence played a role in nine of the sinkings, accounting for 69 percent of the total tonnage sunk. The Axis forces received only 45,698 tons of supplies in October, just 56 percent of the 81,603 tons shipped.[8]

The Axis lost 148,646 tons of shipping during August, September, and October 1942. Submarines sank 68 percent of this total. Malta-based boats accounted for thirteen of the thirty-seven ships lost to submarines and 31 percent of the total tonnage lost. Aircraft flying out of Egypt sank five vessels displacing 25,149 tons while Malta-based air accounted for six vessels of 18,068 tons. More antishipping sorties were flown from Egypt than from Malta (approximately 300 to 200). Signals intelligence was a factor in 80 percent of the tonnage lost. Malta-based forces accounted for nineteen of the forty-one freighters and tankers (displacing more than 500 GRT) sunk during the period and 47 percent of the total tonnage lost. Overall, the impact of Malta on Axis traffic increased throughout this period as more submarines operated from the island.[9]

The Italians delivered nearly three-quarters of the materiel shipped to North Africa in the four months August through November 1942. To this should be added 42,000 troops and 15,000 tons of fuel and ammunition flown in by the Luftwaffe and approximately half that amount by the Regia Aeronautica.

Rommel's last serious attempt to breach the British defenses at El Alamein failed on 30 August. Despite the general's vitriolic condemnation of his Italian allies, particularly the Regia Marina, he was defeated by superior ground and air strength and by the enemy's possession of his plan of attack. In fact, poor German security contributed to many of the military difficulties that Rommel attributed to Italian treason. For the rest, Rommel was his own worst enemy. Operating in the European war's most logistically demanding theater, he set unrealistic objectives and expected the impossible from his support services.

Table 9.1. Percentage of Materiel Shipped to and Unloaded in North Africa, August–December 1942

Month	Fuel			Ammunition & Materiel			Total		
	Shipped	Arrived	Percent	Shipped	Arrived	Percent	Shipped	Arrived	Percent
August	38,384	22,500	58.6%	38,750	29,155	75.2%	77,134	51,655	67.0%
September	40,200	31,061	77.3%	56,703	46,465	81.9%	96,903	77,526	80.0%
October	25,771	13,208	51.3%	57,924	33,490	57.8%	83,695	46,698	55.8%
November	51,902	33,678	64.9%	68,407	64,397	94.1%	120,309	98,075	81.5%
December	31,861	16,896	53.0%	65,924	49,874	75.7%	97,785	66,770	68.3%

Source: *Data statistici*, Tables LI and LVI

Field Marshal Kesselring wrote, "The Comando Supremo and C-in-C South (OBS) had moved heaven and earth to assemble an adequate provision of petrol.... The defeat may be attributed to causes of a more psychological nature."[10]

On 10 October the Axis began another aerial offensive against Malta to ease the growing pressure being exerted against African traffic. By 17 October Malta's air commander described the situation as serious, saying that seventy-three Spitfires were grounded awaiting repairs. However Kesselring ended the assault on 19 October because of heavy losses and the need to transfer units back to North Africa to face the impending Allied attack. Precious space on the few blockade runners reaching the island was an issue of contention between the island's governor, the RAF, and the chiefs of staff, with Gort anxious to maintain enough fuel reserves to give fighter coverage of the next convoy scheduled for the November dark period.[11]

On 23 October the British 8th Army attacked at El Alamein, and in two weeks of heavy fighting it cracked the Axis line and forced a general retreat. However, most of the enemy's mobile force slipped away, and, as the British army methodically followed, Rome and Berlin regarded Rommel's defeat as another swing in the desert pendulum of advance, retreat, advance, retreat. Kesselring and Cavallero intended to stand at Sollum/Halfaya Pass, but on 6 November Comando Supremo realized that losses had been too great to permit such a forward defense and agreed with Rommel's request to hold at El Agheila. By 8 November the Germans had just evacuated Mersa Matruh, and Cavallero was in the process of mustering fresh Italian divisions and arranging for new supplies to be shipped from Italy. On this date, however, the Allies took decisive action that finally broke the two-year desert stalemate.[12]

TORCH

By 8 November Malta's food reserves had dropped to critical levels, and London was considering measures, such as slaughtering the island's draft animals, to extend into December the date when all reserves would be exhausted. That day an Anglo-American army invaded French Algeria and Morocco. As one British historian has correctly noted, "the American commitment to a campaign in North Africa would have closed down Axis operations in Cyrenaica even without the defeat at El Alamein." To give an idea of the operation's scale compared to previous efforts, the Royal Navy alone deployed 124 warships to cover the assaults on Oran and Algiers, including two battleships, seven carriers, eight cruisers, and forty-eight destroyers. This was only possible by "removing a substantial part of the Home Fleet's strength, by stopping the Russian convoys, by reducing Atlantic escort forces and by temporarily suspending the mercantile convoys running between Britain and the south Atlantic."[13]

Torch marked the first significant appearance of American forces in the Mediterranean and the end of the British Empire's last major independent campaign against the European Axis. London's assessment of September 1940 was that Italy's morale was fragile and Rome could be driven from the war with relative ease. Although this became the British Empire's main military effort, it could not conquer Libya without a major commitment from its powerful ally. Henceforth London's ability to set strategy and conduct its own operations was increasingly subject to Washington's dictates.[14]

The Allied conquest of Morocco and Algeria and the reoccupation of Cyrenaica raised the siege of Malta. On 16 November Operation Stoneage, or Convoy MW13, got under way from Suez. This involved the passage of four transports, the American *Mormacmoon* and *Robin Locksley,* the British *Denbighshire,* and the Dutch *Bantam.* The escort included five light cruisers, seven fleet destroyers, and ten Hunt-class destroyers. Axis intelligence failed to detect the sailing until 18 November. Ju 88s operating as torpedo-bombers severely damaged the light cruiser *Arethusa,* which lost 155 men. Inclement weather and improved fighter cover, assisted by better ship-to-plane control and newly captured airfields in Cyrenaica (the 8th Army entered Tobruk unopposed on 12 November and occupied the airfields at Martuba on 15 November), helped the convoy escape further damage. It made port early on the morning of 20 November.

On the same day advance units of the 8th Army captured Benghazi while to the west the British 1st Army entered Tunisia. There it confronted Axis units that had been airlifted across the Sicilian Straits and supplied by a series of convoys from Italy. Against this critical movement of men and materiel, the forces on Malta did nothing for three critical weeks. In part this was a command failure: British intelligence estimated it would take up to seven weeks before one complete German division could become operational in Tunisia. In part the importance of ensuring the November convoy's safety commanded the island's attention. However, it still required a week after the convoy's arrival before a reconstituted Force K anchored in Grand Harbour. From 20 to 30 November, Italy dispatched twenty-seven vessels to Tunisia from Italian ports in twelve groups or convoys, several of which were completely unescorted. Submarines attacked two of these convoys and aircraft another two, but without results. Only one vessel, the German *Menès*, failed to arrive.[15]

This delay in acting against the late November traffic to Tunisia was deadly because Axis troops barely repulsed the British spearheads, and the campaign dragged on for another six months.

A convoy called Portcullis, consisting of five transports and a tanker, reached Malta unopposed from the east on 5 December as Axis air forces were fully engaged in Tripolitania and Tunisia. These two convoys delivered 56,000 tons of cargo not including oil and raised the siege of Malta.

November 1942 was a critical month. On the Eastern Front the Soviet defense of Stalingrad erased German hopes for a decision in the east and kept Stalin in the war (or, at least, it raised his price for a separate peace, in feelers extended in December 1942, to a level Hitler declined to pay). In the Pacific, American victories at Guadalcanal frustrated Japanese ambitions and compelled their eventual retreat from that island. The Axis summer of promise had become an autumn of ruin.

TO THE END OF THE WAR

For six months an Italo-German army maintained an African bridgehead in Tunisia, and the naval war's focus shifted to the Sicilian Channel. As small Italian convoys plied these heavily mined waters, Malta once again—as in April and September–December 1941—became important as a base for offensive, antishipping operations and only experienced small-scale nuisance raids conducted by the Regia Aeronautica.

Tunis finally fell on 8 May 1943. In the face of overwhelming Allied naval strength, the Axis made no effort to evacuate their troops by sea. Another consequence of this victory was the arrival in Egypt that month of a direct convoy from Gibraltar—the first since early 1941. The breaking of the Axis blockage of the Sicilian narrows theoretically freed a million tons of shipping, although in the event, escalating military commitments in the Mediterranean "diverted far more merchant ships to that region in autumn and winter 1943 than had been saved by TORCH when it opened the Mediterranean." Only the phenomenal production of American shipyards made this situation possible. For

London, the problem was that because Washington was paying the band, it wanted to call the tune, ultimately frustrating Churchill's ambitions in the Aegean and Balkans.[16]

Operation Husky, the Anglo-American invasion of Sicily in July 1943, ended the need for the WS convoys around Africa and returned the Mediterranean to its pre-war position as the shortcut between India and Britain. This decisive event occurred more than three years into the Mediterranean war and nineteen months after Great Britain first entertained hopes of conducting such an operation as a part of the November 1941 Crusader offensive. Malta provided an important base for Husky, and had the island fallen to an Axis invasion in July 1942, the Allies almost certainly would have needed to retake Malta before attacking Sicily, seriously delaying that operation.

On July 25 while the battle for Sicily still raged, Italy's King Victor Emmanuel III sanctioned Mussolini's arrest, and on 8 September an armistice between Italy and the Allies went into effect. This armistice caught the Regia Marina by surprise—in fact the fleet was raising anchor to attack the Allied beachheads at Salerno—and it was swept up in a series of actions against its erstwhile ally that cost it the battleship *Roma* and several destroyers and smaller vessels. After German forces captured La Maddelena and threatened Taranto, the naval command ordered the battle fleet to concentrate at Malta but to not surrender control to the Allies, which it never did. At the time of the Armistice the Regia Marina had operational six battleships, nine cruisers, eighteen destroyers, thirty-three torpedo boats, seventeen corvettes, and forty-two submarines. The navy had one battleship, four cruisers, nine destroyers, ten torpedo boats, six corvettes, and seventeen submarines under repair.[17]

After Italy's government switched sides the Reich proceeded to collect a surface fleet, mostly ex-Italian or French vessels that the Germans repaired or finished constructing, that deployed at one time or another sixty-three warships displacing more than 500 tons. Germany fought distinct naval campaigns in the Aegean to keep Turkey neutral and deny the Allies access to the Black Sea, and in the Adriatic to protect its flanks and to use that sea as a supply corridor to support its Balkan and Italian armies. In the Aegean campaign fought from September to November 1943 the British attempted to capture the Dodecanese Islands without American support using locally available forces. The result was a fiasco that recalled the worse defeats of 1940 and truly demonstrated the end of Britain's ability to fight independently of its more powerful ally.

In the Western Mediterranean German flotillas of torpedo boats and MTBs, supported by a small Italian fascist navy, fought in the Tyrrhenian Sea to protect the seaward flanks of their armies, transport supplies, and to maintain Spanish imports. The Allies tried to break the stalemated Italian campaign with an amphibious assault at Anzio on 22 January 1944. This operation, however, only yielded an isolated beachhead that tied up shipping.

Giant Allied convoys now traversed the Mediterranean. Between the Italian armistice and December 1944 fifty convoys averaging sixty-nine ships each entered the Middle Sea. The strength of their escorts foiled German submarines, and the last Axis submarine success in the Mediterranean occurred on 18 May 1944.

On 15 August Allied forces landed in the French Riviera. An armada consisting of 9 escort carriers, 5 battleships, 24 cruisers, and 111 destroyers supported this assault. However, even the conquest of southern France did not end Mediterranean naval operations, as fighting continued in the Adriatic and Ligurian Seas up to the war's end. In fact, the last surface action fought in European waters pitted British destroyers against German torpedo boats and a destroyer in the Ligurian Sea on 18 March 1945.[18]

More surface actions were fought in the Mediterranean than anywhere else in the war. Submarine operations were costly for both sides. There were five major Allied, multidivisional amphibious landings and dozens of smaller landings by both Allied and Axis forces. For the first three years, Italy largely realized its naval objectives. Not until the capture of Sicily did the Allies reclaim the ability to navigate the length of the Mediterranean while troop transports and tankers circumnavigated Africa until September 1943. Germany's final campaigns in the Adriatic, Tyrrhenian, and Ligurian seas were instrumental in preventing the Reich from ever facing a threat from the south. This was not the war that Mussolini anticipated when he joined Germany's war of aggression, and it was not the war that Churchill envisioned when he ordered Malta to be held at all costs.

CONCLUSION

[We] have committed the grave mistake of despising the enemy.

William Sims, RN, after the Battle of Coronel

WHY DID THE British Empire fight in the Mediterranean? The usual answer is that it fought to protect its vital interests: Malta and the Middle East. In fact, in August 1940 these interests faced a negligible threat; the fact was that the British Empire had nowhere else to fight. Given the demonstrated power of Germany's war machine and the priorities of the new Churchill administration, which considered "defence" a dirty word, where could the British win victories? The only answers were North Africa, East Africa, and the Mediterranean. The War Cabinet appraisal of September 1940 stated the rationale succinctly: "Owing to the uncertain state of the morale of the Italian people and the lower fighting value of their forces, Italy is the soft spot in the enemy's front and it will be an objective of our offensive policy to increase the pressure on Germany through the elimination of Italy."[1]

Holding Malta and reinforcing it so it could serve as an offensive base was central to the British War Cabinet plan for defeating Italy. The expressed hope was that a series of sharp blows delivered from England by air, from Egypt by land and sea, and ultimately from Malta by air and sea would eventually drive Italy from the war.[2] In fact, this is exactly what happened, but it required thirty-eight months and American participation. During those three years Great Britain deployed a great portion of its military strength in the Mediterranean and Middle East. The Royal Navy maintained, on the average, four battleships, one and a half carriers, and sixteen cruisers in the Mediterranean and Red seas (including Gibraltar). The RAF based between a quarter to a third of its strength there while fifteen British and Empire divisions—generally the best available—fought in the Mediterranean and Middle East.

The price of eliminating Italy proved far greater than Great Britain's decision makers calculated in September 1940. The distances involved in establishing and maintaining a Middle Eastern front increased the resource and shipping requirements exponentially, and the lengthy duration of the Mediterranean closure—from April 1940 to July 1943—made this a long-term burden. London's single-minded emphasis on offensive warfare, even after its original assumptions about Italy's fragile morale repeatedly proved false, represented a case of pursuing secondary goals to the neglect of vital interests. For example, the defense of the Middle Eastern oil fields was a vital interest of the British Empire. Retention of Ceylon and Singapore were vital interests. Control of the North Atlantic sea-lanes was a vital interest. With the Mediterranean passage closed, possession of the Libyan coast and the island of Malta were not matters that affected the British Empire's survival. In the absence of a North African campaign, and as long as Great Britain retained Aden, the Suez Canal was only a cul-de-sac at the end of a long blind alley leading back to India.

In this situation, the loss of Malta or even Suez would not have severely impacted the Empire's global situation. As demonstrated in these pages, Malta served an immediate purpose only so long as the North African shoreline was a battle zone; but even then, Malta's actual contribution to the blockage of Axis North African traffic was minor, except for three short periods. A lack of transportation infrastructure, natural resources, and harbor capacity impeded Axis African operations more than Malta-based submarines and aircraft.

These observations do not deny the island's effectiveness as a base when it was fully supplied and garrisoned strongly or its potential as a springboard for future offensive operations against Italy. They assert, however, that over the course of the two-and-a-half-year siege, the cost of maintaining Malta outweighed the island's overall contributions to the British Empire's war effort. Great Britain shortchanged Singapore's defense and subjected the home population to impoverishment because it allocated to the Mediterranean so much shipping and so many warships that might have been productively employed on the more vital North Atlantic routes. First-class Australian, New Zealand, and Indian divisions were deadlocked fighting a few Italians and Germans in Africa and not protecting Malaya, Burma, and the East Indies.

In defense of the British government's September 1940 decision to launch an offensive war against Italy in Africa and the Mediterranean, the cabinet was fighting the war they were in; they were not preparing to fight a future war. It is difficult to characterize as shortsighted the decision of men engaged in a life-and-death struggle who are suffering daily bombardments of their great cities and who are preparing their nation for invasion.

Italy's decision to enter the war proved ill-advised, but given the situation in June 1940 it would have taken supernatural foresight to realize that. While it is easy to assert that Mussolini would have been wiser to copy General Franco's fence-straddling policy, the much different situation of the two nations—not to mention Mussolini's personal ambitions—did not allow such a strategy. Italy's reasons for fighting included predatory, opportunistic, and legitimate elements, but they were sufficient to win the cooperation of most of the nation's population and sustain its morale through more than three years of war.

To counter Great Britain's Mediterranean offensive, Italy used the vast majority of its navy, most of its air force, and a small portion of its army. Germany deployed three divisions for most of the campaign—less than 2 percent of its army and as much as, depending upon the period, 15 percent of its air force. Sixty-three German submarines served in the Mediterranean, and although Dönitz condemned this deployment as a diversion from the traffic war, the number of boats there was a small fraction of the total available: 22 of 252 in January 1942 and 23 of 399 in January 1943. Moreover, these diversions were partially offset by the contributions of large Italian cruiser submarines to the Atlantic war.[3] Germany's vital interests lay in the European heartland and in Russia. Every day it could deflect its enemy's main effort with tiny forces in Africa or anywhere along the Mediterranean shoreline was a successful day for the Reich.

Italy's hopes for empire may have resided in Africa, but its economic interests lay in the Balkans and the home peninsula. Italy's very entry into the war accomplished, without any other effort, the worst damage it could inflict on the British Empire by forcing the need for the WS convoys with their attendant cost in shipping and time and by providing the British a seductively attractive foe they believed they could defeat. Italy had no vital military need to fight an offensive war in North Africa, but, contrary to pre-war plans, it did so for reasons of politics and prestige.

This analysis downplays political factors. Politically, it may have been impossible for Great Britain to fight its war according to the cold dictates of military necessity. Politically, it may have been impossible to surrender Malta and the Mediterranean to Axis control and focus on greater needs. One can measure, after the fact, the economic cost and military consequences of the Mediterranean campaign and the battle to retain Malta. The political aspects, on the other hand, are less quantifiable and it is easy to predict this consequence or that to suit a particular point of view. However, Great Britain's government survived the political consequences of France's collapse; it survived three desperate evacuations of its armies from the continent; it survived the loss of Singapore; and it survived three years of almost uninterrupted defeat. The British government's political resilience was remarkable.

This leads to the question of the mid-June 1942 operations. Although the war was going poorly, the Allied leadership remained confident of ultimate victory. As originally conceived in Whitehall, the massive replenishment of Malta scheduled for June 1942 would make the island unassailable and—in conjunction with a successful offensive toward Tripoli—provide it with the means to serve as a springboard for further operations against Italy. A strong Malta unsheathed by the capture of Tripoli would permit a rapid thrust from Africa into Sicily, Sardinia, or even the Balkans (if Turkey could be enticed to participate). Such an Imperial triumph would have given weight to Churchill and the cabinet's belief that the United Kingdom was the senior member of the Anglo-American alliance with the right to set policy and direct strategy before a rising flood of American materiel and troops made such a notion ludicrous.

By this time, with nearly three years of wartime experience and having successfully conducted similar operations in 1940, 1941, and 1942, the British commands in London and Cairo were confident that Harpoon and Vigorous would likewise succeed. Instead these operations were failures, and as such they illuminated some seldom-explored corners in both the Italian and British military systems.

The reasons why the mid-June 1942 convoys failed are not to be found in a laundry list of things this admiral or that general failed to do or did poorly. It misses the larger point to say, for example, that Admiral Harwood should not have ordered Rear Admiral Vian to turn back while he waited to hear whether his air strikes had succeeded, or that Captain Hardy should have waited at "Point Z" for Lieutenant Commander Doran's minesweepers to catch up. The British military suffered from systemic problems that contributed to its defeat. The decisions made by Harwood or Hardy were symptoms of these problems, not their cause.

Moreover, there are always two sides to a story. The mid-June 1942 battles are as much the story of Italian success as they are of British failure. In June

1940 the Royal Navy outclassed the Regia Marina in terms of experience, self-confidence, and its war-making skills and techniques. Defeat is a harsh but effective tutor, as long as the loser can absorb the lesson and continue the struggle, which the Regia Marina did after Taranto, Matapan, and the Beta Convoy disaster. The results of the mid-June battles suggest that the Regia Marina had, since 1940, evolved faster than the Royal Navy and was, by mid-1942, demonstrating skills on a par with or even superior to its enemy.

COMPARISONS

There are several areas where comparisons between British and Italian performance illustrate these points.

Command and Planning

British plans were rapidly drafted by operational officers, not by specialized staff. Contingency plans were inadequate or nonexistent, as demonstrated by the minefield disaster that befell the Harpoon convoy when it arrived at Malta behind schedule. One history noted that "The Royal Navy, Army and R.A.F. planned in unison but retained individual operational control."[4] Operationally, this structure bred situations where one service acted to meet their priorities and not the priorities of their sister service, or the larger mission. For example, the reallocation of fighter escorts to a ground support mission compromised the crucially important air strike against the Italian battleships on the morning of 15 June. The diversion of four antiaircraft destroyers to accompany a damaged cruiser rather than protect the convoy facing a day of air attacks and perhaps a surface attack as well demonstrates confused priorities. The British lacked a supreme command to balance the interests of the navy, air force, and army in a fast-moving, tactical situation. The Italian services planned separately, but their command system was more hierarchical with Comando Supremo overseeing and coordinating the actions of Supermarina and Superaereo. The Italians had a reaction plan and implemented it in a timely fashion.

Intelligence

Given Italy's hand-to-mouth situation with its fuel oil supplies, the timing of the battle fleet's sortie against the Vigorous Convoy was critical. If the convoys had been detected late—as happened so often in the past—or if one of the deceptions the British practiced to disguise their true intentions had succeeded, one or both of the convoys would have won through. The various Italian headquarters correctly evaluated their signals and human intelligence and made the right decisions at the proper time. Italy's ability to routinely intercept and rapidly decipher British radio traffic—particularly from reconnaissance aircraft—gave Supermarina an immediate picture of what the enemy knew and facilitated its operations. The British, on the other hand, allowed poorly supported assumptions to override concrete intelligence and thus permitted a surface task force to surprise a convoy. They failed to properly gauge their enemies' strength and capabilities. Ultra did not offset these failures as, unlike Italian decrypts, it provided little intelligence of direct operational use during these battles.

Communications

Supermarina was practiced in its supervision of operations, and, after resolving a series of problems during the first year of war, it had an effective system run by Admiral Sansonetti and a competent staff. Tactical communications were accomplished by short-range, VHF voice radio using a system similar to the U.S. Navy's "Talk-Between-Ships" (TBS). The navy had developed strict procedures regulating this system's use. The British generally carried out major operations by issuing orders and then allowing the senior officer afloat to carry out those orders as he determined best. During the May 1941 operations off Crete Admiral Cunningham had exercised command from Alexandria with poor results due to delays receiving and relaying information. Vigorous was the next occasion when the fleet's commander in chief attempted to follow the Italian model of onshore management. It failed for the same reasons it had failed before: communication breakdowns. The lack of a practiced staff and a system to coordinate the flow of information between Malta, Alexandria, and the convoys, not to mention between services, was deadly. Ship-to-ship communications were largely conducted with flags due to a lack of effective procedures regulating the use of potentially more efficient short-range radios. The number of ships involved in the convoy operations and volume of traffic they generated overwhelmed the system in times of stress.

Experience

The Italian officers and crew were veterans of many operations, and they fought in stable formations. Admiral Iachino had led or participated in nearly a dozen fleet operations against the British. Many of the Allied vessels supporting Harpoon had been in service for months, not years. Acting Admiral Harwood was commanding his first major operation. Acting Captain Hardy was leading his first independent command. The commander of Harpoon's fleet destroyers had never experienced surface combat. The crews were diluted and the formations ad hoc. The British deployed rookie carrier pilots flying inferior machines; they conducted critical strikes with pilots who had never dropped a torpedo in action. These men fought bravely and often with great enthusiasm, but they did not always fight effectively.

Aerial-Naval Cooperation

This was generally a weakness in Italian operations, and during the mid-June operations problems remained. Nonetheless strategically, if not tactically, the coordination between air and surface forces was adequate. The quality and accuracy of aerial reconnaissance was consistently better than in past operations. The impact that air forces had against a convoy facing surface action was clearly demonstrated by comparing the different experience of Harpoon and Pedestal after they passed the Sicilian narrows. Pedestal was not delayed nor were its escorts distracted by major surface forces, and it delivered proportionally more transports to Malta than did Harpoon, which faced Da Zara's cruisers. The British also suffered from cooperation breakdowns between the RAF and the Royal Navy. Admiral Vian was particularly harsh in his judgment of air cooperation.

Intangibles

Finally, there were the intangibles. The British fought the battle as victims of their own propaganda regarding the fighting qualities of the Italian armed forces. Harwood's plan relied upon the Italian fleet to react either too soon or too late. When he received favorable (and inaccurate) reports from bombers and submarines, he expected the Italian fleet to withdraw "on past form." Curteis did not reinforce Force X because, judging from past encounters, he believed a 4-inch cruiser and five fleet destroyers were enough to deter a pair of enemy 6-inch cruisers and five destroyers.

THE SUM OF THEIR ACTIONS

In this text, Acting Admiral Harwood is described as competent. Rear Admiral Vian and Vice Admiral Curteis were experienced officers who knew their jobs. Yet the sum of the actions of these skilled, courageous, and experienced professionals can be described as amateur in that the details required to improve the odds of a successful operation were rushed or not considered. For example, in his postwar correspondence Vian admitted that he let his disapproval of the operation influence his conduct. The efforts of admirals to shift blame to captains and captains to point the finger at lieutenant commanders, as in the mining disaster off Malta, were unprofessional. At sea refueling was not practiced sufficiently in advance to ensure properly working equipment and good results in action. The attentive reader may compile a long list of similar examples. On the Italian side Iachino and Da Zara demonstrated dogged determination and a sense that they had the advantage and could not let their opportunity pass.

Overall, the Axis response to the mid-June operations was competent rather than brilliant. They made fewer mistakes than the British. They persisted, and the reasonable risks taken by the fleet and air force were rewarded. The Italians, with aid from the Germans, did what was necessary to win. However, the failure of Mussolini and Comando Supremo to grasp the opportunity to completely defeat the British mid-August operation by recalling the cruiser surface strike force in the face of a perceived risk generated by inaccurate intelligence demonstrates how fragile the margin of victory can be and how quickly a model for success can be disregarded.

Appendix

CONVERSIONS

1 nautical mile = 2,205 yards, 1,852 meters, or 1.151 statute miles

1 knot = 1.852 km/hour or 1.151 statue mile/hour

1 meter = 1.094 yards

1 yard = 0.9144 meters

1 centimeter = 0.3937 inches

1 inch = 2.54 centimeters

1 kilogram = 2.205 pounds

1 pound = 0.4536 kilograms

1 tonne = .9842 long tons

1 long ton = 1.016 tonnes

ABBREVIATIONS

General

AA	anti-aircraft
AP	armor-piercing
ASV	air surface-vessel (radar)
ASW	antisubmarine warfare
BR	British
Capt.	Captain
Cdr.	Commander
CS	cruiser squadron
DC	depth charge
DEMS	defensively equipped merchant ship
DP	dual-purpose
F	flagship
FAA	Fleet Air Arm
Flot.	flotilla
GE	German
GK	Greek
GRT	gross registered tons
HA	high-angle
HE	high-explosive (or high effect)
LA	low-angle
OBS	*Oberbefehlshaber Süd*
PO	Polish
RAF	Royal Air Force
RN	Royal Navy
SA	South African
SLC	*Siluro a Lenta Corsa*
TBS	talk between ships
UP	unguided projectile
US	United States
USN	United States Navy
VHF	very high frequency

Ship Types

AMC	armed merchant cruiser
AO	oiler
BB	battleship
BC	battle cruiser
BM	monitor
CA	heavy cruiser
CB	coastal battleship (obsolete)

CL	light cruiser
CLA	antiaircraft light cruiser
CM	minelayer (large)
CV	aircraft carrier
CVE	escort carrier
DD	destroyer
DE	destroyer escort or "Hunt" type destroyer
DC	corvette
GB	gunboat
MAS	Italian motor torpedo boat (*motoscafi armati siluranti* or *motoscafi anti sommergibili*)
MFP	*marinefährprahm* (German armed barge or "F" lighter)
ML	motor launch
MMS	motor minesweeper
MS	minesweeper (British) or *motosiluranti* (large Italian MTB)
MTB	motor torpedo boat
O	old
PB	patrol boat
RS	rescue ship
S-boat	*schnellboot* (German motor torpedo boat or "E" boat)
SC	submarine chaser
SS	submarine
TB	torpedo boat
TS	target ship
U-boat	*unterseeboot* (German submarine)
UJ-boat	*unterseebootsjäger* (German submarine chaser)
V-boat	*vorpostenboot* (German patrol boat)

Aircraft Types

DB	dive bomber
F	fighter
FB	fighter-bomber
HB	heavy bomber
LB	level bomber

Table Appendix. Malta Convoys and Independent Sailings

Operation Name — Convoy	Date Arrived	Transports	Loss	From
Hats—MF2	2-Sep-40	3	1 damaged	East
MF3	11-Oct-40	4	0	East
MW3	10-Nov-40	5	0	East
MW4	26-Nov-40	4	0	East
Collar	26-Nov-40	2	0	West
MW5A & 5B	20-Dec-40	7	0	East
MW5.5	10-Jan-41	2	0	East
Excess	11-Jan-41	1	0	West
MW6	23-Mar-41	4	0	East
MD2	21-Apr-41	1	0	East
Temple (SS)	28-Apr-41 (sailed)	1	1 sunk	West
MW7	9-May-41	6	0	East
Substance—GM1	24-Jul-41	6	1 damaged	West
Propeller (SS)	19-Sep-41	1		West
Halbard—GM2	28-Sep-41	9	1 sunk	West
Astrologer (SS)	11/12 Nov (sailed)	2	2 sunk	West
MF1	18-Dec-41	1	0	East
MF2	8-Jan-42	1	0	East
MF3—MW8/8A	19-Jan-42	4	1 sunk	East
MF4	27-Jan-42	1	0	East
MF5—MW9	12-Feb-42 (sailed)	3	2 sunk, 1 damaged and turned back	East
MG1—MW10	23-Mar-42	4	2 sunk, 1 damaged	East
Vigorous—MW11	11-Jun-42 (sailed)	11	2 sunk, 3 damaged, 9 turned back	East
Harpoon—GM4	11-Jun-42	5	3 sunk, 1 damaged	West
Pedestal	10-Aug-42	14	9 sunk, 3 damaged	West
Independent (SS)	1-Nov-42	1	0	East
Crupper (SS)	8-Nov-42 (sailed)	2	2 captured	West
Stoneage—MW13	20-Nov-42	4	0	East
Portcullis—MW14	5-Dec-42	5	0	East
MW15	10-Dec-42	2	0	East
MW16	14-Dec-42	3	0	East
MW17	21-Dec-42	2	0	East
MW18	31-Dec-42	2	0	East

Notes: SS indicates single ship(s) sailing unescorted. Operation Excess only includes the portion of the operation bound for Malta.

THE MEDITERRANEAN TRAFFIC WAR 1940–43

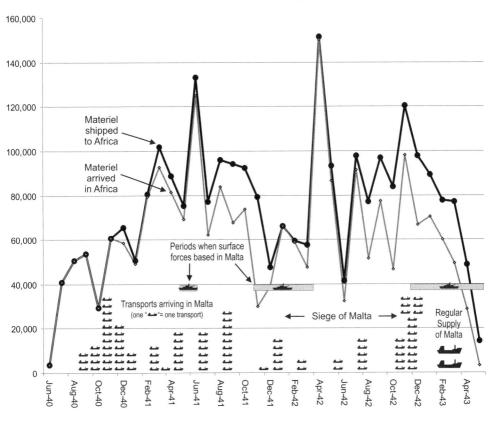

Notes

PREFACE

1. Mussolini, *My Rise and Fall,* 59.

2. Moses, *At All Costs,* 304. Roskill, *The War at Sea,* Vol. 2, 71. Woodman, *Malta Convoys,* 347. Ireland, *The War in the Mediterranean,* 135. Flooding in one vessel reduced the amount of supplies delivered to 13,500 tons.

1. THE VITAL SEA

1. Roskill, *War at Sea,* Vol. 1, 271. He gives distance in statute miles. The net gain in nautical miles is 17,400 miles.

2. Lord (Maurice) Hankey observed in his diary that in speaking to the House of Lords he "would be addressing most of the members of the Fifth Column." Hastings, *Winston's War,* 32.

3. Budden, "Defending the Indefensible?" 453.

4. Simpson, *Cunningham Papers,* Vol. 1, 75.

5. Quotes from War Cabinet W. P. (40) 362, September 4, 1940, 39, 5, and 46. Hastings, *Winston's War,* 104. Churchill, *Their Finest Hour,* 390, also identifies inferior "fighting values" of the Italian fleet as a reason to undertake a naval offensive in the Mediterranean.

6. Simpson, *Cunningham Papers,* Vol. 1, 76. Schreiber, et al., *Germany and the Second World War,* Vol. III, 128.

7. Smith, *Conflict over Convoys,* 1. Coakley, *Global Logistics and Strategy,* 47.

8. Hastings, *Winston's War,* 102.

9. Salerno, *Vital Crossroads,* 205.

10. See Harrison, *The Economics of World War II,* 186. *Foreign Relations,* 1940, Volume II, 694.

11. Knox, *Mussolini Unleashed,* 102. Ciano, *Diaries,* 236.

12. Gooch, *Mussolini and his Generals,* 487.

13. *Fuehrer Conferences on Naval Affairs,* 134. Schreiber, et al., *Germany and the Second World War,* Vol. III, 3.

14. Schreiber, et al., *Germany and the Second World War,* Vol. III, 146.

15. Ibid., 151. Payne, *Franco and Hitler,* 72.

2. MALTA AND THE MEDITERRANEAN WAR TO 1942

1. Allied intentions are stated in a series of letters to the Admiralty written between 6 and 9 June. See Simpson, *Cunningham Papers,* Vol. 1, 48–51; also Auphan and Mordal, *The French Navy in World War II,* 98. Iachino, *Tramonto di una grande marina,* 155, summarizes Italian plans.

2. *Foreign Relations,* 1940, Vol. III, 38.

3. Cernuschi, *Fecero tutti il loro dovere,* 91–93. See Sullivan, "Downfall of the Regia Aeronautica," for a discussion of the poor interservice cooperation and its impact on Italy's war effort.

4. See Roskill, *Churchill and the Admirals,* 150, and Barnett, *Engage the Enemy More Closely,* 211–12.

5. Austin, *Churchill and Malta,* 84.

6. Schreiber, et al., *Germany and the Second World War,* Vol. III, 130. Austin, *Malta and Churchill,* 84.

7. Willmott, *The Last Century of Sea Power,* Vol. 2, 226.

8. The Action off Calabria is cited in nearly every English-language account as having established the Royal Navy's "moral ascendency" over the Regia Marina. For a discussion of this belief and its association with wartime propaganda, see O'Hara, "Action off Calabria," *Warship,* 2008.

9. Cab. W. P. (40) 330, August 22, 1940. Page, ed., *Royal Navy and the Mediterranean,* Vol. I, 100.

10. Fioravanzo, USMM, Vol. IV, *Le azioni navali,* 187.

11. Simpson, *Cunningham Papers,* Vol. 1, 143. Simpson, *Somerville Papers,* 139.

12. See O'Hara, *Struggle for the Middle Sea,* 57–61.

13. *Foreign Relations,* 1940, Volume III, 16. Bauer, *World War II,* 129.

14. Bradagin, *Italian Navy in World War II,* 15. Austin, *Churchill and Malta's War,* 73.

15. "The morale of the Italian navy is uncertain and might deteriorate rapidly if we could engage it successfully." Cab. W. P. (40) 27; also, 5, 24, 45.

16. Austin, *Malta and Churchill,* 91.

17. Rohwer, *Allied Submarine Attacks,* 126–29, and Kemp, *The Admiralty Regrets,* 121–36. Padfield, *War beneath the Sea,* 331, discusses why British submarines were so unsuccessful. For air strengths see Shores, et al., *Malta: The Hurricane Years,* 396, and Playfair, *Mediterranean and the Middle East,* Vol. I, 312.

18. For examples see Smith, *Pedestal,* 18; Macintyre, *Battle for the Mediterranean,* 44–45; Woodman, *Malta Convoys,* 108, and Ruge, *Der Seekrieg,* 146–48. Quote: *Fuehrer Conferences,* 155.

19. Sullivan, "Downfall of the Regia Aeronautica," 146.

20. Iachino was a prolific author. In addition to the works cited herein, he wrote books about Matapan, the battles of First and Second Sirte, and other operations of the naval war.

21. Simpson, *Cunningham Papers*, Vol. 1, 327. Page, ed., *The Royal Navy and the Mediterranean*, Vol. 2, 68.

22. Submarines damaged several other vessels. See Rohwer, *Allied Submarine Attacks*, 131–32; Hezlet, *Submarine Operations*, Patrolgram 7 and Chapter 9; and Shores, *Malta: The Hurricane Years*, 399. Also Marcon, "Malta difesa," 10. For ammunition expenditures, see Austin, *Churchill and Malta's War*, 84.

23. Iachino, *Tramonto di una grande marina*, 245.

24. Van Creveld, *Supplying War*, 183.

25. Woodman, *Malta Convoys*, 168. Simpson, *Somerville Papers*, 262, 265.

26. Churchill, *The Grand Alliance*, 223.

27. Page, ed., *The Royal Navy and the Mediterranean*, Vol. 2, 132. Austin, *Churchill and Malta's War*, 89.

28. Playfair, *Mediterranean and the Middle East*, Vol. II, 58. Austin, *Churchill and Malta's War*, 110.

29. USMM, Vol. I, *Dati statistici*, 126.

30. Gwyer and Butler, *Grand Strategy*, Vol. III, 6. Howarth and Law, *Battle of the Atlantic*, 38.

31. Gwyer and Butler, *Grand Strategy*, Vol. III, 6.

32. Hinsley, et al., *British Intelligence*, Vol. 2, 283–84.

33. Ibid., 277. Liddell Hart, *History of the Second World War*, 182. Gwyer and Butler, *Grand Strategy*, Vol. III, 405. Smith, *Conflict over Convoys*, 67–68.

34. Hezlet, *Submarine Operations*, Chapter 11. Rohwer, *Allied Submarine Attacks*, 138–41. USMM, Vol. I, *Dati statistici*, 232–33. Playfair, *Mediterranean and the Middle East*, Vol. II, 281. Submarine attacks include gun as well as torpedo actions. Losses only consider vessels displacing more than 500 tons.

35. *MAS 213* torpedoed the light cruiser *Capetown* on 8 April 1941 off Massawa in the Red Sea.

36. Austin, *Churchill and Malta's War*, 115.

37. Hezlet, *Submarine Operations*, Chapter 11. Rohwer, *Allied Submarine Attacks*, 141–42. USMM, Vol. I, *Dati statistici*, 232–33. Aircraft also sank the hospital ship *California* (13,060 GRT).

38. Iachino, *Operazione mezzo giugno*, 184.

39. See Playfair, *Mediterranean and the Middle East*, Vol. II, 276.

40. Hezlet, *Submarine Operations*, Chapter 11. Rohwer, *Allied Submarine Attacks*, 143–44. USMM, Vol. I, *Dati statistici*, 232–33, and Vol. III, *Navi perdute*, 40–42. Malta-based bombers also sank the French freighter *Monselet*.

41. Schreiber, et al., *Germany in the Second World War*, Vol. III, 711.

42. Greene and Massignani, *Rommel's North African Campaign*, 95.

43. Hazlet, *Submarine Operations*, Patrolgram 11. Rohwer, *Allied Submarine Attacks*, 144–46. USMM, Vol. I, *Dati statistici*, 232–33, and Vol. III, *Navi perdute*, 42–43. Playfair, *Mediterranean and the Middle East*, Vol. II, 281.

44. Austin, *Churchill and Malta's War*, 136 and 138.

45. Hinsley, et al., *British Intelligence*, Vol. 2, 284.

46. See Cocchia, USMM, Vol. VII, *La difesa del traffico*, 368–73.

47. *Fuehrer Conferences*, 243. Shores, et al., *Malta: The Hurricane Years*, 399.

48. See O'Hara, *Struggle for the Middle Sea*, 143–47, for an account of this action.

49. Woodman, *Malta Convoys*, 250.

50. Simpson, *Cunningham Papers*, Vol. 1, 519.

51. Hazlet, *Submarine Operations*, Chapter 11. Rohwer, *Allied Submarine Attacks*, 144–46. USMM, Vol. I, *Dati statistici*, 232–33, and Vol. III, *Navi perdute*, 44–45.

52. In November and December Italian submarines delivered to Bardia and Derna 535 tons of gasoline and 21 tons of munitions. See Cocchia, USMM, Vol. VII, *La difesa del traffico*, 475–81.

53. Hinsley et al., *British Intelligence*, Vol. 2, 324. Playfair, *Mediterranean and the Middle East*, Vol. III, 96.

54. Hezlet, *Submarine Operations*, Chapter 11. Rohwer, *Allied Submarine Attacks*, 148–50. USMM, Vol. I, *Dati statistici*, 232–33, and Vol. VII, *La difesa del traffico*, 478–85.

55. Playfair, *Mediterranean and the Middle East*, Vol. II, 281. USMM, Vol. I, *Dati statistici*, 126. Austin, *Churchill and Malta's War*, 126 and 144.

56. Bennett and Bennett, *Hitler's Admirals*, 119–20. Gwyer and Butler, *Grand Strategy*, Vol. III, 18.

57. Churchill, *Grand Alliance*, 539.

3. THE MEDITERRANEAN WAR JANUARY TO MAY 1942

1. Deakin, *Brutal Friendship*, 16–17. Ciano, *Diaries*, 417.

2. Churchill, *Grand Alliance*, 621. Operation Gymnast was a plan to "send aid" in the form of an armored division, three infantry divisions, and a strong air contingent to French North Africa at short notice. Super-Gymnast included an American component. It evolved into Operation Torch.

3. This account is based upon Supermarina, "Convegno italo-tedesco di Garmisch, relazione sommaria."

4. Austin, *Churchill and Malta's War*, 147. Biagini and Frattolillo, *Diario Storico del Comando Supremo*, Vol. VI, 467.

5. Playfair, *Mediterranean and the Middle East*, Vol. 3, 156.

6. Jellison, *Besieged*, 150. Hezlet, *Submarine Operations*, Chapter 14.

7. Hinsley, et al., *British Intelligence*, Vol. 2, 330. Hezlet, *Submarine Operations*, Chapter 14. Rohwer, *Allied Submarine Attacks*, 150–51. USMM, Vol. III, *Navi perdute*, 48–49.

8. USMM, Vol. I, *Dati statistici*, 128.

9. Gwyer and Butler, *Grand Strategy*, Vol. III, 439. The British used the word "administration" in the same sense that the Americans used the word "logistics."

10. See Santoni and Mattesini, *La partecipazione tedesca*, 156–58.

11. Cull and Galea, *Spitfires over Malta*, 10.

12. Hezlet, *Submarine Operations*, Chapter 14. Rohwer, *Allied Submarine Attacks*, 152–53. USMM, Vol. III, *Navi perdute*, 48–49. For traffic statistics see Cocchia, USMM, Vol. VII, *La difesa del traffico*, 398–403, and Vol. I, *Dati statistici*, 128.

13. See Jordan, *Merchant Fleets*, 447. Rohwer, *Chronology*, 150, misidentifies *Cuma* as displacing 8,260 tons. There was an Italian *Cuma* (6,463 GRT) that was mined on 18 October 1940. USMM, Vol. III, *Navi perdute*, 24.

14. Vian, *Action This Day*, 84.

15. Supermarina, "Invio di un convoglio inglese a Malta. 20–23 Marzo 1942." Hinsley, et al., *British Intelligence*, Vol. 2, 347.

16. ADM 234/353, *Malta Convoys 1942*, 5. Playfair, *Mediterranean and the Middle East*, Vol. 3, 164.

17. ADM 234/353, *Malta Convoys 1942*, 5. Cunningham, *A Sailor's Odyssey*, 451. Simpson, *Cunningham Papers*, Vol. I, 584.

18. Fioravanzo, USMM, Vol. V, *Le azioni navali*, 202.

19. Ibid., 204 fn.

20. Santoni and Mattesini, *La partecipazione tedesca*, 168. ADM 235/324, *Malta Convoys 1942*, 6.

21. Supermarina, "Relazione riassuntiva sulla missione del 22 e 23 marzo 1942."

22. ADM 235/324, *Malta Convoys 1942*, 6. Fioravanzo, USMM, Vol. V, *Le azioni navali*, 204.

23. London Gazette, "Battle of Sirte," 4375. Vian, *Action This Day*, 90. Roskill, *War at Sea*, Vol. 2, 53.

24. ADM 234/325, *Malta Convoys 1942*, 9.

25. Supermarina, "Relazione riassuntiva sulla missione del 22 e 23 marzo 1942."

26. Ibid.

27. Thompson, *War at Sea*, 184.

28. Winton, ed., *War at Sea*, 224.

29. Supermarina, "Relazione riassuntiva sulla missione del 22 e 23 Marzo 1942."

30. Santoni and Mattesini, *La partecipazione tedesca*, 169.

31. Bartimeus, *East of Malta*, 199. Jellison, *Besieged*, 163. Whelan, *Malta Airman*, 23.

32. Cunningham, *A Sailor's Odyssey*, 454.

33. Supermarina, "Considerazioni," April 9, 1942.

34. Hezlet, *Submarine Operations*, Chapter 14. Rohwer, *Allied Submarine Attacks*, 153–54. USMM, Vol. III, *Navi perdute*, 49–50, and Vol. VII, *La difesa del traffico*, 404–409. The other ship lost to an air attack, the German transport *Achaia* (1,778 GRT), actually hit a mine while avoiding an FAA Albacore's torpedo.

35. USMM, Vol. I, *Dati statistici*, 128 and 234.

36. Austin, *Churchill and Malta*, 116. Gwyer and Butler, *Grand Strategy*, Vol. III, 450 and 451. Austin, *Churchill and Malta's War*, 152.

37. Simpson, *Cunningham Papers*, Vol. I, 584. Gwyer and Butler, *Grand Strategy*, Vol. III, 459.

38. Richards and Saunders, *The Fight Avails*, 193–94. Playfair, *Mediterranean and the Middle East*, Vol. 3, 179. Jellison, *Besieged*, 167.

39. Simpson, *Cunningham Papers*, Vol. 1, 582. Roskill, *Churchill and the Admirals*, 188. Stephen, *Fighting Admirals*, 156–57.

40. Playfair, *Mediterranean and the Middle East,* Vol. 3, 181 and 186.

41. Many histories state that the award of the cross led to an "upsurge of loyalty to the Crown." Reportedly graffiti also appeared on the walls of burned-out buildings: *"Hobz, mux George Cross."* Bread, not George Cross. Jellison, *Besieged,* 213–14 and 182. Quote, Austin, *Churchill and Malta's War,* 182.

42. Cull and Galea, *Spitfires over Malta,* 66. Richards and Saunders, *The Fight Avails,* 194. Jellison, *Besieged,* 173.

43. Playfair, *Mediterranean and the Middle East,* Vol. 3, 183.

44. Ibid., 188. Cull and Galea, *Spitfires over Malta,* 105.

45. Ibid., 117.

46. Ansel, *Hitler and the Middle Sea,* 479. Boog, et al., *Germany and the Second World War,* Vol. VI, 656–57.

47. Kesselring, *Kesselring,* 144. Ciano, *Diaries,* 478.

48. See Greene and Massignani, *Naval War in the Mediterranean,* 226–29.

49. Wilt, *War from the Top,* 188. Boog, et al., *Germany and the Second World War,* Vol. VI, 658.

50. Cocchia, USMM, Vol. VII, *La difesa del traffico,* 410–19.

51. Hinsley, et al., *British Intelligence,* Vol. 2, 348–49. Hezlet, *Submarine Operations,* Chapter 14. Rohwer, *Allied Submarine Attacks,* 155–56. USMM, Vol. III, *Navi perdute,* 50–51; *Dati statistici,* 128.

52. Cocchia, USMM, Vol. VII, *La difesa del traffico,* 420–28.

53. Hezlet, *Submarine Operations,* Chapter 14. Rohwer, *Allied Submarine Attacks,* 157–58. USMM, Vol. III, *Navi perdute,* 50–51; *Dati statistici,* 128. Quotes from Fioravanzo, USMM, Vol. V, *Le azioni navali,* 260. Hezlet, *Submarine Operations,* Chapter 14.

54. Spertini and Bagnasco, *Mezzi d'assalto,* 51.

55. Roskill, *War at Sea,* Vol. 2, 60.

56. Playfair, *Mediterranean and the Middle East,* Vol. 3, 203. Hinsley, et al., *British Intelligence,* Vol. 2, 362.

57. Ibid., 366.

58. *Fuehrer Conferences,* 285.

4. GLOBAL SNAPSHOT—JUNE 1942

1. Supermarina, "L'obiettivo strategico principale," March 10, 1942.

2. Hastings, *Winston's War,* 217.

3. Ellis, *World War II,* 175–78.

4. Lyon, "The British Order of Battle," in Howarth and Law, *The Battle of the Atlantic,* 273.

5. See Hague, *The Allied Convoy System;* www.convoyweb.org.uk; and Willmott, *The Last Century of Sea Power,* Vol. 2, 86.

6. Dear, ed., *Oxford Companion to World War II,* 1067.

7. Ibid., 1070.

8. Roskill, *War at Sea,* Vol. 2, 78.

9. Simpson, *Somerville Papers,* 355.

10. Hastings, *Winston's War*, 202.

11. Bennett and Bennett, *Hitler's Admirals*, 153.

5. OPERATION VIGOROUS

1. Playfair, *Mediterranean and the Middle East*, Vol. 3, 299.

2. RAF, *RAF Review*, 65.

3. Playfair, *Mediterranean and the Middle East*, Vol. 3, 299–300; Richards and Saunders, *The Fight Avails*, 204.

4. For air strengths see Santoro, *L'aeronautica italiana*, Vol. II, 378, and Fioravanzo, USMM, Vol. V, *Le azioni navali*, 272–73.

5. Roskill, *Churchill and the Admirals*, 189. Hastings, *Winston's War*, 258. Austin, *Churchill and Malta*, 77. Kennedy, *The Business of War*, 164.

6. Roskill, *Churchill and the Admirals*, 30. Stevens, *The Fighting Admirals*, 80. Cunningham felt he had a good staff. In his 15 March 1942 response to the news of his reassignment, he stated, "With my strong staff team behind him he [his temporary replacement] won't go far wrong." Simpson, *Cunningham Papers*, Vol. 1, 583.

7. ADM 199/1244, "M.V. Potaro 18th June, 1942," 1.

8. Ibid., "Commander in Chief, Report," 2. For the commando actions see Messenger, *Middle East Commandos*, 113, and Santoni and Mattesini, *La partecipazione tedesca*, 205.

9. ADM 234/353, *Malta Convoys 1942*, 26. Hezlet, *Submarine Operations*, Patrolgram 13.

10. Simpson, *Somerville Papers*, 421.

11. Stephens, *Fighting Admirals*, 152. Royal Navy Flag Officers, http://www.admirals .org.uk/admirals/fleet/vianpl.php. Barnett, *Engage the Enemy*, 511.

12. ADM 199/1244, "Operation Vigorous Plans Launch and Marshal."

13. Capo di Stato Maggiore della Regia Marina, "Una lettera da consegnare personalmente al Grande Ammiraglio RAEDER," 23 May, 1942; Supermarina, "Situazione della nafta," June 8, 1942.

14. SIS, "Intercettazioni estere e informazioni, No. 6," 21821 and 21878. Hinsley, et al., *British Intelligence*, Vol. 2, 347.

15. Supermarina, "Promemoria N. 46," Comando Supremo, Appunto, June 12, 1942.

16. Santoni and Mattesini, *La partecipazione tedesca*, 207. ADM 199/1244, "Report of Proceedings of Coventry," 1.

17. ADM 199/1244, "Report of Proceedings Fourteenth Destroyer Flotilla," 1.

18. Ibid., "Commander in Chief, Report," 2; "Operational Orders, 15th C.S.," 12.

19. Ibid., "S.S. *Bhutan* Report of Proceedings."

20. Santoni and Mattesini, *La partecipazione tedesca*, 207. ADM 199/1244, "Report of Proceedings Fourteenth Destroyer Flotilla," 2; "S.S. Bhutan Report of Proceedings."

21. ADM 199/1244, "Report, Rear Admiral Commanding 15th C. S.," 2. Radtke, *Kampfgeschwader 54*, 122.

22. Pugsley, *Destroyer Man*, 117. ADM 199/1244, 4th Cruiser Squadron, "Report of Proceedings," 1.

23. ADM 199/1244, "Air Co-operation," 1.

24. Ibid., "Tetcott, Report of a Bombing Attack," 1. ADM 234/353, *Malta Convoys 1942,* 28. Santoni, *La partecipazione tedesca,* 207. See also Taghon, *Die Geschichte des Lehrge- schwader,* 1. Band 2, 29–31.

25. Woodman, *Malta Convoys,* 355. ADM 199/1244, "Tetcott, Report of a Bombing At- tack," 1.

26. Supermarina, "Conversazioni telefoniche del giorno 14 giugno 1942."

27. Pugsley, *Destroyer Man,* 119. Radtke, *Kampfgeschwader 54,* 122.

28. ADM 199/1244, "Air Co-operation," 4. *People's War,* http://www.bbc.co.uk /ww2peopleswar/stories/42/a7819842.shtml.

29. ADM 199/1244, "Rescue of Survivors from S.S. Bhutan," 2; "Operational Orders 15th C.S.," 12.

30. Radtke, *Kampfgeschwader 54,* 123.

31. Archivio dell'Ufficio Storico dell'Aeronautica Militare, "Relazione operative Co- mando del 106° Gruppo B.T"; ibid., "Relazione operative Comando del 41° Gruppo Sil."

32. ADM 199/1244, "Casualties Inflicted on Enemy Aircraft by Gunfire," 1.

33. Pugsley, *Destroyer Man,* 119.

34. ADM 199/1244, "Birmingham, Report of Operations"; "Analysis of Air Attacks," 3. Frank, *German S-Boats in Action,* 80. Quote from ADM 199/1244, "Report, Rear Admiral Commanding 15th C. S.," 4.

35. Fioravanzo, USMM, Vol. V, *Le azioni navali,* 328. ADM 199/1244, "Report, Rear Admiral Commanding 15th C. S.," 4.

36. ADM 199/1244, "Operational Orders 15th C.S.," 9. Iachino, *Operazione mezzo giugno,* 286. Fioravanzo, USMM, Vol. V, *Le azioni navali,* 341.

37. ADM 199/1244, "Commander in Chief, Report," 2.

38. Ibid., "Newcastle Report," 2.

39. Ibid., "Loss of *Hasty,*" 1.

40. Ibid., "4th Cruiser Squadron, Report of Proceedings," 2.

41. Fioravanzo, USMM, Vol. V, *Le azioni navali,* 332.

42. ADM 199/1244, "Commander in Chief, Report," 4.

43. According to their account cited in Hanable, *Case Studies,* 61. Fioravanzo, USMM, Vol. V, *Le azioni navali,* 335, has all five aircraft dropping their torpedoes from the star- board side.

44. Fioravanzo, USMM, Vol. V, *Le azioni navali,* 338. Hanable, *Case Studies,* 61. One of the Beauforts in the last group reported that he dropped his torpedo at *Trento* but missed because he did not know the cruiser had lost so much way.

45. Fioravanzo, USMM, Vol. V, *Le azioni navali,* 340.

46. Giorgerini and Nani, *Gli incrociatori italiani,* 467.

47. Fioravanzo, USMM, Vol. V, *Le azioni navali,* 341.

48. ADM 199/1244, "Commander in Chief, Report," 4.

49. The U.S. aircraft came from a group of thirteen B-24Ds that bombed Ploesti on 11 June, the first strategic mission undertaken by the USAAF in Europe. They caused neg- ligible damage and lost six bombers (including four interned in Turkey). The other two

belonged to 160 Squadron RAF. One of the RAF craft had to turn back before contact, leaving only eight planes to conduct the raid. See Craven and Cate, eds., *Army Air Forces in World War II,* Vol. II, 12.

50. SIS, "Intercettazioni estere e informazioni, No. 7," 22339.

51. Fioravanzo, USMM, Vol. V, *Le azioni navali,* 342.

52. Ibid., 344.

53. Ibid., 345.

54. See Hanable, *Case Studies,* 61.

55. Fioravanzo, USMM, Vol. V, *Le azioni navali,* 350.

56. ADM 199/1244, "Operation Vigorous Report, Narrative," 6.

57. ADM 234/353, *Malta Convoys 1942,* 33. ADM 199/1244, "Commander in Chief, Report," 5. "On past form it seemed unlikely that the enemy would continue southward."

58. Fioravanzo, USMM, Vol. V, *Le azioni navali,* 352.

59. ADM 234/353, *Malta Convoys 1942,* 33. ADM 199/1244, "Report, Rear Admiral Commanding 15th C. S.," 6.

60. Iachino, *Operazione mezzo giugno,* 291.

61. SIS, "Intercettazioni estere e informazioni, No. 7," 22387.

62. Fioravanzo, USMM, Vol. V, *Le azioni navali,* 359.

63. ADM 199/1244, "Loss of Airedale," 1.

64. Santoni and Mattesini, *La partecipazione tedesca,* 212.

65. ADM 234/353, *Malta Convoys 1942,* 33–34.

66. "Diari di guerra, 5ª Squadra," 15 June 1942. ADM 199/1244, "Report of Loss of H.M.A.S. *Nestor,*" 1; "Analysis of Air Attacks," 5. This incorrectly states that two BR.20s, He.111s, Do.17s, and Ju 88s attacked.

67. "Diari di guerra, 5ª Squadra," 15 June 1942. ADM 199/1244, "Analysis of Air Attacks," 5.

68. ADM 199/1244, "Report of loss of H.M.A.S. *Nestor,* 4." The torpedo attack was likely, but according to Axis records, the high-level and dive-bombing attacks were long over by this time.

69. ADM 199/1244, "Report Operation Vigorous, Analysis of Air Attacks," 6. Santoni and Mattesini, *La partecipazione tedesca,* 215. Santoro, *L'aeronautica italiana,* Vol. II, 377.

70. ADM 234/353, *Malta Convoys 1942,* 33–34.

71. Iachino, *Operazione Mezzo Giugno,* 308.

72. Ibid., 309. Supermarina, "Relazione sulle operazioni navali svoltesi dal 12 al 16 Giugno 1942."

73. ADM 199/1244, "Report, Rear Admiral Commanding 15th C. S.," 8. Ibid., "Report of Loss of *Hermione,*" 2.

74. Woodman, *Malta Convoys,* 348. Barrett, *Engage the Enemy,* 515. ADM 199/1244, "Commander in Chief, Report," 6.

75. Iachino sailed from Taranto to intercept the March convoy forty-two hours after it left Alexandria. His interception point for the June operation was two hundred miles farther east than in March, which complicated Harwood's plan. However, for Harwood's

decoy convoy to work, the Italians would have needed to get the fleet to sea within twenty hours of the convoy's departure. In other words, he wanted the Italians to sortie far too early or too late.

76. Playfair, *Mediterranean and the Middle East,* Vol. 2, 313.

6. OPERATION HARPOON

1. ADM 199/1110, "Orders for Harpoon, Enemy Information."
2. Rice, "M.V. *Orari,*" 1.
3. SIS, "Intercettazioni estere e informazioni, No. 7," 21821 and 21878.
4. Ibid., 22173 and 22188. Supermarina, "Promemoria N. 46."
5. Rice, "M.V. *Orari,*" 1.
6. ADM 199/1110, "Report of Proceedings, *Eagle,*" 1–2.
7. Supermarina, "Apprezzamento situazione ore 20."
8. SIS, "Intercettazioni estere e informazioni, No. 7," 22247 and 22251.
9. ADM 199/1110, "Report of Proceedings, *Eagle*"; Rohwer, *Axis Submarine Successes,* 234.
10. Supermarina, "Conversazioni telefoniche del giorno 14 Giugno"; Da Zara, *Pelle d'ammiraglio,* 389.
11. Santoro, *L'aeronautica italiana,* Vol. 2, 379.
12. ADM 199/1110, "*Kenya,* Report of Attack by Enemy Aircraft." ADM 234/358, *Malta Convoys 1942,* 17.
13. Supermarina, "Verbale della riunione tenuta presso il Comando Supremo." Fioravanzo, USMM, Vol. V, *Le azioni navali,* 278. Santoro, *L'aeronautica italiana,* Vol. 2, 380. *Eagle's* report estimated there were fifty torpedo-bombers.
14. ADM 239/489, *H.M. Ships Damaged or Sunk, Liverpool,* and ADM 234/353, *Malta Convoys 1942,* 18.
15. ADM 199/1110, "Report of Proceedings, *Wrestler.*"
16. Fioravanzo, USMM, Vol. V, *Le azioni navali,* 280. Rocca, *I disperati,* 229.
17. Supermarina, "Verbale della riunione tenuta presso il Comando Supremo."
18. ADM 199/1110, "Report of Proceedings, *Westcott.*"
19. Ibid., "Report of Proceedings, *Liverpool,*" 2.
20. Santoro, *L'aeronautica italiana,* Vol. 2, 381, and Supermarina, "Verbale della Riunione tenuta presso il Comando Supremo."
21. Da Zara, *Pelle d'ammiraglio,* 390.
22. ADM 199/1110, "Report of Proceedings, *Argus,*" 3. Santoni and Mattesini, *La partecipazione tedesca,* 210; Santoro, *L'aeronautica italiana,* Vol. 2, 381.
23. Santoro, *L'aeronautica italiana,* Vol. 2, 381; ADM 199/1110, "Report of Proceedings," *Eagle,* 5. *London Gazette,* "Mediterranean Convoy Operations," 4496.
24. ADM 234/353, *Malta Convoys 1942,* 19. Quote from ADM 199/1110, "Narrative of Air Attacks which affected *Wrestler.*" British accounts identify the level bombers as Ju 88s. Also see Santoro, *L'aeronautica italiana,* Vol. 2, 381.
25. ADM 199/1110, "Report of Proceedings, *Argus,*" 4.
26. Ibid., "D.17, Report of Proceedings," 2.

27. Santoro, *L'aeronautica italiana*, Vol. 2, 381, and Santoni and Mattesini, *La partecipazione tedesca*, 217–18.

28. ADM 199/1110, "Chronological Sequence of Events."

29. Ibid., *"Speedy*, Report of Attack on U-Boat," and *London Gazette*, "Mediterranean Convoy Operations," 4496.

30. Quote from ADM 194/449, "Admiralty: Officers' Service Records, Hardy, Cecil Campbell." For the orders see ADM 199/1110, "Orders for Operation Harpoon, Instructions for Force X."

31. *London Gazette*, "Mediterranean Convoy Operations," 4497.

32. ADM 199/1110, "Report of Proceedings of Passage of Force X," 7, and "Report of Proceedings, *Ithuriel*," 1.

33. Da Zara, *Pelle d'ammiraglio*, 391.

34. Ibid., 392.

7. THE BATTLE OF PANTELLERIA

1. *London Gazette*, "Mediterranean Convoy Operations," 4498; RAF, *RAF Review No. 1*, 67.

2. Bagnasco, *Le armi delle navi italiane*, 52–53, and Campbell, *Naval Weapons*, 394.

3. ADM 199/1110, "Report of Passage of M.L. 135"; "Report of Proceedings of Convoy W"; and "War Log, *Kujawiak*," 3.

4. Da Zara, *Pelle d'ammiraglio*, 395. ADM 199/1110, "Report of Proceedings, H. M. S. *Marne*"; "Report of Proceedings, *Matchless*"; and "Report of Proceedings of Convoy W. S. 19 Z." Territorial waters meant the African coast.

5. ADM 199/1110, "Report of Proceedings, *Marne*." Da Zara, *Pelle d'ammiraglio*, 395. Campbell, *Naval Weapons*, 46–58. *Marne* also stated her first round was an over. At 0645 the range would have been more than twenty thousand yards.

6. Quotes from Winton, *War at Sea*, 225–26. This account was written to his wife from an Italian prison camp. Also, ADM 199/1110, "Report of Proceedings, *Ithuriel*."

7. Da Zara, *Pelle d'ammiraglio*, 395. Quote, Winton, *War at Sea*, 226. Supermarina, "Azione a Fuoco, Azione mattinale dei CC.TT, *Ascari* e *Oriani*."

8. *London Gazette*, "Mediterranean Convoys," 4498.

9. Supermarina, "Azione a Fuoco, Azione mattinale dei CC.TT. *Malocello*." Also Cocchia, *Hunters and the Hunted*, 130. ADM 199/1110, "*Blankney*, Narrative of Action," and "Report of Proceedings, *Matchless*." War Log, *Kujawiak*, 4.

10. See Cernuschi, "Acque di Pantelleria," Part 2, 12–13.

11. *London Gazette*, "Mediterranean Convoys," 4499. ADM 199/1110, "*Blankey*, Narrative of Action"; "Report of Passage of *M.L. 135*"; "Report of Proceedings of Convoy W. S. 19 Z"; "Report on the loss of *Kentucky*"; "War Log, *Kujawiak*," 4. ADM 199/835, "*Speedy* Report of Proceedings." Rice, "M.V. *Orari*," 5.

12. Santoro, *L'aeronautica Italiana*, Vol. II, 384.

13. Ibid., 385. Weal, *Junkers Ju 88*, 65, states that only two Ju 88s from I./ KG 54 attacked that morning. Shores, et al., *Malta: The Spitfire Year, 1942*, 337–38, identifies the attackers as seven Ju 88s from I./KG 54. Radtke, *Kampfgeschwader 54*, does not men-

tion any attacks by this unit on the Harpoon convoy during the 15th. I./KG 54 was flying shuttle bombing missions between Derna and Crete against the Vigorous convoy on the 14th.

14. Da Zara, *Pelle d'ammiraglio*, 396. On the nameplate "One hundred eyes" thus became "One hundred asses."

15. Supermarina, "Relazione sulle operazioni navali svoltesi dal 12 al 16 giugno 1942." *London Gazette*, "Mediterranean Convoy Operations," 4498.

16. Winton, *War at Sea*, 226–27. Rudolf men referred to radar operators. ADM 199/1110, "Report of Proceedings, *Ithuriel*." The range was nearer twelve than five thousand yards.

17. ADM 199/1110, "Report of Proceedings, *Matchless*."

18. Ibid., "Report of Proceedings, *Ithuriel*."

19. Supermarina, "Azione a Fuoco, Azione mattinale dei CC.TT. *Malocello*"; Fioravanzo, USMM, Vol. V, *Le azioni navali*, 297; quote from Cocchia, *Hunters and the Hunted*, 131. ADM 199/1110, "Report of Proceedings, *Marne*."

20. Da Zara, *Pelle d'ammiraglio*, 397.

21. Ibid., 398.

22. ADM 199/1110, "Report of Proceedings, *Marne*." Da Zara, *Pelle d'ammiraglio*, 399.

23. ADM 199/1110, "Enclosure No. 9 to Malta No. 330/692/1 of 21st July, 1942." Joseph Caruana, correspondence, 29 January 2010. Some histories state that *Kentucky* was given a British crew and that they did not know how to make the simple repairs required to get the ship under way. See Moses, *At All Costs*, 69, for an example. "The Yanks were yanked and put on a tub back to New York, and a crew from the British Merchant Navy moved into the luxurious quarters on the new tanker." In fact, the American crew stayed aboard.

24. Fioravanzo, USMM, Vol. V, *Le azioni navali*, 297–98.

25. Supermarina, "Azione a Fuoco, Azione mattinale dei CC.TT. *Malocello*." ADM 199/1110, "Report of Proceedings, *Blankney*."

26. ADM 199/1110, "Report of Proceedings, *Partridge*." Fioravanzo, USMM, Vol. V, *Le azioni navali*, 297.

27. Supermarina, "Osservazioni sulla Battaglia di Pantelleria."

28. ADM 234/353, *Malta Convoys 1942*, 22. ADM 199/1110, "Report of Proceedings, *Matchless*."

29. Fioravanzo, USMM, Vol. V, *Le azioni navali*, 299.

30. ADM 199/1110, "Report of Proceedings, *Blankney*."

31. Da Zara, *Pelle d'ammiraglio*, 400–401. Santoro, *L'aeronautica italiana*, Vol. II, 385. By Italian standards this was good cooperation. The hour it took Air Sicily to respond to Da Zara's call can be compared to the four hours Malta required to meet Hardy's more urgent appeal.

32. ADM 199/1110, "Report on the Loss of *Bedouin*." *London Gazette*, "Mediterranean Convoy Operations," 4499. He must have experienced more difficulty with the tow than reported because his progress did not reflect a speed of seven knots.

33. Fioravanzo, USMM, Vol. V, *Le azioni navali*, 302. SIS, "Intercettazioni estere e informazioni, No. 7," 22353 and 22355.

34. ADM 199/1110, "Report of Proceedings, *Speedy.*" *London Gazette,* "Mediterranean Convoy Operations," 4499.

35. RAF, *RAF Review No. 1,* 68.

36. Massimello, "Bombe sul Convoglio Harpoon," 16.

37. Cull and Galea, *Spitfires over Malta,* 163. Da Zara, *Pelle d'ammiraglio,* 401. Note the disparity in the number of Spitfires assigned to convoy protection compared to the number assigned to escort the air strikes.

38. Taghorn, *Die Geschichte des Lehrgeschwaders 1,* 31–32.

39. *London Gazette,* "Mediterranean Convoy Operations," 4499. ADM 199/1110, "Report of Proceedings, *Marne*"; "War Log, *Kujawiak,* 4."

40. Da Zara, *Pelle d'ammiraglio,* 401–402.

41. ADM 199/1110, "Report of Proceedings, *Speedy.*" Supermarina, "Azione a fuoco, Azione meridiana e pomeridiana."

42. Cull and Galea, *Spitfires over Malta,* 164–65. Santoro, *L'aeronautica italiana,* Vol. 2, 387.

43. Fioravanzo, USMM, Vol. V, *Le azioni navali,* 307.

44. *London Gazette,* "Mediterranean Convoy Operations," 4499, and ADM 199/1110, "Report of Proceedings, *Marne*"; "War Log, *Kujawiak,* 4."

45. ADM 199/1110, "Report of Proceedings, *Partridge.*"

46. Santoro, *L'aeronautica italiana,* Vol. 2, 386.

47. Da Zara, *Pelle d'ammiraglio,* 403. Fioravanzo, USMM, Vol. V, *Le azioni navali,* 310.

48. Santoro, *L'aeronautica italiana,* Vol. 2, 387.

49. ADM 199/1110, "Report of Proceedings, *Marne*"; "Report of Proceedings, *Matchless*"; "Report of Proceedings, *Cairo.*" Cull and Galea, *Spitfires over Malta,* 167.

50. Supermarina, "Relazione sulle operazioni navali svoltesi dal 12 al 16 giugno 1942."

51. ADM 199/1110, "Enclosure No. 13 to Malta No. 330/682/1 of 21st July, 1942"; "Report of Proceedings, *Cairo.*" The *London Gazette* version of this report deletes Hardy's assertion that he passed along the correct information about the swept channel.

52. ADM 199/1110, "Report of Proceedings, *Cairo.*" J. Caruana, correspondence.

53. Ibid., "Report of Proceedings, *Speedy.*" Position Z was three miles off St. Thomas Bay.

54. Ibid., "Report of Sinking of *Kujawiak,*" and "Loss of *Kujawiak* and Mining of *Badsworth.*"

55. ADM 199/1110, "Report of Proceedings, Convoy Commodore." Rice, "M.V. *Orari,*" 5. ADM 199/1110, "Report of Proceedings, *Matchless,*" and ADM 234/444, *H.M. Ships Damaged or Sunk by Enemy Action. Matchless.* ADM 199/1110, "Loss of *Kujawiak* and Mining of *Badsworth.*"

56. Playfair, *Mediterranean and the Middle East,* Vol. 3, 307. Correspondence with Joseph Caruana, 29 January 2010.

57. ADM 199/1110, Report of Proceedings, "*Marne*" and "*Ithuriel.*"

58. Ibid., Report of Proceedings, "Passage of Force X," "*Marne,*" and "*Ithuriel.*" ADM 234/444, *H.M. Ships Damaged or Sunk by Enemy Action.* Destroyers 1942, 207.

59. Churchill, *Hinge of Fate,* 336 and 343.

60. ADM 199/1110, "Report of Proceedings, *Eagle,* Inadequacy of Fighter Protection in Operation Harpoon."

61. Ibid., "Enclosure No. 13 to Malta No. 330/682 of 21st July, 1942."

62. Ibid., "D.17, Report of Proceedings," 3.

63. Macintyre, *Battle for the Mediterranean*, 157. Supermarina, "Osservazioni sulla Battaglia di Pantelleria." Barnett, *Engage the Enemy More Closely*, 508, writes, "The enemy destroyers followed the customary Italian pattern of discretion before valour, and retired." Also that the cruisers "displayed a reluctance to engage more closely."

8. THE AUGUST CONVOY

1. Austin, *Churchill and Malta's War*, 206. Playfair, *Mediterranean and the Middle East*, Vol. 2, 316.

2. Naval Cypher 1209C/21. Jellison, *Besieged*, 220–21 (this excludes bread and locally grown foodstuffs). Hastings, *Winston's War*, 251.

3. Greene and Massignani, *Rommel's North African Campaign*, 168. Also Playfair, *Mediterranean and the Middle East*, Vol. 2, 277.

4. Barnett, *Engage the Enemy*, 516.

5. See Cocchia, USMM, Vol. VII, *La difesa del traffico*, 440–447.

6. Barnett, *Engage the Enemy*, 517.

7. ADM 234/353, *Malta Convoys 1942*, 37.

8. Woodman, *Malta Convoys*, 376.

9. Simpson, *Somerville Papers*, 438.

10. Woodman, *Malta Convoys*, 370.

11. Seventeen aircraft per week. See Vego, "Major Convoy Operation to Malta," 116.

12. Austin, *Churchill and Malta's War*, 211.

13. For air, ibid., 212; for submarines, Hezlet, *Submarine Operations*, Chapter 15.

14. "Intercettazioni estere e informazioni, No. 10," 24751. Hinsley, et al., *British Intelligence*, Vol. 2, 418. Vego, "Major Convoy Operation to Malta," 111.

15. Smith, *Pedestal*, 92.

16. See Woodman, *Malta Convoys*, 389.

17. Santoro, *L'aeronautica italiana*, Vol. 2, 399.

18. Vego, "Major Convoy Operation to Malta," 128–29. Fioravanzo, USMM, Vol. V, *Le azioni navali*, 405.

19. Santoro, *L'aeronautica italiana*, Vol. 2, 398.

20. ADM 234/353, *Malta Convoys 1942*, 39. A total of three cruisers and twenty-four destroyers fueled from the tankers.

21. Thompson, *War at Sea*, 192.

22. Santoro, *L'aeronautica italiana*, Vol. 2, 399.

23. Fioravanzo, USMM, Vol. V, *Le azioni navali*, 422–23.

24. The British timed the attack at 0915 whereas the German report stated it started at 0830. See Santoro, *L'aeronautica italiana*, Vol. 2, 400. Also, Santoni and Mattesini, *La partecipazione tedesca*, 238.

25. The *motobomba* FFF had been dropped over Alexandria and Gibraltar in small quantities since June 1941, but without effect.

26. Admiral Syfret commented in his report, "It will be a happy day when the fleet is equipped with modern fighter aircraft." *London Gazette*, "Malta Convoys," 4503.

27. Santoro, *L'aeronautica italiana*, Vol. 2, 402, and Fioravanzo, USMM, Vol. V, *Le azioni navali*, 424, specify that the Re.2001s were armed with "special penetration bombs." Fioravanzo speculates that these bombs were probably dropped at too low an altitude to permit the detonators to function properly. Smith, *Pedestal*, 106, and Greene and Massignani, *Naval War in the Mediterranean*, 248–49, say that the special bombs were not available and the aircraft used antipersonnel bombs instead; they also state that the other bomb hit the carrier, broke up on impact, and sprayed the deck with splinters, killing six men and wounding two. The summary of damage in ADM 234/444 only mentions the bomb that fell over the side.

28. ADM 234/353, *Malta Convoys 1942*, 41. *London Gazette*, "Malta Convoys," 4503.

29. ADM 234/353, *Malta Convoys 1942*, 41. Thompson, *War at Sea*, 194. Woodman, *Malta Convoys*, 407. The claims and numbers of Axis aircraft are based on Santoro, *L'aeronautica italiana*, Vol. 2, 402–404.

30. *London Gazette*, "Malta Convoys," 4503.

31. Santoro, *L'aeronautica italiana*, Vol. 2, 405.

32. Quoted in Smith, *Pedestal*, 144.

33. SIS, "Intercettazioni estere e informazioni, No. 10," 24850.

34. Quoted in Smith, *Pedestal*, 145. Also Moses, *At All Costs*, 188. He identifies the destroyer as *Ledbury*.

35. Quoted in Smith, *Pedestal*, 153.

36. Quoted in ibid., 157.

37. See Fioravanzo, USMM, Vol. V, *Le azioni navali*, 437; Woodman, *Malta Convoys*, 427; and Frank, *German S-Boats*, 180. German claims are vastly exaggerated. Quotes from Woodman, *Malta Convoys*, 429, and *London Gazette*, "Malta Convoys," 4503.

38. Bragadin, *Italian Navy*, 211–12. Fioravanzo, USMM, Vol. V, *Le azioni navali*, 408. Woodman, *Malta Convoys*, 419.

39. Biagini and Frattolillo, *Diario Storico del Comando Supremo*, Vol. VII, 914–17.

40. Santoni and Mattesini, *La partecipazione tedesca*, 246.

41. Quoted in Smith, *Pedestal*, 185.

42. Quoted in ibid., 187. Santoro, *L'aeronautica italiana*, Vol. 2, 408.

43. Smith, *Pedestal*, 187, and Woodman, *Malta Convoys*, 439.

44. *London Gazette*, "Malta Convoys," 4511.

45. Santoro, *L'aeronautica italiana*, Vol. 2, 408.

46. Moses, *At All Costs*, 247–48. ADM 234/353, *Malta Convoys 1942*, 44.

47. Santoni and Mattesini, *La partecipazione tedesca*, 248. Moses, *At All Costs*, 278.

48. Vego, "Major Convoy Operation to Malta," 139. *London Gazette*, "Malta Convoys," 4512.

49. Churchill, *The Hinge of Fate*, 455. Thompson, *War at Sea*, 195. Maugeri, *From the Ashes of Disgrace*, 83.

9. TORCH TO THE END OF THE WAR

1. RAF, *RAF Review No. 1*, 74. Ciano, *Diaries*, 510.

2. Austin, *Churchill and Malta's War*, 225. Playfair, *The Mediterranean and Middle East*, Vol. 4, 196.

3. Hinsley, et al., *British Intelligence*, Vol. 2, 423.

4. Statistics regarding losses include only ships displacing more than 500 tons. They are complied from Rohwer, *Allied Submarine Attacks*; Hezlet, *Submarine Operations*; Hinsley, et al., *British Intelligence*, Vol. 2; USMM, Vol. III, *Navi perdute*; and USMM, Vols. VII and VIII, *La difesa del traffico*. One ship, *Paolina* (4,894 GRT), foundered on an Italian mine off Cape Bon.

5. Austin, *Churchill and Malta*, 139. Hinsley, et al., *British Intelligence*, Vol. 2, 730–32.

6. See note 4.

7. Playfair, *Mediterranean and the Middle East*, Vol. 4, 20–23.

8. See note 4.

9. RAF, *RAF Review No. 1*, 58. Hinsley, et al., *British Intelligence*, Vol. 2, 730–37.

10. "The protection of our convoys at sea was the responsibility of the Italian Navy. A great part of its officers, like many other Italians, were not supporters of Mussolini and would rather have seen our defeat than our victory. Hence they sabotaged wherever they could." Liddell Hart, *Rommel Papers*, 244. Kesselring, *Kesselring*, 152.

11. Austin, *Churchill and Malta's War*, 228.

12. See Biagini and Frattolillo, *Diario Storico del Comando Supremo*, Vol. VIII, 625, 637, and 652.

13. Willmott, *Last Century of Sea Power*, Vol. 2, 270. Roskill, *War at Sea*, Vol. 2, 315.

14. Although it mostly operated in the Atlantic, the U.S. Navy's contribution to Torch included three battleships, five carriers, seven cruisers, and thirty-eight destroyers.

15. Hinsley, et al., *British Intelligence*, Vol. 2, 466. Fioravanzo, USMM, Vol. VIII, *La difesa del traffico*, 301–308.

16. Smith, *Conflict over Convoys*, 207.

17. O'Hara and Cernuschi, *Dark Navy*, 75–79.

18. Ironically, the German destroyer was the ex-*Premuda* fighting as *TA32*. Supply difficulties forced the Germans to discard her 5.5-inch guns and arm her with 4.1-inch weapons.

CONCLUSION

The epigraph comes from http://www.quotationspage.com/quote/1359.html

1. Cab. W.P. (40) 362, September 4, 1940, 45.

2. In this hope's most extreme form the British leadership, with a firm memory of how the Kaiser's regime unexpectedly collapsed in 1918, dared to hope that Hitler's personal rule might also be swept away by defeats on the periphery, uprisings of the subjected peoples of Europe, and popular discontent caused by the strategic bombing campaign.

3. In January 1942, 89 submarines were in frontline service; thus, the Mediterranean had 25 percent of Germany's operational boats. In January 1943, 11 percent of operational boats were deployed in the Middle Sea. See O'Hara, et al., *On Seas Contested*, 74.

4. RAF, *RAF Review No. 1*, 49.

Bibliography

PRIMARY SOURCES AND OFFICIAL HISTORIES

Admiralty. *British Merchant Vessels Lost or Damaged by Enemy Action during Second World War: 3rd September 1939 to 2nd September 1945.* London: HMSO, 1947.

———. *Ships of the Royal Navy Statement of Losses during the Second World War: 3rd September 1939 to 2nd September 1945.* London: HMSO, 1947.

Archivio Centrale dello Stato, Rome. Ministero della Marina. "Condotta del tiro navale." January 1941.

———. "Direttive e Norme per l'impiego della Squadra nel conflitto attuale." January 1942.

———. "Norme di massima per l'impiego in guerra." January 1942.

———. Servizio Informazione Segreto (SIS). "Intercettazioni estere e informazioni." No. 6, a 18 dal 24-5-1942 al 8-1-1943.

Archivio dell'Ufficio Storico della Marina Militare, Rome. Capo di Stato Maggiore della Regia Marina. "Una lettera da consegnare personalmente al Grande Ammiraglio RAEDER." May 23, 1942.

———. Comando Supremo. "Appunto. 12 Giugno 1942—Ore 13." June 12, 1942.

———. Supermarina. "Azione a fuoco delle unita' della VII Divisione nella Battaglia di Pantelleria del 15 giugno 1942." June 18, 1942.

———. Supermarina. "Convoglio da Alessandria apprezzamento della manovra eseguita."

———. Supermarina. "Ufficio statistica operativa, danni inflitti al nemico Scontro di Capo Matapan." March 31, 1941.

———. Supermarina. "Elogio del Duce alla VII Divisione Navale. Comunicato dall'ammiraglio Riccardi all'ammiraglio Iachino Il 16 Giugno 1942." June 16, 1942.

———. Supermarina. "Osservazioni sulla Battaglia di Pantelleria. Lettera privata dell'ammiraglio Angelo Iachino all'ammiraglio Alberto Da Zara." January 9, 1943.

———. Supermarina. "Avviso N. Progressivo 7003. Apprezzamento situazione ore 20. 13/6/1942-XX Ore 2100." June 13, 1942.

———. Supermarina. "Conversazioni telefoniche del giorno 14 giugno 1942 fra l'ammiraglio Sansonetti e gli ammiragli Iachino e Da Zara." June 14, 1942.

———. Supermarina. "Possibilità d'impiego della VII Divisione." June 13, 1942.

———. Supermarina. "Promemoria N. 46." June 12, 1942.

———. Supermarina. "Relazione sulle operazioni navali svoltesi nel Bacino Centro Oc-
cidentale ed Orientale del Mediterraneo dal 12 al 16 Giugno 1942." June 16, 1942.

———. Supermarina. "Situazione della nafta." June 8, 1942.

———. Supermarina. "Verbale della riunione tenuta presso il Comando Supremo il 14
giugno 1942 alle ore 1300." June 14, 1942.

Archivio dell'Ufficio Storico dell'Aeronautica Militare, Rome. "Diari di guerra, 5ª
Squadra." June 1942.

———. "Diari di guerra, Comando Egeo." June 1942.

Biagini, Antonello, and Fernando Frattolillo. *Diario Storico del Comando Supremo.*
Rome: Ufficio Storico dello Stato Maggiore dell'Esercito, 1999.

Coakley, Robert W. *Global Logistics and Strategy, 1940–1943.* Washington, DC: Office of
the Chief of Military History, 1955.

Craven, Wesley Frank, and James Lea Cate, eds. *The Army Air Forces in World War II.*
Volume II, *Europe: Torch to Pointblank August 1942 to December 1943.* Chicago: University of Chicago Press, 1949.

Foreign Relations of the United States. http://uwdc.library.wisc.edu/collections/FRUS
(June 11, 2011).

Fueher Conferences on Naval Affairs, 1939–1945. London: Chatham, 2005.

Garland, Albert N., and Howard McGaw Smyth. *Sicily and the Surrender of Italy.* Washington, DC: U.S. Government Printing Office, 1965.

Gill, G. Hermon. *Royal Australian Navy 1942–1945.* Adelaide: Griffin, 1968.

Giorgerini, Giorgio, and Augusto Nani. *Le navi di linea italiane.* Rome: Ufficio Storico
della Marina Militare, 1962.

———. *Gli incrociatori italiani 1861–1964.* Rome: Ufficio Storico della Marina Militare,
1964.

Gwyer, J. M. A., and J. R. M. Butler. *Grand Strategy.* Volume III, *June 1941–August 1942.*
London: HMSO, 1964.

Hinsley, F. H., et al. *British Intelligence in the Second World War: Its Influence on Strategy
and Operations.* Volume 1. New York: Cambridge University Press, 1979.

———. *British Intelligence in the Second World War: Its Influence on Strategy and Operations.* Volume 2. New York: Cambridge University Press, 1981.

———. *British Intelligence in the Second World War: Its Influence on Strategy and Operations.* Volume 3, Part 1. New York: Cambridge University Press, 1984.

The London Gazette. "Mediterranean Convoy Operations." Supplement, 11 August 1948.

———. "The Battle of Sirte of 22nd March, 1942." Supplement, 18 September 1947.

Militärgeschichtliches Forschungsamt. *Germany and the Second World War.* Volume III.
The Mediterranean, South-east Europe, and North Africa 1939–1941. Schreiber, Gerhard,
Bernd Stegemann, and Detlef Vogel. Oxford, Clarendon Press, 1995.

———. Volume VI. *The Global War.* Boog, Horst, Werner Rahn, and Reinhard Stumpf.
Oxford, Clarendon Press, 2001.

The National Archives, Kew, England. ADM 194/449, Admiralty: Officers' Service Records, Hardy, Cecil Campbell.

———. ADM 199/835. Harpoon Military Convoy Reports.

———. ADM 199/1110. Operation Harpoon.

———. ADM 199/1244. Operation Vigorous.

———. ADM 234/353. *Battle Summaries. No. 32, Malta Convoys 1942.*

———. ADM 234/359. *Operation "Torch" Invasion of North Africa November 1942 to February 1943.*

———. ADM 234/444. *H.M. Ships Damaged or Sunk by Enemy Action 3 Sept. 1939 to 2 Sept. 1945.*

———. Cabinet Papers, 1915–1980. Total War at http://www.nationalarchives.gov.uk /cabinetpapers/themes/total-war.htm

Page, Christopher, ed. *The Royal Navy and the Mediterranean.* Volume 1, *September 1939– October 1940.* Naval Staff Histories. London: Frank Cass, 2002.

———. *The Royal Navy and the Mediterranean.* Volume 2, *November 1940–December 1941.* Naval Staff Histories. London: Frank Cass, 2002.

Playfair, I. S. O. *The Mediterranean and Middle East.* Volume 1, *The Early Successes against Italy (to May 1941).* Uckfield, England: Naval and Military, 2004.

———. *The Mediterranean and Middle East.* Volume 2, *The Germans Come to the Help of Their Ally (1941).* Uckfield, England: Naval and Military, 2004.

———. *The Mediterranean and Middle East.* Volume 3, *British Fortunes Reach Their Lowest Ebb (September 1941 to September 1942).* Uckfield, England: Naval and Military, 2004.

———. *The Mediterranean and Middle East.* Volume 4, *The Destruction of the Axis Forces in Africa.* Uckfield, England: Naval and Military, 2004.

Rice, Nelson. "M.V. *Orari* in a Malta Convoy. June, 1942." Confidential letter for N.Z.S. Co's records.

Richards, Dennis, and Hilary St. George Saunders. *The Royal Air Force 1939–1945.* Volume 2, *The Fight Avails.* London: HMSO, 1954.

Roskill, S. W. *The War at Sea 1939–1945.* Volume 1, *The Defensive.* London: HMSO, 1954.

———. *The War at Sea 1939–1945.* Volume 2, *The Period of Balance.* London: HMSO, 1956.

———. *The War at Sea 1939–1945.* Volume 3, *The Offensive Part I.* London: HMSO, 1960.

———. *The War at Sea 1939–1945.* Volume 3, *The Offensive Part II.* Nashville, TN: Battery, 1994.

Royal Air Force, Headquarters Middle East. *RAF Review No. 1.* Printing and Stationery Services MEF, 1943.

Santoro, Giuseppe. *L'Aeronautica italiana nella Seconda Guerra Mondiale.* Rome: Danesi, 1957.

Simpson, Michael, ed. *The Cunningham Papers: Selections from the Private and Official Correspondence of Admiral of the Fleet Viscount Cunningham of Hyndhope, O.M, K.T., G.C.B., D.S.O. and Two Bars.* Volume 1, *The Mediterranean Fleet, 1939–1942.* Aldershot, England: Ashgate, 1999.

———. *The Cunningham Papers.* Volume 2, *The Triumph of Allied Sea Power 1942–1946.* Aldershot, England: Ashgate, 2006.

———. *The Somerville Papers: Selections from the Private and Official Correspondence of Admiral of the Fleet Sir James Somerville, G.C.B., G.B.E., D.S.O.* Aldershot, England: Scolar, 1996.

Ufficio Storico della Marina Militare (USMM). *La Marina Italiana nella Seconda Guerra Mondiale.* Volume I. Giuseppe Fioravanzo. *Dati statistici.* Rome, 1972.

———.Volume II. Luigi Castagna, et al. *Navi militari perdute.* Rome, 1965.

———. Volume III. *Navi perdute—Navi mercantili.* Rome, 1952.

———. Volume IV. Giuseppe Fioravanzo. *Le azioni navali in Mediterraneo dal 10 giugno 1940 al 31 marzo 1941.* Rome, 1976.

———. Volume V. Giuseppe Fioravanzo. *Le azioni navali in Mediterraneo dal 1 aprile 1941 al'8 settembre 1943.* Rome, 1970.

———. Volume VII. Aldo Cocchia. *La difesa del traffico con L'Africa settentrionale: dal 1 Ottobre 1941 al 30 Settembre 1942.* Rome, 1962.

———. Volume VIII. Giuseppe Fioravanzo. *La difesa del traffico con L'Africa settentrionale: dal 1 Ottobre 1942 alla caduta della Tunisia.* Rome, 1964.

Whelan, J. A. *Malta Airman.* Wellington: Historical Publications Branch, 1950.

BOOKS

Ansel, Walter. *Hitler and the Middle Sea.* Durham, NC: Duke University Press, 1972.

Auphan, Paul, and Jacques Mordal. *The French Navy in World War II.* Westport, CT: Greenwood, 1976.

Austin, Douglas. *Churchill and Malta: A Special Relationship.* The Mill, England: Spellmount, 2006.

———. *Churchill and Malta's War 1939–1945.* Stroud, England: Amberley, 2010.

Bagnasco, Erminio. *Le armi delle navi italiane nella seconda guerra mondiale.* Parma: Ermanno Albertelli, 2007.

———. *In Guerra sul mare: navi e marinai italiani nel secondo conflitto mondiale.* Parma: Ermanno Albertelli, 2005.

Bagnasco, Erminio, and Achille Rastelli. *Sommergibili in guerra: centosettantadue battelli italiani nella seconda guerra mondiale.* Parma: Ermanno Albertelli, 2007.

Bagnasco, Erminio, and Enrico Cernuschi. *Le navi da guerra italiane 1940–1945.* Parma: Ermanno Albertelli, 2003.

Bagnasco, Erminio, and Mark Grossman. *Regia Marina: Italian Battleships of World War Two.* Missoula, MT: Pictorial Histories, 1986.

Bagnasco, Erminio, and Maurizio Brescia. *Cacciatorpediniere classi "Freccia/Folgore" "Maestrale" "Oriani" Parti seconda e terza.* Rome: Ermanno Albertelli, 1997.

Barnett, Correlli. *Engage the Enemy More Closely: The Royal Navy in the Second World War.* New York: W. W. Norton, 1991.

Bartimeus. *East of Malta, West of Suez: The Dramatic Inside Story of the Winning of Naval Control of the Mediterranean 1939–1943.* Boston: Little, Brown and Company, 1944.

Bauer, Eddy. *The History of World War II.* New York: Galahad Books, 1979.

Bennett, G. H., and R. Bennett. *Hitler's Admirals.* Annapolis, MD: Naval Institute Press, 2004.

Bennett, Ralph. *Ultra and Mediterranean Strategy: The Never-Before-Told Story of How Ultra First Proved Itself in Battle.* New York: William Morrow, 1989.

Borghese, Valerio J. *Sea Devils: Italian Navy Commandos in World War II.* Annapolis, MD: Naval Institute Press, 1995.

Bragadin, Marc' Antonio. *The Italian Navy in World War II*. Annapolis, MD: Naval Institute Press, 1957.

Brown, David. *Warship Losses of WWII*. Annapolis, MD: Naval Institute Press, 1995.

Cameron, Ian. *Red Duster, White Ensign: The Story of Malta and the Malta Convoys*. New York: Bantam Books, 1983.

Campbell, John. *Naval Weapons of World War II*. Annapolis, MD: Naval Institute Press, 2002.

Cernuschi, Enrico. *Fecero tutti il loro dovere*. Rome: Rivista Marittima, 2006.

Churchill, Winston S. *The Second World War*. Volume 3, *The Grand Alliance*. Boston: Houghton Mifflin, 1950.

Ciano, Galeazzo. *The Ciano Diaries 1939–1943*. Safety Harbor, FL: Simon Publications, 2001.

Cocchia, Aldo. *The Hunters and the Hunted*. New York: Arno, 1980.

Cull, Brian, and Frederick Galea. *Spitfires over Malta: The Epic Air Battles of 1942*. London: Grub Street, 2005.

Cunningham, Andrew Browne. *A Sailor's Odyssey*. London: Hutchinson, 1951.

Da Zara, Alberto. *Pelle d'ammiraglio*. Verona, Italy: Mondadori, 1949.

Deakin, F. W. *The Brutal Friendship: Mussolini, Hitler and the Fall of Italian Fascism*. New York: Harper and Row, 1962.

Dear, I. C. B., ed. *The Oxford Companion to World War II*. New York: Oxford University Press, 1995.

De Belot, Raymond. *The Struggle for the Mediterranean 1939–1945*. Princeton, NJ: Princeton University Press, 1951.

Dunning, Chris. *Courage Alone: The Italian Air Force 1940–1943*. Manchester, England: Hikoki Publications, 2009.

Ellis, John. *World War II: A Statistical Survey*. New York: Facts on File, 1995.

Felmy, Hellmuth. *The German Air Force in the Mediterranean Theater of War*. U.S. Air Force Historical Study 161. Washington DC: U.S. Air Force, 1955.

Frank, Hans. *German S-Boats in Action in the Second World War*. Annapolis, MD: Naval Institute Press, 2007.

Friedman, Norman. *Naval Firepower: Battleship Guns and Gunnery in the Dreadnought Era*. Annapolis, MD: Naval Institute Press, 2008.

Gardiner, Robert, ed. *Conway's All the World's Fighting Ships 1922–1946*. New York: Mayflower, 1980.

———. *Conway's All the World's Fighting Ships 1906–1921*. Annapolis, MD: Naval Institute Press, 1986.

Gooch, John. *Mussolini and His Generals: The Armed Forces and Fascist Foreign Policy 1922–1940*. New York: Cambridge University Press, 2007.

Greene, Jack. *Mare Nostrum: The War in the Mediterranean*. Watsonville, CA: Typesetting, Etc., 1990.

Greene, Jack, and Alessandro Massignani. *Rommel's North African Campaign: September 1940–November 1942*. Cambridge, MA: Da Capo, 1994.

———. *The Naval War in the Mediterranean 1940–1943*. London: Chatham, 1998.

Gröner, Erich. *German Warships 1815–1945*, Volume 1. London: Conway Maritime, 1990.

———. *German Warships 1815–1945,* Volume 2. London: Conway Maritime, 1991.

Grove, Eric. *Sea Battles in Close-Up: World War II,* Volume 2. Annapolis, MD: Naval Institute Press, 1993.

Hague, Arnold. *The Allied Convoy System 1939–1945.* Annapolis, MD: Naval Institute Press, 2000.

Hanable, William S. *Case Studies in the Use of Land-Based Aerial Forces in Maritime Operations, 1939–1990.* Washington DC: Air Force History & Museums Program, 1998.

Harrison, Mark, ed. *The Economics of World War II: Six Great Powers in International Competition.* Cambridge: Cambridge University Press, 2000.

Hastings, Max. *Winston's War: Churchill 1940–1945.* New York: Alfred A. Knopf, 2010.

Hezlet, Arthur. *British and Allied Submarine Operations in World War II.* Portsmouth, UK: The Royal Navy Submarine Museum. No date.

Howard, Michael. *The Mediterranean Strategy in the Second World War.* London: Greenhill, 1993.

Howarth, Stephen, and Derek Law, eds. *The Battle of the Atlantic 1939–1945: The 50th Anniversary International Naval Conference.* London: Greenhill, 1994.

Iachino, Angelo. *Operazione mezzo giugno: episodi dell'ultima guerra sul mare.* Verona: Arnoldo Mondadori, 1955.

———. *Tramonto di una grande marina.* Verona: Arnoldo Mondadori, 1966.

Ireland, Bernard. *The War in the Mediterranean 1940–1943.* London: Arms and Armour, 1993.

Jellison, Charles A. *Besieged: The World War II Ordeal of Malta, 1940–1942.* Hanover, NH: University Press of New England, 1984.

Jordan, Roger. *The World's Merchant Fleets 1939.* Annapolis, MD: Naval Institute Press, 1999.

Kemp, P. K. *H.M. Destroyers.* London: Herbert Jenkins, 1956.

———. *Key to Victory: the Triumph of British Sea Power in WWII.* Boston: Little, Brown, 1957.

Kemp, Paul. *The Admiralty Regrets: British Warship Losses of the 20th Century.* Phoenix Mill, England: Sutton, 1999.

Kennedy, John. *The Business of War: The War Narrative of Major-General Sir John Kennedy.* New York: William Morrow, 1958.

Kesselring, Albert. *Kesselring: A Soldier's Record.* New York: William Morrow, 1954.

Knox, MacGregor. *Hitler's Italian Allies.* London: Cambridge University Press, 2000.

———. *Mussolini Unleashed 1939–1941.* London: Cambridge University Press, 1982.

Langtree, Christopher. *The Kellys: British J, K and N Class Destroyers of World War II.* Annapolis, MD: Naval Institute Press, 2002.

Levine, Alan J. *The War against Rommel's Supply Lines 1942–1943.* Westport, CT: Praeger, 1999.

Liddell Hart, B. H. *The German Generals Talk.* New York: Quill, 1979.

———. *The Rommel Papers.* New York: Harcourt, Brace, 1953.

Macintyre, Donald. *The Battle for the Mediterranean.* New York: W. W. Norton, 1965.

MacKay, Ron. *Junkers Ju 88.* Marlborough, UK: Crowood Press, 2001.

Marcon, Tullio. *C.R.D.A. Cant Z.501*. Turin, Italy: La Bancarella Aeronautica, 2001.

———. *Imam RO 43/44*. Turin, Italy: La Bancarella Aeronautica, 1999.

Mars, Alastair. *British Submarines at War 1939–1945*. Annapolis, MD: Naval Institute Press, 1971.

Martienssen, Anthony. *Hitler and His Admirals*. New York: E. P. Dutton, 1949.

Maugeri, Franco. *From the Ashes of Disgrace*. New York: Reynal and Hitchcock, 1948.

Messenger, Charles, et al. *The Middle East Commandos*. Wellingborough, England: William Kimber, 1988.

Mollo, Andrew. *The Armed Forces of World War II: Uniforms, Insignia and Organization*. New York: Crown, 1981.

Morison, Samuel Eliot. *The Two Ocean War*. Boston: Little, Brown, 1963.

———. *History of United States Naval Operations in World War II*. Volume I, *The Battle of the Atlantic 1939–1943*. Boston: Little, Brown, 1984.

———. *History of United States Naval Operations in World War II*. Volume 2, *Operations in North African Waters, October 1942–June 1943*. Boston: Little, Brown, 1984.

Moses, Sam. *At All Costs*. New York: Random House, 2006.

Mussolini, Benito. *My Rise and Fall*. Cambridge, MA: Da Capo, 1998.

O'Hara, Vincent P. *The German Fleet at War 1939–1945*. Annapolis, MD: Naval Institute Press, 2004.

———. *Struggle for the Middle Sea: The Great Navies at War in the Mediterranean Theater, 1940–1945*. Annapolis, MD: Naval Institute Press, 2009.

———. *The U.S. Navy against the Axis: Surface Combat 1941–1945*. Annapolis, MD: Naval Institute Press, 2007.

O'Hara, Vincent P., W. David Dickson, and Richard Worth, eds. *On Seas Contested: The Seven Great Navies of the Second World War*. Annapolis, MD: Naval Institute Press, 2010.

O'Hara, Vincent P., and Enrico Cernuschi. *Dark Navy: The Regia Marina and the Armistice of 8 September 1943*. Ann Arbor, MI: Nimble Books, 2009.

Padfield, Peter. *War beneath the Sea: Submarine Conflict during World War II*. New York: John Wiley and Sons, 1995.

Parrish, Thomas, ed. *The Simon and Schuster Encyclopedia of World War II*. New York: Simon and Schuster, 1978.

Paterson, Lawrence. *U-Boats in the Mediterranean 1941–1945*. Annapolis, MD: Naval Institute Press, 2007.

Payne, Stanley G. *Franco and Hitler: Spain, Germany, and World War II*. New Haven, CT: Yale University Press, 2008.

Pugsley, A. F. *Destroyer Man*. London: Weidenfeld and Nicolson, 1957.

Radtke, Siegfried. *Kampfgeschwader 54—von der Ju 52 zur Me 262: Eine Chronik nach Kriegstagebüchern, Dokumenten und Berichten 1935–1945*. Munich: Schild Verlag, 1990.

Raeder, Erich. *Struggle for the Sea*. London: Kimber, 1959.

———. *Grand Admiral*. Cambridge, MA: Da Capo, 2001.

Ricciardi, Enrico. *Mediterraneo 1940–1943: Recordi di guerra di un giovane ufficiale di Marina*. Parma: Ermanno Albertelli, 2004.

Robertson, Stuart, and Stephen Dent. *Conway's The War at Sea in Photographs 1939–1945*. London: Conway Maritime, 2007.

Rocca, Gianni. *I disperati: la tragedia dell'Aeronautica italiana nella seconda guerra mondiale*. Milan: Arnoldo Mondadori, 1991.

Rohwer, Jürgen. *War at Sea 1939–1945*. Annapolis, MD: Naval Institute Press, 1996.

———. *Allied Submarine Attacks of World War II*. Annapolis, MD: Naval Institute Press, 1997.

———. *Axis Submarine Successes of World War II*. Annapolis, MD: Naval Institute Press, 1999.

Rohwer, Jürgen, and Gerhard Hummelchen. *Chronology of the War at Sea 1939–1945*. Annapolis, MD: Naval Institute Press, 2006.

Roskill, S. W. *Churchill and the Admirals*. New York: William Morrow, 1978.

Ruge, Friedrich. *Der Seekrieg: The German Navy's Story 1939–1945*. Annapolis, MD: Naval Institute Press, 1957.

Sadkovich, James J. *The Italian Navy in World War II*. Westport, CT: Greenwood, 1994.

Salerno, Reynolds M. *Vital Crossroads: Mediterranean Origins of the Second World War 1935–1940*. Ithaca, NY: Cornell University Press, 2002.

Santoni, Alberto, and Francesco Mattesini. *La partecipazione aeronavale tedesca alla Guerra nel Mediterraneo*. Rome: Ateneo e Bizzarri, 1980.

Shores, Christopher, Brian Cull, and Nicola Malizia. *Malta: The Hurricane Years*. London: Grub Street, 1987.

Showell, Jak. *The German Navy in WWII*. Annapolis, MD: Naval Institute Press, 1979.

Smith, Peter C. *Pedestal: The Convoy That Saved Malta*. Manchester, England: Crecy, 1999.

Spertini, Marco, and Erminio Bagnasco. *I mezzi d'assalto della Xa Flottiglia MAS*. Parma: Ermanno Albertelli, 2005.

Stephen, Martin. *The Fighting Admirals: British Admirals of the Second World War*. Annapolis, MD: Naval Institute Press, 1991.

Stephen, Martin, and Eric Grove. *Sea Battles in Close-Up*. Annapolis, MD: Naval Institute Press, 1993.

Stitt, George. *Under Cunningham's Command 1940–1943*. London: George Allen and Unwin, 1944.

Taghorn, Peter. *Die Geschichte des Lehrgeschwaders 1*. Band 1: *1936–1942*. Zweibrücken, Germany: Nickel, Heinz, 2004.

Thompson, Julian. *The War at Sea: The Royal Navy in the Second World War*. Osceola, WI: Motorbooks International, 1996.

Tomblin, Barbara Brooks. *With Utmost Spirit: Allied Naval Operations in the Mediterranean, 1942–1945*. Lexington, KY: University of Kentucky Press, 2004.

Van Creveld, Martin. *Supplying War: Logistics from Wallenstein to Patton*. Cambridge: Cambridge University Press, 1977.

Vian, Philip. *Action This Day*. London: Frederick Muller, 1960.

Von der Porten, Edward P. *The German Navy in World War II*. New York: Thomas Y. Crowell, 1968.

Von Senger und Etterlin, Frido. *Neither Fear Nor Hope.* New York: E. P. Dutton, 1964.

Wade, Frank. *A Midshipman's War: A Young Man in the Mediterranean Naval War 1941–1943.* Victoria, Canada: Trafford, 2005.

Weal, John. *Junkers Ju 88* Kampfgeschwader *in North Africa and the Mediterranean.* Botley, UK: Osprey Press, 2009.

Whitley, M. J. *Battleships of World War Two.* Annapolis, MD: Naval Institute Press, 1998.

———. *Cruisers of World War Two.* Annapolis, MD: Naval Institute Press, 1995.

———. *Destroyers of World War Two.* Annapolis, MD: Naval Institute Press, 1998.

Willmott, H. P. *The Last Century of Sea Power Volume 2: From Washington to Tokyo, 1922–1945.* Bloomington, IN: Indiana University Press, 2010.

Winton, John, ed. *The War at Sea: The British Navy in World War II.* New York: William Morrow, 1968.

Woodman, Richard. *Malta Convoys 1940–1943.* London: John Murray, 2000.

Worth, Richard. *Fleets of World War II.* Cambridge, MA: Da Capo, 2001.

Wynn, Kenneth. *U-Boat Operations of the Second World War.* Annapolis, MD: Naval Institute Press, 1997.

Zorini, Decio. *C.R.D.A. Cant Z 506.* Turin, Italy: La Bancarella Aeronautica, 1997.

MAGAZINES AND CHAPTERS

Aylwin, Ken. "Malta's Years of Siege." *Naval Review* 82 (October 1994): 397–403.

Barker, Edward L. "War without Aircraft Carriers." U.S. Naval Institute *Proceedings* 80 (March 1954): 281–89.

Bernotti, Romeo. "Italian Naval Policy under Fascism." U.S. Naval Institute *Proceedings* 82 (July 1956): 722–31.

Budden, Michael J. "Defending the Indefensible? The Air Defence of Malta, 1936–1940." *War in History* 6(4) (1999): 447–67.

Burtt, John D., Hans Roolvink, and Albert Zorge. "Operation Herkules." *Military Chronicles* 1(2) (Spring 2006): 30–41.

Caruana, Joseph. "Fighters to Malta." *Warship International* 43(4) (2006): 383–93.

———. "I convogli britannici per Malta." *Storia Militare* 43 (April 1997): 15–24.

Cernuschi, Enrico. "Acque di Pantelleria, 15 giugno 1942." *Storia Militare* 205 (October 2010): 4–18, and 206 (November 2010): 12–26.

———. "Guerra di mine intorno a Malta." *Storia Militare* 184 (January 2009): 26–38.

Cernuschi, Enrico, and Vincent O'Hara. "The Breakout Fleet: The Oceanic Programmes of the Regia Marina, 1934–1940." *Warship 2006.* London: Conway Maritime, 2006, 86–101.

———. "In Search of a Flattop: The Italian Navy and the Aircraft Carrier 1907–2007." *Warship 2007.* London: Conway Maritime, 2007, 61–80.

———. "Taranto: The Raid and the Aftermath." *Warship 2010.* London: Conway Maritime, 2010, 77–95.

Colliva, Giuliano. "Questioni di tiro . . . e altre. Le artiglierie navali italiane nella Guerra nel Mediterraneo." *Bollettino d'archivio dell'Ufficio Storico della Marina Militare* 17(3) (September 2003).

De Toro, Augusto. "La crisi del traffico con la Libia nell'autunno 1941 e il carteggio Weichold-Sansonetti." *Bollettino d'archivio dell'Ufficio Storico della Marina Militare* 23(1) (March 2009).

Donolo, Luigi, and James J. Tritten. "The History of Italian Naval Doctrine." *Naval Doctrine Command* (June 1995).

Fioravanzo, Giuseppe. "Italian Strategy in the Mediterranean, 1940–43." U.S. Naval Institute *Proceedings* 84 (September 1958): 65–72.

Freivogel, Zvonimir. "Siluranti ex italiane sotto bandiera tedesca." *Storia Militare* 36 (September 1996): 18–29, and 37 (October 1996): 22–35.

———. "*Vasilefs Georgios* and *Vasilissa Olga:* From Sister-Ships to Adversaries." *Warship International* 40(4) (2003): 351–64.

Hervieux, Pierre. "German Auxiliaries at War 1939–45: Minesweepers, Submarine Chasers and Patrol Boats." *Warship 1995.* London: Conway Maritime, 1995, 108–23.

———. "German TA Torpedo Boats at War." *Warship 1997–1998.* London: Conway Maritime, 1998, 133–48.

Lynn, Henry. "Malta: Effort and Sacrifice, 1940–42." *Naval Review* 86 (July 1998): 240–49.

Mancini, Renato. "I porti della Libia." *Storia Militare* 54 (February 1998): 20–27.

Marcon, Tullio. "Malta difesa a oltranza sinonimo di vittoria." *Storia Militare* 46 (July 1997): 4–16, and 47 (August 1997): 35–45.

Massimello, Giovanni. "Bombe sul convoglio 'Harpoon.'" *Storia Militare* 37 (October 1996): 15–20.

Nailer, Roger. "Aircraft to Malta." *Warship 1990.* Annapolis, MD: Naval Institute Press, 1990, 151–65.

Poynder, C. F. T. "Midshipman 1942." *Naval Review* 84 (July 1996): 256–61.

Prideaux, A. G. "With 'A.B.C.' in the Med." *Naval Review* 65 (April 1977): 133–40; (July 1977): 270–77; (October 1977): 351–60; 66 (January 1978): 46–54.

Roucek, Joseph S. "The Geopolitics of the Mediterranean." *American Journal of Economics and Sociology* 12 (July 1953): 347–54, 13 (October 1953): 71–86.

Salerno, Reynolds M. "The French Navy and the Appeasement of Italy, 1937–39." *English Historical Review* 112 (February 1997): 66–104.

Short, Edward C. "Malta: Strategic Impact During World War II." U.S. Army War College, April 2000.

Sullivan, Brian R. "A Fleet in Being: The Rise and Fall of Italian Sea Power, 1861–1943." *International History Review* 10 (February 1980): 106–24.

———. "Downfall of the Regia Aeronautica, 1933–1945." In *Why Air Forces Fail: The Anatomy of Defeat,* edited by Robin Higham and Stephen J. Harris. Lexington, KY: The University Press of Kentucky, 2006.

———. "Prisoner in the Mediterranean: The Evolution and Execution of Italian Naval Strategy, 1919–42." In *Naval History: The Seventh Symposium of the U.S. Naval Academy,* edited by William B. Cogar. Wilmington, DE: Scholarly Resources, 1988.

Vego, Milan. "Major Convoy Operation to Malta, 10–15 August 1942 (Operation Pedestal)." *Naval War College Review* (Winter 2010): 107–153.

INTERNET

Convoy Web. http://www.convoyweb.org.uk/ (May 28, 2011).

Hyperwar: A Hypertext History of World War II. http://www.ibiblio.org/hyperwar (March 6, 2011).

Naval History.net. http://www.naval-history.net (March 6, 2011).

Naval Weapons, Naval Technology and Naval Reunions. http://www.navweaps.com (March 6, 2011).

New Zealand Electronic Text Center. http://www.nzetc.org/tm/scholarly/subject -000001.html (March 6, 2011).

People's War. http://www.bbc.co.uk/ww2peopleswar (March 6, 2011).

Regia Marina. www.regiamarina.net (March 6, 2011).

Royal Navy Flag Officers 1904–1945. http://www.admirals.org.uk/ (June 24, 2011).

Index

Page numbers in italics indicate illustrations.

TWENTIETH-CENTURY BATTLES
Edited by Spencer C. Tucker

Vincent P. O'Hara is a naval historian and the author of five books including *Struggle for the Middle Sea: The Great Navies at War in the Mediterranean Theater 1940–1945* (2009). He serves on the editorial review board of *Global War Studies* and is a *Collaboratore* for *Storia MILITARE* magazine. Mr. O'Hara contributed introductions to two volumes of Samuel E. Morison's *History of United States Naval Operations in World War II,* which has been recently republished by the Naval Institute; he is an assistant editor of *World War II at Sea: An Encyclopedia;* and a regular contributor to publications such as the respected British annual *Warship.* O'Hara holds a history degree from the University of California, Berkeley, and resides in southern California.